I0410539

100 YEARS OF THE MIDDLE EAST

Adnan Khan

مكتبة اسلامية MaktabaIslamia

MaktabaIslamia Publications

www.maktabaislamia.com
info@maktabaislamia.com
www.facebook.com/everythingislamic
www.twitter.com/maktabaislamia

2016 CE – 1437 H

Translation of the Qur'ān

It should be perfectly clear that the Qur'ān is only authentic in its original language, Arabic. Since perfect translation of the Qur'ān is impossible, we have used the translation of the meaning of the Qur'ān throughout the book, as the result is only a crude meaning of the Arabic text.

Qur'ānic verses appear in speech marks proceeded by a reference to the Surah and verse number. Sayings (*Hadith*) of Prophet Muhammad ﷺ appear in inverted commas along with reference to the Hadith Book and its Reporter.

ﷺ - صلى الله عليه وسلم (Peace be upon him)

ﷻ - سبحانه وتعالى (Glory to Him, the Exalted)

"I think the Sykes-Picot agreement is falling apart, which is an interesting phenomenon. That is a century. But, the Sykes-Picot agreement was just an imperial imposition that has no legitimacy; there is no reason for any of these borders — except the interests of the imperial powers.

I think as far as Sykes-Picot is concerned, it is beginning to erode. Whatever happens in Syria — it's hard to imagine — but if anything survives, parts of Syria will be separated. The Kurdish areas are almost autonomous now and they are beginning to link up with the almost-autonomous parts of Northern Iraq Kurdish areas, and may spill over to some extent to south-eastern Turkey. What will happen in the rest of the country is hard to say."[i]

[Noam Chomsky]

"We must face the truth; Iraq no longer exists and Syria no longer exists whilst Lebanon is virtually a failed state and it is probable that Libya will be likewise. We now have the Islamic State, Al-Qaeda, Kurds, Sunnis, Shia and Alawites in what was previously called Syria and Iraq."[ii]

[Michael Hayden, former Director of the CIA]

CONTENTS

PREFACE

The year 2016 marks 100 years since the Middle East was carved up by the Sykes-Picot agreement. Today the Middle East is in disarray; chaos, anarchy and instability characterise the region. This has been the story of the Middle East for the last 100 years, a period in which many of the nations in the region were conceived and eventually created out of thin air. On the centennial anniversary of the Sykes-Picot agreement many misconceptions, stereotypes and outright lies still exist regarding the Middle East, so much so that I felt compelled to dispel and clarify the air of misconception that clouds this complex region.

Oil, Gas, the Suez Canal, Islam, Sunni-Shia and history are all reasons why so much is written about the region. There is no shortage of books, reports, articles and other media trying to understand the Middle East. However, much of this literature looks at the region with preconceived positions which only add to the confusion about the region rather than clarify it.

External interference and influence is seldom given attention and is one of the key reasons the region continues to be marred in chaos. It was not the people of Jordan, Syria, Saudi Arabia or Iraq that determined their borders but the governments of Britain and France. It was not the people of Egypt who concluded the 1979 peace treaty with Israel, but their unelected leader Anwar Sadat. It was however Britain, France and the US who have maintained cordial relations with the region's dictators, autocrats, unelected elite and monarchs despite the oppression of their own people. The ruling elites in the Gulf States and Jordan owe a great debt to Britain who brought them to power and maintained them ever since.

The rulers in the Middle East from Gamal Abdul Nasser to

9

Yasser Arafat to Bashar al-Assad and the Saudi monarchs have maintained the status quo that Sykes-Picot created. Sykes-Picot aimed to divide the Muslim world. It aimed to create new nationalities in the hope that weaker and smaller states would no longer be a threat to the west. The rulers in the region one after the other protected this architecture, and was rewarded with aid, defence deals and political cover. This legitimacy has been afforded by Western governments to dictators, monarchs and autocrats in the region. Their justification is a false pretext, namely that the general public need a "strong leader" to maintain law and order. These figures and institutions which represent the Middle East ruling class are themselves deeply corrupt, inefficient and rule with brutal means. In reality, their only purpose is to further give life to the system that was established by the Sykes-Picot agreement.

There are still many who want to reshape the Middle East based upon their own worldview- they view the Middle East just as those who did before them as their own geopolitical playground. Shaped by their own Western version of history they believe, rather arrogantly, that all peoples would choose democracy, secularism and freedom given the opportunity. The articles, reports and books by these individuals and organisations examine the region and seek to influence policy and political activity in it according to their preconceived ideas about what constitutes progress. They do this, regardless of whether or not what they desire for the region actually agrees with the values and aspirations of the people that live within it. Furthermore, there are still a significant number of such individuals and organisations that accept vastly outdated orientalist preconceived notions that are so far removed from the reality on the ground that it makes their position farcical and untenable.

A mere 7% of the Middle East is not Muslim.[iii] And yet, the Muslim view on their own region is seldom given airtime or coverage. On the Centennial anniversary of Sykes-Picot, the Middle East and the people of the region face numerous, multifaceted and unprecedented trends which will impact its 317 million inhabitants. If these trends can be harnessed for the benefit of the people of the region, the next 100 years will be very different to the last 100 years. Accordingly, U.S. think tanks and policy makers are analysing how they can benefit from these emerging trends and maintain their foreign policy grip on this strategic region. Furthermore, British and French policy makers are also looking to maintain the influence they have for the foreseeable future by utilising these trends.

Despite Islam being indigenous to the region, and the fact that democracy and liberal values are a European export, Islam is viewed as the problem and something that is holding the region back. Islam is considered the cause of fanaticism, extremism and dogmatic division amongst the people. The U.N. Arab Human Development Reports have found there are less than 53 circulating newspaper copies per 1,000 Arab citizens, compared with 285 per 1,000 in developed countries. There are 18 computers per 1,000 people in Arab countries, compared with a global average of 78.3 per 1,000. Access to a telephone line in the region is barely one-fifth that of developed countries. Just 4.4 translated books per 1 million people were published between 1980 and 1985. The corresponding rate for Hungary was 519 books per 1 million people, and in Spain, 920 books. The number of scientists and engineers working in research and development is 371 per 1 million people, compared with the global average of 979. The production of literary and artistic books in 1996 did not exceed 1,945 books, representing just 0.8 percent of world production. Religious books account for 17% of the total.[iv] It is these issues that give rise to many in the West calling for a "reformation" (another European construct) in the Middle East. Much of the literature written on the Middle East looks at the region from a liberal lens and through the history of the West. The fact that Islam revived the Arabs and the region, and that the removal of Islam precipitated the decline of the people as a power, is seldom acknowledged.

I have studied the intricacies of the Middle East for over a decade and have travelled across the region. Throughout this period I have written, researched, analysed and proposed policies for the Middle East. On this Centennial anniversary of the Sykes-Picot agreement, that created the Middle East, an interpretation of the past is needed; one which is free from the baggage of western history and experience.

This book analyses the emerging trends the Middle East will need to navigate and where the region stands after being constructed 100 years ago. This book is, however, more than a history book. It looks at some key historical events – the effects which remain with the region today and presents an alternative to the conventional and sometimes simplistic assumptions of the region.

INTRODUCTION

100 years ago in 1916 there was no place called Jordan, Iraq did not exist and Syria as we know today had not been invented yet. Anyone asking for directions to Saudi Arabia would have been met with some confusion as there was no place on the planet with such a name because the tribe with the name had not yet risen to power. 100 years ago, there was no nation called Lebanon, there was just a mountain range by that name. There were no Jordanians, Iraqis or Lebanese, these nationalities simply did not exist.

The major powers of the day – Britain, France, Germany, Russia and Austria-Hungary were slugging it out in WW1 from July 1914. After the German march on Paris came to a halt, what became known as the Western Front settled into a battle of attrition, with a trench line that would change little until 1918, when the war finally ended. However, it was events in the East, i.e. Russia that would change the Middle East forever. A show of national unity had accompanied Russia's entrance into WW1, with defence of the Slavic Serbs, the main battle cry. Tsar Nicholas II presided over a backward nation by pretty much every standard at the time, but saw the emergence of a powerful Germany as a strategic threat. However, military reversals and the Tsar's incompetence soon soured much of the population's view towards him. Inept Russian preparations for war and ineffective economic policies hurt the country financially, logistically and militarily. By February 1917, public support for the Tsarist regime had virtually evaporated and with troops refusing to fire on rioting crowds in St. Petersburg, Emperor Nicholas II was overthrown, the Russian government collapsed and three centuries of Tsarist rule come to a bloody end.

By November 1917 the Bolshevik Revolution in Russia was in full swing and the ransacking of the foreign ministry brought to light an agreement by two civil servants from the British Empire and France, Sir Mark Sykes and Francois Georges-Picot. On behalf of their governments they had secretly agreed in clandestine meetings from November 1915 to May 1916 to carve up the Muslim world for themselves, despite it being under Ottoman leadership. In the middle of WW1, France and Britain were bargaining which pieces of the Middle East they would take as spoils of war. The pre-communist government had a copy of the agreement as it was promised the Caucuses including Turkish Armenia and northern Kurdistan, in another secret deal conducted with Britain.

Britain made numerous deals with various individuals, groups and tribes to revolt against the Ottomans in return for their own nation, power and leadership in a new future Middle East. The Sykes-Picot agreement was the only agreement that Britain stuck to despite promises made to numerous individuals. By drawing artificial lines in the desert sand, they created nations and borders that we refer to as the "Middle East" today. These borders and nations have managed to survive a century intact not because of nationalism, patriotism or loyalty but due to significant engineering, intervention, interference and handouts.

With the demise of both Britain and France as global powers after WW2, questions have continued on the sustainability of the Sykes-Picot borders in the Middle East. Nevertheless, in 2016 on the 100-year anniversary of the Anglo-French creation, the question is not on the legacy, but how this artificial construct has survived for so long.

Despite 100 years of volatility and instability, the self-immolation of Mohamed Bouazizi in 2010 at a marketplace in Tunisia spread to thousands on the streets in Cairo and evolved to hundreds of thousands demanding political change for the entire region. His desperate act created a sweeping wave, which crossed the artificial borders to Egypt then to Libya, Yemen and Bahrain until it engulfed most of the Middle East. Despite 100 years of being told how to live, govern and organise the people of the Middle East, the people erupted to take their destiny into their own hands. Contradicting every theory and opinion the world had of the region they even voted in Islamic parties. This was a critical moment in the regions 100 year history as it showed the people in the region rejecting socialism, nationalism, Arabism and all the other value systems that had previously been imposed upon them. Whilst these so called Islamic governments turned out to be even more secular than their predecessors the region remains in flux, 100 years on since Sykes-Picot.

The Middle East today stands at an epoch. The artificial architecture created by the British and French is tearing apart at the seams and no amount of stitching can keep it together. The Muslim rulers, who have long played the role of maintaining the artificial architecture in the Middle East, have lost their most potent weapon; fear. This was their only method of maintaining Sykes-Picot as well as themselves in power. Looking forward there are huge unprecedented demographic, economic, political, social, technological and geopolitical trends taking shape that will subsume everything standing in its way and sweep away those who try to maintain the status quo.

Today's rulers in the Middle East are the descendants of the Sykes-Picot creation 100 years ago and are not in power due to their track record or merit. They are all more interested in maintaining the status quo and securing their own power, rather than taking care of their people's affairs. Egypt, which is at the centre of the Middle East and one of the significant powers in the region, has a population of 90 million. A quarter of a century ago in 1980 the country's population was half of this at 45 million. The country's population is forecasted to exceed 121 million by 2050. All of this has been possible because between 2006 and 2012 there was a 40% increase in the number of births, this also means over a million people enter the country's workforce employment every year to jobs that do not exist.

Successive governments in Egypt have failed to develop any policies for this time bomb. This is a common pattern across the region.

In order to understand the present, the past needs to be evaluated. The actions, intrigues, plots and plans of the past have come to shape the Middle East today and understanding them will give us a better idea of the current situation of the region. To comprehend the Middle East of the future, an accurate assessment of the region today is necessary in order to place the emerging trends in their correct context.

This book looks to provide answers to a number of questions. How did the Muslims, led by the Ottomans, go from a global power to the sick man of Europe? Was the Sykes-Picot agreement a folly by the French and British empires and poor strategic planning? Or part of a carefully constructed plan to divide the Muslim world in order to control it? Does the Arab spring confirm the end of Sykes-Picot and a new dawn for the people of the region? What are the most important emerging trends going forward? What do these mean for the region and beyond? What myths exist of the region which are simply untrue and upon closer scrutiny, do not stack up to the facts?

Adnan Khan
18th July 2015 CE
13th Ramadan 1437 AH

THE 'SICK MAN OF EUROPE'

On the 3rd March 1924 the Caliph, Abdul-Mejid II earned the title of the last Caliph of the Muslims. He was bundled into a car with a suitcase of clothes and money and exiled from Turkey never to return. For the Muslim world, even today, 1924 holds great significance as over thirteen centuries of Islamic rule that began with the Prophet Muhammed ﷺ himself, back in the 7th century, was forcefully brought to an end. Siding with Germany in WW1 was a disastrous policy, but the writing was on the wall for the Ottomans well before Yugoslav nationalist, Gavrilo Princip, shot and assassinated Archduke Franz Ferdinand of Austria, heir to the throne of Austria-Hungary Empire on 28th June 1914 in Sarajevo.

The term 'sick man' was used to describe the declining situation of the Ottomans by Tsar Nicholas I of Russia in 1853. The Ottoman territories were being swallowed by rival world powers and its debts were out of control due to a series of catastrophic wars. Nicholas I of Russia described the Ottomans as:

> *"a sick man – a very sick man, a man who has fallen into a state of decrepitude, or a sick man … gravely ill.'*

The Ottomans had drastically lost control of its economy, its political prowess had all but disappeared and it had turned into a subordinate state being swallowed up by the European powers who were also trying to carve out a new Middle East. In a period of 300 years things had completely fallen apart for the Ottomans. Although the Ottomans had taken Constantinople over 200 years earlier in 1453, and no doubt this was a seminary event in history, it was developments that began in the 1600's that are central to what would take place in the 20th century.

WHAT WAS THE INTERNATIONAL SITUATION IN THE 17TH CENTURY?

Europe was Christian, the region where Jesus Christ was worshipped. Christianity had a long and tumultuous history by this point. However, the adoption of Christianity by the Roman Empire is what preserved it on the continent. The adoption of Christianity by the Roman Empire was in order to build a common mentality and loyalty among citizens. Despite this, Christianity could not sustain or preserve the Empire. In 476 CE, Romulus, the last of the western Roman emperors, was overthrown by the Germanic tribes. The demise of the Romans as a force meant the Church was able to dominate much of Europe. The Eastern Roman Empire, better known as the Byzantine Empire, would last for another 1000 years until the Ottomans conquered it in 1453. The Fall of Roman Empire in Rome left a power vacuum which the Church filled as the sole identifiable central authority and enabling it to dominate Europe. The dominance of the Church meant that all affairs of life had to conform to the dogma of the Church. This caused countless problems given that the Bible, which the Church used as its authoritative text, only dealt with very limited matters. This meant there was a huge gap in Europe's political landscape and subsequently was an area of constant conflict of interests between Kings, feudal barons and priests.

Christianity ruled Europe, but Islam dominated a far larger region stretching from Morocco in the West to Indonesia in the East and Central Asia in the north to as far south as Zanzibar in Africa. Islam had created one of the most widespread civilisations in history, despite periods of instability and rival Muslim empires. A western critic once wrote that a visitor from Mars in the 16th century would have probably concluded that the world was on the verge of

18

becoming Muslim. With Muslim empires in the Indian sub-continent in the East, the Safavid dynasty in the centre and the Ottoman Empire in the West, this would have been the opinion of every visitor, not just from Mars.[v]

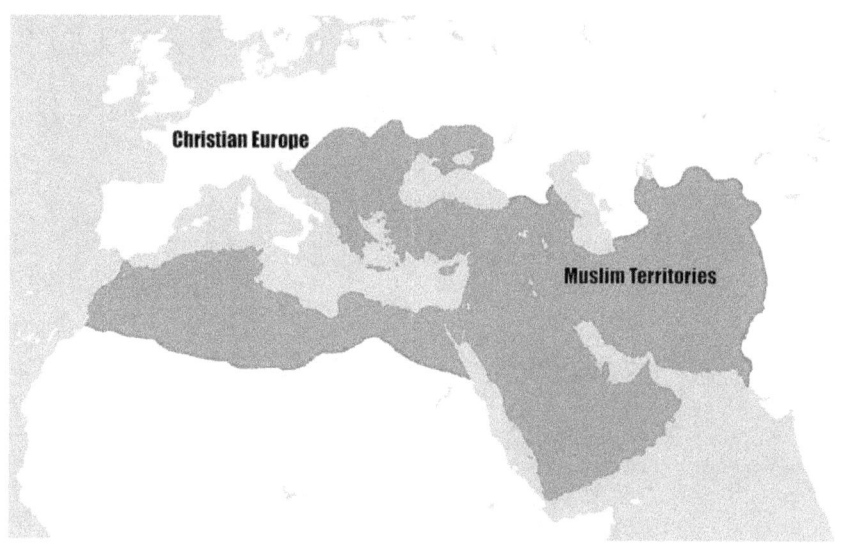

Christianity existed in the Arab territories before the Prophethood of Muhammad (saw). Nestorians and other Christian denominations were already present, and as the two religions grew it was inevitable that there would be a contest for power; confrontation between Islam and Christianity emerged from the outset. Christianity ruled over the Northern Mediterranean shore, whilst Islam dominated the Southern one. In 711, the Berber general turned Muslim, Tariq ibn Zayid, began the conquest of Spain. After occupying Spain they turned north into France across the Pyrenees. In the 732 Battle of Tours, a defining battle, Charles Martel defeated the Muslim advance and forced them back behind the mountains and confined the Muslims to the Iberian Peninsula. This battle was a defining moment in history because Europe was politically divided. All western historians agree the Muslims would have conquered the rest of Europe. Edward Gibbon the 18th century historian remarked:

"If Charles Martel had been defeated at Tours-Poitiers, the Qur'an

19

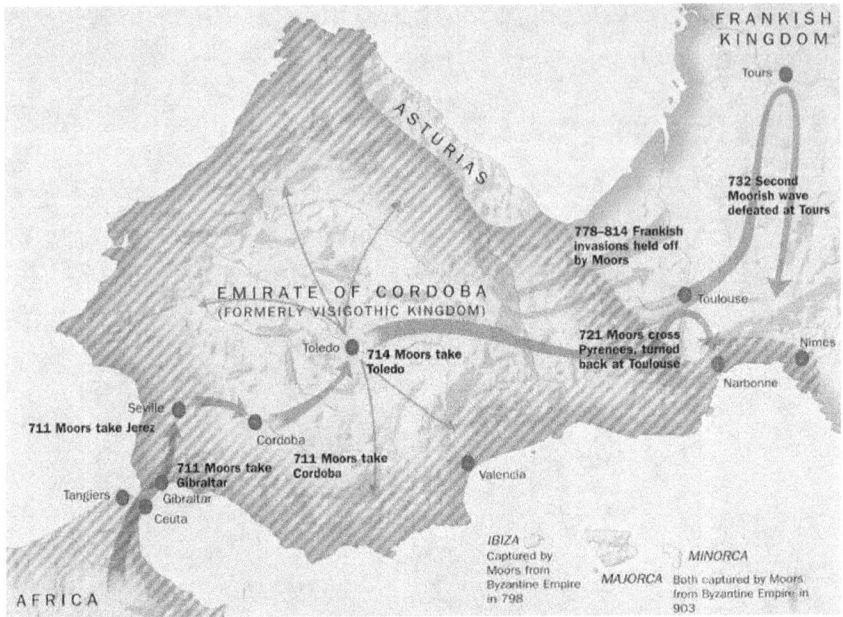

Islam's major encounter with European Christians was with the Crusades during the 12th century. Despite losing Jerusalem for 88 years, it was liberated by the forces of Salah ad-Din in 1187 in the decisive Battle of Hattin, which effectively took the wind out of the Crusades. Through to the end of the 13th century, groups of Crusaders sought to gain ground in the Holy Land through short-lived raids. When the Mamluks became the leaders of the Muslims in 1260, Egypt with its war economy halted the advance of the Mongols, an invading force led by Genghis Khan and his descendants. Under the Sultan Baybars, the Mamluks demolished Antioch in 1268, prompting Louis IX to set out on another Crusade which ended in his death in North Africa. By the end of the 13th century, the Mamluks had provided the final reckoning for the Crusaders, toppling the coastal stronghold of Acre and driving the European invaders out of Palestine and Syria in 1291. The Europeans never forgot this humiliation even when they returned over 700 years later during WW1.

OTTOMANS

When the Ottomans conquered Constantinople in 1453, the Byzantine capital, it represented a mortal threat to Europe. The fall of Constantinople led to the Ottomans conquering much of Christian Europe. This remained the trend into the 17th century.

The Ottomans in the 13th century first took control of some lands in what is today western Turkey. At that time, they were on the northern frontier of the Abbasid Caliphate with the Byzantine Empire. The Muslim world then was ruled by many competing dynasties and military elites such as the Fatimid's in Egypt, who were replaced by the Mamluks. The Abbasids retained the Caliphate but the actual power was in the hands of their military, the Seljuks. The Ottomans were one of the many bands of Turkmen horsemen who began to come into the Islamic lands as a result of the Mongol invasions in the 13th century. These Turkmen warriors, who had converted to Islam, were sent to the frontiers of the Caliphate by the Seljuks, who themselves were of Turkish origin. This was partly because it was feared that they would have a destabilising effect on the society, due to their wildness. But also, they had excellent fighting skills and zeal, which the Seljuks wanted them to apply along the frontier with the Byzantines. The House of Osman proved to be one of the most successful of these bands, taking many towns and villages from the control of the Byzantines, they then unified the other ghazis under their banner.

The position of the Ottomans, on the frontier of the Islamic lands, bordering Europe, had a great influence on their strength. Regional emirs in other areas immersed themselves in petty local rivalries and disputes amongst themselves. The Ottomans kept the momentum of Jihad going as they continued to attract those who wanted to fight for Islam, or perhaps for booty, from across the Islamic world. So from the early rulers such as Osman Ghazi, Orhan

Bey and Murad the Exalted, the Ottomans had retained the Jihadi characteristics that would propel them forward for centuries.

The Ottomans constructed a regime that was dedicated to propagating Islam via Jihad. Whilst much

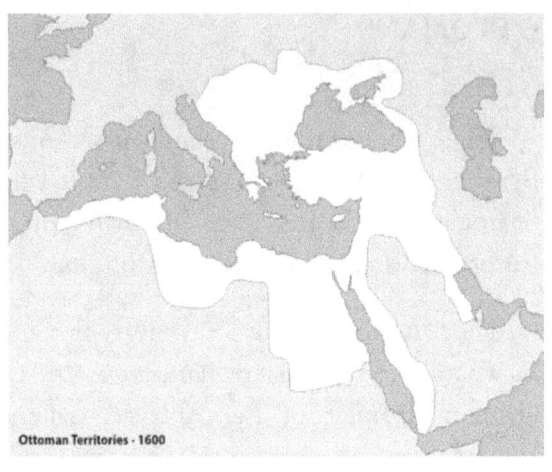

Ottoman Territories - 1600

propaganda exists about Jihad today, Jihad from an Islamic perspective is the removal of the obstacles which prevent the propagation of Islam, not the indiscriminate slaughter of people. The Ottomans would go to war every year, beginning their campaign each year on 23rd April. Each campaign would usually last for five months and the entire palace would move with the Sultan including key officials such as the "Sadr-i-A'zam," the second in charge. The falconers, gardeners, dog handlers and the oarsmen of the palace would return to their regiments. The head gardener of the palace would resume his seasonal role as executioner, for those causing disorder during the march to war. The young servant boys of the palace formed the Sultan's personal guard. There was even a special regiment for the insane, called the 'deli,' which would be used as human battering rams or to form human bridges during sieges. Georgius de Hungaria, was captured by the Ottoman army in 1438 and remained with them for 20 years. Upon his return to Christian Europe, he described the Muslims' eagerness for Jihad in the following way:

"When recruiting for the army is begun, they gather with such readiness and speed you might think they are invited to a wedding and not to war. They gather within a month in the order they are summoned, the infantry separately from the cavalrymen, all of them with their appointed chiefs, in the same order

22

which they use at encampments and when preparing for battle ... with such enthusiasm that men put themselves forward in place of their neighbours, and those left at home feel an injustice has been done to them ... Those who die in war like this are not mourned but are hailed as saints and victors, to be set up as an example and given high respect."[xii]

In comparison to this, when the European rulers wanted to wage war, they would have to spend months, sometimes years bribing and pleading with their barons and dukes.

One of the key factors in the strength of the Ottoman caliphate, as a rising power in the world, was that it took Islam as a basis and upon this basis it established institutions to guarantee success. In every era the Ottomans were able to creatively establish institutions in the face of changing environments. Two of the main institutions were the army and the bureaucracy. As early as Murad I, in 1365, the Ottomans recognised the importance of transforming the army into a solidly grounded professional institution. Until that point, under Osman himself and then Orhan, the army had been organised on a clan basis; when the Ottomans took control of lands held by other rival emirs, they would incorporate the defeated army into their own ranks. These armies would form and disband as the need arose, returning back to farming or trading, or whatever else might have been their preferred pastime post-war. Sultan Murad I, instituted the new troop, or Jeni Ceri, who we know in English as the Janissaries, a standing infantry that would only admit into its ranks captured non-Muslims. These troops would be trained and then, after converting to Islam, they would be fully enrolled into the Janissary order. The usual source for these troops was the captured nobles of whichever people the Ottomans had defeated, especially taking their young sons as slaves. For centuries onwards from this time, they were the only standing army in Europe, a professional corps of fighters always prepared and ready for battle. The upkeep for the Janissaries was paid for through the basic state revenues. This meant that the Ottomans would always have the advantage of being able to immediately deploy their forces, at no extra cost. In contrast, the feudal states of Europe would have to impose hefty taxes on their peasant population in order to generate the needed funds.

Another vital aspect that has tremendous importance when we speak of the benefits of the standing army was that it cemented the power of the Caliphates legitimate authority. If we look to the Europeans, their kings, dukes or other potentates would have to rely on their nobles to provide troops. When this wasn't sufficient, they would have to hire foreign forces or enter into pacts, treaties and other political agreements that could all in themselves lead to more of a threat than the menace of the Ottomans army itself. On the other hand, the Sultan could count on the fact that the Janissaries had no loyalty to anyone other than himself. So the Caliph had no rivals or other centres of power to placate because his authority in the Caliphate was absolute. This led to continued political stability in the Caliphate and gave the Caliph the ability to engage in long term plans to expand power.

In 1432, Sultan Murad II, introduced the *devshirme* or boy-tribute system. According to this system a tribute officer would set out across the Balkans and Greece, and from the villages a number of young boys, usually less than a handful from each village, would be taken for training. These youths were effectively the Sultan's personal slaves; they were trained physically and put through an education system that would enable them to proceed into the state's administrative system. Part of their education was conversion to Islam. Those who showed good intellectual aptitude would proceed on this track, while those were not considered suitable for administrative tasks would be drafted into the Janissaries, or other positions serving the Sultan.

Leaving aside the issue of the Caliphate taking its own citizens as slaves, which was a deviation from Islamic texts, there were certain benefits that could be obtained by having such a system for bringing officials into high office. Firstly, the Caliphate could constantly guarantee that the only basis for people to obtain posts in the Caliphate was the personal qualities that shone through under examination. These officials were literally the best of the best. Alongside that, the administrative system was only open to slaves of the sultan, since the sons of all officials were Muslims, they could not be enslaved. Hence, it could be assured that any official, no matter what post he reached, would not be able to pass on all that he had earned, or try and get his son into power after him. Once again, this had the effect of not allowing power to be cemented in the hands of anyone other than the Sultan. The importance of this system cannot be underestimated. From the time of Muhammad al-Fatih in the 1450s, 34 of the next 36 *Mu'aawin Tafweedh* or grand *Wazeers* (second only to the Caliph himself), were converts to Islam, who had come through this same system.

A Flemish noble, Ogier Ghiselin De Busbecq, who served as an ambassador in Istanbul from 1554 to 1562 reported regarding this system, in memoirs of his time in the Caliphate: *"These are not our ideas; with us there is no opening left for merit; birth is the standard for everything; the prestige of birth is the sole key to advancement in the public service."*[xviii] So the Caliphate owed a great deal of its strength, in relation to the European states, to the fact that in terms of its administrative system, there was a rigid meritocracy. From 1453 to well into the 17th century the Ottomans were storming Europe. Sulayman the Magnificent conquered Belgrade in 1521 and evicted the Knights Hospitallers, remnants of the Crusades, from Rhodes in 1522. He smashed the Hungarians and its European allies at Mohács in 1526, besieged Vienna in 1529, and entered alliances in Europe with Francis I against the Habsburgs.

By the 17th century the Muslims controlled and dominated the silk trade routes and the Ottomans dominated the routes into the Mediterranean. Asia and Europe were linked by land and sea. Ships brought spices from India by sea and silk from China reached

Europe from land routes to Europe, but the sea and land routes terminated at Constantinople where another sea route made its way to Italian ports for further distribution of goods to the rest of Europe. The Caliph in the 10th century, who ruled from Cairo, founded the city as a trading hub in order to control the spice trade to Europe. It quickly became the single point were spices passing through the Red Sea were collected for shipping to the Mediterranean. The Ottomans, as the leaders of the Muslims, globally dominated the sea and land routes linking Europe with Asia also controlled the profits and with profits came political power. There were, however, events already taking place on the edge of Europe in the Iberian Peninsula (Portugal and Spain) that would change the global balance of power and the world forever.

NEW WORLD

Iberia was cut off from the rest of Europe by the Pyrenees and in effect was a self-contained land in the Atlantic. Muslims first came to Iberia in 711 when the forces of Tariq ibn Ziyad began the conquest of Europe. Within seven years, most of the Iberian Peninsula was under Muslim control. Parts of this land would remain dominated by Muslims for over 700 years. When the Umayyad's were overthrown and murdered in 750 in Damascus, a few survivors managed to reach Andalusia and the Umayyad Abd al-Rahman al-Dakhil ruled independently from there. Whilst Islamic Spain was strictly outside the fold of the Caliphate from this point onwards, it was nevertheless viewed by Christian Europe as Islamic rule. Although Andalus did not declare total independence from Caliphate in the Middle East, it was, nevertheless, ruled separately for most of its history.

By the mid-900s, Islam had reached its zenith in Andalus. Over 5 million Muslims lived there, making up over 80% of the population. A strong united Caliphate ruled the land and was by far the most advanced and stable society in Europe. The capital, Cordoba, attracted those seeking education from all over the Muslim world and Europe. By the 1000s, the Caliphate broke up and divided into numerous small states called "taifas". The Muslim taifas were disunited and susceptible to invasion from Christian kingdoms in the north. For the next 200 years, the taifas fell one by one to the Christian "Reconquista". By the 1240s, one kingdom remained in the south: Granada.

During the Reconquista, Muslim states fell one by one to Christian kingdoms invading from the north. The major cities of Cordoba, Seville, and Toledo fell from the 1000s to the 1200s. Only Granada was able to escape conquest by Christians in the 1200s. After the fall of Cordoba in 1236, the rulers of the Emirate of Granada signed a special agreement with the Kingdom of Castile, one of the most powerful Christian kingdoms. Granada had agreed to become a tributary state to Castile. This meant they were allowed to remain independent as the Emirate of Granada, but in exchange for not being invaded by Castile, they had to pay a yearly sum (usually in gold) to the Castilian monarchy. This created a detrimental situation for the Muslims of Granada as they paid regularly to strengthen their enemies. For over 250 years, Granada remained as a tributary state to the stronger Kingdom of Castile but surrounded by unfriendly Christian nations, Granada was constantly at risk of being exterminated. This all changed in 1469, when King Ferdinand of Aragon and Queen Isabella of Castile married. This united the two most powerful Christian kingdoms of the Iberian Peninsula. With a united front, the Christians set their sights on removing the last Muslims from the peninsula.

Granada experienced huge political upheaval. Muslim leaders and governors were commonly at odds and scheming different plans to undermine each other. Many of them were even secretly working with the Christian kingdoms in exchange for wealth, land, and power. But in 1483, one year into the war, the sultan's son, Muhammad, rebelled against his father and sparked a civil war in Granada just as Spanish forces began to attack from outside. Right after solidifying his rule over Granada, however, Muhammad was sent a letter by King Ferdinand that demanded he immediately surrender the city. Clearly, Muhammad realised too late that he had been just a pawn used by Ferdinand to weaken Granada. Muhammad's resistance was futile; he was forced to sign a treaty which gave over control of the city in November 1491.

In 1492, Spain's monarchs signed an edict which required Muslims to convert to Christianity and forced the Jews out of the country, the Muslims were also eventually expelled. From a geopolitical perspective Spain was now united under Spain's monarchs and became a more powerful land force than Portugal. As Portugal was smaller than Spain, it focused on becoming a sea power, whilst Spain the larger country that dominated the Iberian Peninsula needed to become a naval power. This competition between both countries kicked off the age of discovery. The Muslims controlling the region between Europe and Asia and the sea and land routes was a key factor that drove both the Spanish and the Portuguese in the age of discovery. Both nations needed to find ways to circumvent Muslim sea and land routes. Portugal started the process in 1434 and focused on going south around the southern tip Africa. The problem the Portuguese faced was if they sailed too close to the African shore, their boats would be captured by the Muslims. To probe south they would need to navigate further away from the coast, out of the reach of Muslims. In doing so the Portuguese discovered and seized Azores in the Atlantic – 900 miles off the coast of Portugal. The southern route paid off for the Portuguese when Vasco de Gama reached India in 1498. Once the new route to India was established by by-passing the Muslims and the Ottomans, the stage was set for centuries of European domination of India. Outflanking the Muslims around Africa was Prince Henry of Portugal's ultimate aim.

Christopher Columbus provided the Spanish with another option to bypass the Ottomans, which didn't require challenging the Portuguese route around the hump of Africa. Columbus argued India and China could be reached by going west. At the time people did not know how long it would take to reach the other side of the world and even if it was possible. Columbus originally proposed this to the Portuguese who rejected it but what the Spanish found was about to completely change the world order, as it was known at the time.

Despite the disappointment with his first voyage, the Spanish court funded others and what they discovered was far more than spices or sea routes – but the other half of the world. And when they encountered this new world it was filled with gold and silver. The Portuguese found a new route to somewhere that was already known, Columbus stumbled upon an unknown portion of humanity. Discovering this new humanity revolutionised European thinking. The Spanish encountered something for which there was no reference point

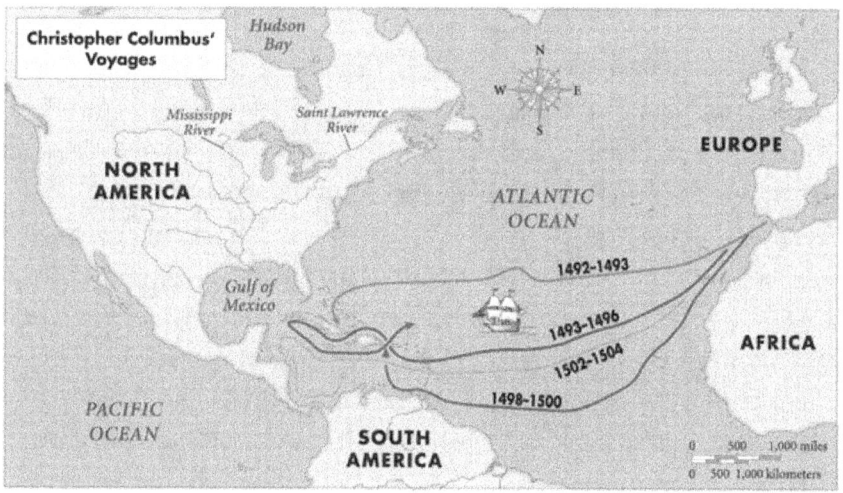

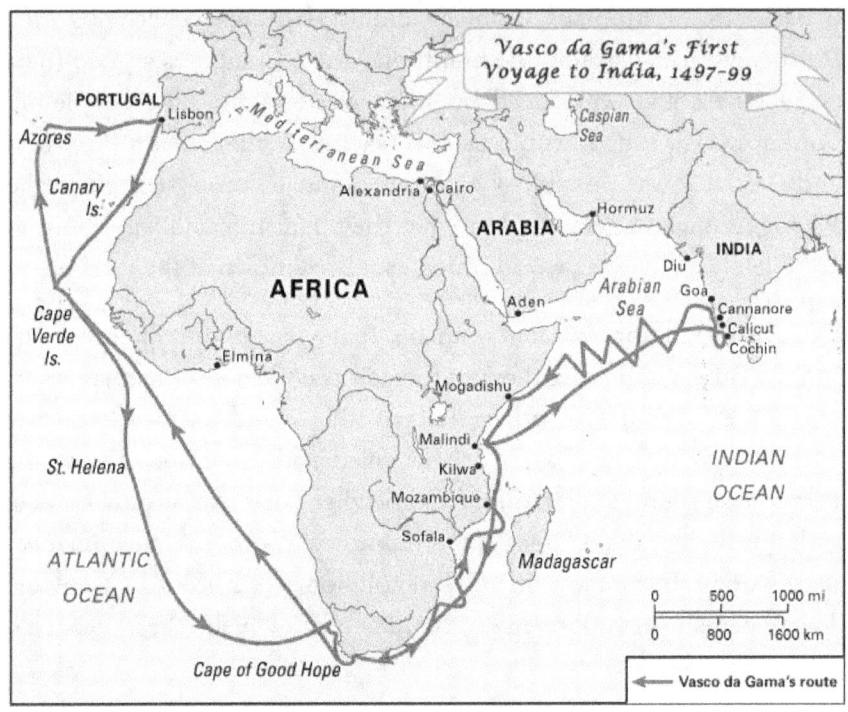

Vasco da Gama's First Voyage to India, 1497-99

These explorers gave way to the next wave of European men – colonialists. Spanish Conquistadors conquered the Incas in Peru, Balboa found Panama and become the first European to lead an expedition to have reached the Pacific from the New World. De Soto went north and discovered Mississippi and Hernán conquered Mexico and the Aztecs. Henry the navigator, Vasco de Gama, Columbus and Cortés are a small part of the conquest of the world by European powers, after the Spanish, the Portuguese, the French, English and Dutch all arrived in the New World. The discovery of the New World kicked off an intellectual awakening in Europe and challenged three certainties that had defined it. These intellectual blows all took place within a 51 year period from 1492 to 1543. Three main certainties were challenged: The Earth is the centre of the universe, Europe is the centre of the world and the Church is the centre of Europe.

Colonisation of the New World

ENLIGHTENMENT

The world being round was not unknown when Columbus undertook his voyage but until Columbus no-one had actually physically proven it was round. Subsequent voyages proved there were other civilisations in the world, including advanced ones that Europe had never heard of. These civilisations had never heard of Christianity and this challenged European thinking. The domination of the Church meant Christ was the saviour but how could a majority of humanity have not received such revelation?

In 1517, 25 years after Columbus, Martin Luther, the German priest nailed his 95 Theses to the door of the church initiating the protestant reformation. In one stroke this challenged the idea that Rome was the centre of Europe and shattered Christian unity. The Churches random practices laid the seeds of direct confrontation between the Church and society. The Reformation began as an attempt to reform the Roman Catholic Church by priests who opposed what they perceived as false doctrines and the selling and buying of clerical offices. Luther challenged the fact that the Bishops of Rome possessed no unique relation to God and that each person could approach on his or her own conclusions. People could read the Bible as individuals guided by their own conscious and the gift of God's grace, reach their own conclusions. Christianity for the first time was being challenged from within Europe itself.

Then in 1543 Copernicus demonstrated that the earth was not the centre of the universe but revolved around the sun. Copernicus argument was so powerful that it raised a question: If God created the world so that He might make men in His own image, why did He not place His masterpiece, the purpose of the entire universe, as its centre? Copernicus' insight proved how insignificant the human race was in the grand scheme of things. This challenged the very basis of

Christianity, that God gave his only son to men. The introduction of individual responsibility, conscious and doubt challenged Christianity and set the stage for a revolution in Europe that had endless consequences.

The Church represented God's word on earth and no individual aside from the Church was allowed to interpret it. Luther introduced the idea of conscious and the individual's right to study the word of God. All of this was taking place in the context of a technical revolution. The printing press had been invented and by 1500 there were approximately one thousand in Europe. Prior to this the written word was rare. With this development the Bible was available for all to read, and more importantly it was now available in the people's mother tongue and not just Latin. This undermined the authority of the Church completely. People could read the Bible rather than waiting for their visit to the Church and for some priest to interpret it for them. Europeans could now read the Bible and disagree on its meaning and break with each other and more importantly with Rome. Whilst the reformation started in Germany it quickly spread throughout the continent. Luther argued that the time of miracles ended with the Church's founding. Divine intrusion no longer interrupted the natural order of things. The world was predictable and stable – the laws of nature governed but the Bible dealt with the supernatural and not with nature. The laws of the universe, i.e. nature could not be studied via the Bible and this led to a revolution in science and the final nail in the coffin for Christianity.

In 1602, the English philosopher and statesman Francis Bacon, published the Great Instauration, where he laid out a systematic way of understanding knowledge – the scientific method. The deductive reasoning or logic that had dominated the middle ages gave way to observation, experimentation and evidence of the scientific method. Where dogma, superstition and faith dominated knowledge, scientific knowledge came to be based upon doubting everything. This doubt, thorough experimentation, was how knowledge would be measured. Bacon created a process where the world could be understood without recourse to God, where the world, universe and everything could be understood. Due to this the individual was elevated to the centre of the world. The scientific method initiated Europe's conquest of nature; the way humans moved, communicated, healed and learned was completely transformed. The scientific method naturally lent itself to the rapid development of technology too.

From 1650 to 1800, a revolution in human thinking took place. The discovery of the New World, the adoption and widening use of the scientific method, advances and proliferation of philosophy amongst the masses was leading to an inevitable clash with the authority of the Church. To preserve its authority, the Church took harsh steps against the emergence of such new ideas. Scientists were branded as heretics, infidels and satanic. In 1633, Galileo was forced to renounce his belief and writings that supported the Copernican theory of heliocentricism claiming the Earth circumvented the Sun. Instead, the Church adamantly maintained the flawed theory of geocentrism, which stated that the Sun circumvented the Earth. Other thinkers, such as Bruno, suffered even worse treatment at the hands of the Church. Bruno was imprisoned for 8 years while questioning proceeded on charges of blasphemy, immoral conduct, and heresy. He was eventually burned at the stake.

There is plenty of evidence that hundreds of thousands of women, alleged to be witches were brutally tortured, burnt and drowned. The response to this oppression from the people, especially the scientists, thinkers and philosophers was equally strong. Many began to highlight the contradictions of the Church and reformers such as Luther and John Calvin called for nothing less than the complete separation of the Church from the state. Desperate measures were taken by the Church to deflect the people's criticism, frustration and anger but these measures failed to halt the desire for change that had galvanised the masses. The Church realised that it could no longer remain dominant without reform. The eventual outcome of the struggle for power between the Church, on the one hand, and the scientists, thinkers and philosophers, on the other, was the complete separation of the Church from state. This compromise solution limited the authority of the Church to preserving morals in society and conducting rituals. It left the administration of worldly affairs to the people themselves. The Reformation led to the enlightenment period that bred secularism as a worldview and finally removed the arbitrary authority of the Christian church. This formed the basis of the secular liberal ideology and sparked the industrial revolution in Europe.

This state of affairs led to an intense intellectual revolution in Europe. European philosophers, writers and intellectuals made considerable efforts for comprehensive change in European ideas with the aim of uniting Europeans under secular liberal democratic thought. Many movements were established and played a great part in the emergence of new opinions about life. One of the most significant events that occurred was the change of the political and legislative systems to the nation state. The spectres of despotic monarchies were gradually replaced by republican systems based on representative rule and national sovereignty. This had the effect of triggering the awakening of Europe from its slumber. The industrial revolution was the centre of the European scene. There were numerous scientific discoveries and inventions springing from Europe. These factors all boosted Europe's intellectual and material progress. This material and scientific progress resulted in Europe finally ridding itself of its medieval culture.

Europe built its navies and began the conquest of the world. Europe became very rich, became engaged in very far-flung empire-building that redefined the human condition and became very good at making war. In short, Europe went from decline to the engine of the world. At home, Europe's growing economic development was exceeded only by the growing ferocity of its conflicts. Abroad,

Europe had achieved the ability to apply military force to gain economic progress. The brutal exploitation of wealth from South America and the thorough subjugation and imposed trading systems in places such as East and South Asia created the foundation of the modern order.

'Sick Man'

The global balance of power that had held for hundreds of years was changing and the Ottomans, who had dominated the global balance of power needed to adapt to this changing political landscape.

It is important to understand the role Islam played in reviving the Arabs before expanding from its original location to incorporate other people, cultures and even empires, eventually reaching the Ottomans. Unlike Christianity and specifically the Church, Islam has never been about superstition, dogma, the supernatural and faith. Islam from its very beginning encouraged people to think and ponder over the created world, universe and everything contained within them. The supernatural is a small component of the Qur'an. A large aspect of the verses of the Qur'an are dedicated to systems of society such as economics, governance, social issues, foreign policy, societal cohesion and law and order. These rules and solutions for society were codified by early Muslim scholars into Jurisprudence. Principles were also derived from these verses making these solutions timeless. So the fact that all citizens of the Caliphate have some basic rights such as food, clothing and accommodation, as well as education, security and health is not restricted to 7th century Arabia, but for all times and places. The fact that Islam allows non-Muslims their own places of worship, courts to deal with their disputes and permits them to eat their own food and dress accordingly is as relevant today as it was in the 7th century. Islamic solutions are timeless. Islam never mandated divine rules when it came to technical issues, administration and science and permitted the adoption of all such developments to progress society. This is why the significant scientific and technological achievements of the Caliphate have been recognised by non-Muslim historians, commentators and experts.

Prior to the age of discovery, Islam propelled the Ottomans. Externally, the Ottomans developed a robust and flexible military to spread Islam and maintain its domination of the Mediterranean. It developed institutions in order to achieve this. Internally the Ottomans institutionalised the Islamic position on non-Muslim citizens into the Millet system. It should be borne in mind that like most of Islamic history, the Muslim territories consisted mostly of non-Muslims and not just Muslims; the same situation prevailed with the Ottomans where non-Muslims represented well in excess of 60% of the population. Large communities of Orthodox Christians, Jews, and Catholics all lived in the Ottomans territories. The Ottomans constructed a system of religious pluralism, known as the Millet system, where each religious group was organised into a Millet, or nation. Each Millet was allowed to run by its own rules, elect its own leaders, and enforce their own laws on their people. For example, after the conquest of Constantinople in 1453, Sultan Mehmed II had the Orthodox Christian community of the city elect a new patriarch, who served as their leader. By not enforcing Islamic laws on non-Muslims in their private beliefs and practices, the Ottoman's ensured social and religious stability and harmony within its borders for much of its history. Contrary to this, throughout the rest of Christian Europe, religious freedom only began to take root in the 1700s and 1800s.

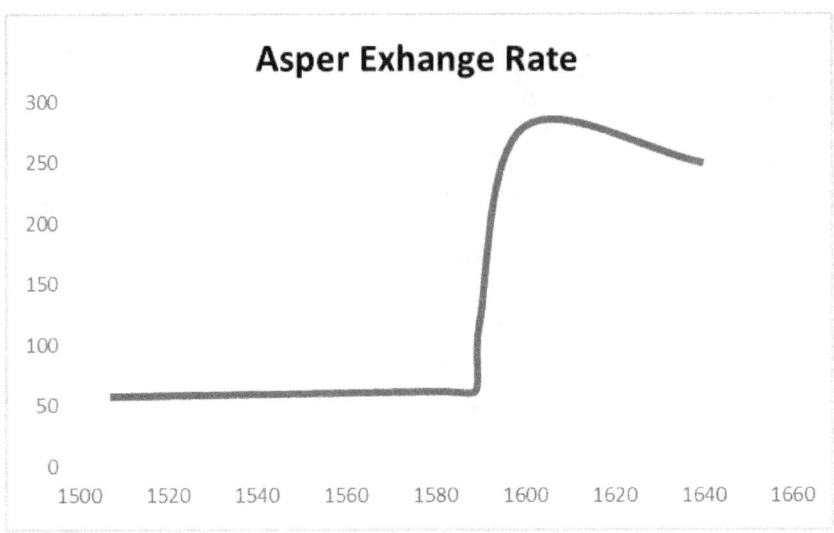

Asper Exhange Rate

Europe's conquest of the New World represented the first major challenge for the Ottomans. Spain, England and France were exploring and conquering the New World across the Atlantic and bringing back with them huge quantities of gold and particularly silver. The Ottoman economy was based on silver. Coins were minted in silver, taxes collected in silver and government officials were also paid in silver. The huge influx of silver coming from America drastically devalued the Ottoman currency and caused massive inflation. Before gold and silver made its way to Europe from the new world, 58 silver aspers, the Ottoman unit of currency, could buy one gold coin in 1507. 82 years later, in 1589, 1 gold coin cost 62 silver aspers, an inflation rate of only 7% over eight decades. By 1600, only 11 years later, the rate was 280 aspers to 1 gold coin, i.e. an inflation of around 350%. In 1580 when the New World gold and silver began to arrive in Europe, 1 gold coin could be bought for 60 silver oncs. 10 years later, in 1590, it would take 120 silver coins to buy one gold coin. And in 1640, it took 250 silver coins in order to buy one gold one. The asper coin itself was reduced in size so it contained less silver. Government salaries which had always been received on time started to be delayed. The inevitable result of this economic crisis was that the Ottoman territories began to see corruption appear at every level, especially the janissaries, who would roam the countryside looking for alternative sources of revenue. The impact of this economic crisis was much deeper as the Ottomans struggled to buy the new emerging tools of war. Thus, the treasures gathered for centuries by the people of the Aztec, Mayan, and Inca cultures were transported to Europe and provided the muscle that was to overwhelm the Ottomans. The circumnavigation around Africa to India had opened a new trade route to Asia, which meant the loss of their monopoly on the spice trade going to Europe, which hurt the Ottoman economy.

These economic challenges needed strong political leadership to tackle them especially given the rapid rate of change that was taking place in the world. Whilst the Ottoman leadership from its early era was extremely strong, creative and made bold decisions, this was mainly due to institutional factors that produced such leaders. This all changed at the dawn of the 17th century. From Uthman Ghazi, who began his rule around 1300, to Sulayman al Qanuni the Magnificent, who died in 1566, i.e. over a 260-year period, the first ten Sultans ruled the Ottoman Empire for an average of about 27 years. During this era, while the Sultan was the Caliph, his sons would be appointed as governors of provinces in Ottoman territories. In course of this time they would have teams of advisers to assist them, so by the time they grasped the keys of power, they were already experienced rulers. This produced a series of strong rulers who had a clear vision of what results they wanted to achieve and what they expected the Empire to be capable of. In contrast to this, the next ten Sultans from Salim II, Suleiman al Qanuni's son who took power in 1566, until Sultan Muhammad IV who was removed from power in 1687, ruled for an average of just 12 years as Sultan. Some of these rulers were in power for just a few months. None of these ten, prior to his rule as Sultan, had had any experience of governing or statecraft at all; so it was not surprising that the Empire, excluding some exceptions, was not able match its earlier glittering achievements. This set the pattern for the general level of the Sultans after this period until the demise of the

Ottomans. This shows that while ruling power can be made hereditary, the qualities that are needed to rule have to be learnt.

In an attempt to solve this problem, Sultan Ahmed I who reigned from 1603 to 1617, instituted a new system for choosing Sultans. Instead of a Sultan's son being a governor within the empire until their father died, they would stay at the palace in Istanbul until their time came. In most cases, they actually were not even allowed to leave the palace. This essentially made them prisoners until they became Sultans. While the intentions of Ahmed I were probably righteous, the effects of his policy were disastrous. Instead of Sultans coming to the throne with experience in governance and policy, they were usually ignorant of anything but the pleasures of palace life. They were completely incompetent as rulers of a powerful empire. The 300 year old tradition of Sultans being the powerful, resourceful, and able leaders of the Ottoman Empire was over. Ottoman Sultans came to see their job primarily as the commander-in-chief of the army. All Ottoman Sultans led their armies into battle and saw that as a central aspect to their job. However, Sultan Murad IV was the last Ottoman Sultan to lead his army into battle in 1638.

Unable to adapt to the new economic and political trends, the military of the Ottomans had long sustained their dominant position in the world, but with incompetent leaders and an economy in decline it was just a matter of time before the effects of this would impact the Ottomans military dominance. It should be very clear the Ottomans prided, above all else, their military prowess and strength in relation to their enemies.

While the defeat of the Ottoman army at the gates of Vienna is looked on as a pivotal event in European and Islamic history, it was not the first defeat the Ottomans had suffered. Their first military defeat was in the sea battle of Lepanto in 1571, in which the Ottoman fleet lost 200 of its 245 ships. Following their defeat at the gates of Vienna in 1683, the next 16 years were full of military defeats for the Ottomans. They lost Hungary to the Austrians. Venetian troops took the Peloponnese, today in Southern Greece. The Ottomans were again defeated at Mohacs by the Austrians in 1688, in 1689 they lost Belgrade, and then in 1690, they lost Nis. The grand *wazeer* Fazil Mustafa managed to regain Serbia for the Ottomans, dying in battle at Peterwaradin in 1691. But by 1699, the Ottomans were forced to sign the treaty of Karlowitz. This treaty between the Ottomans, the Austrians and the Russians was based on the principle of *uti posseditis,* meaning things should be left as they stood. So the Austrian Emperor was recognised as sovereign of Transylvania and most of Hungary. Poland regained Podolia, Russia kept the Sea of Azov and lands north of the Crimea. By the signing of this treaty, the Ottomans lost half of her lands in Europe. Throughout the 18th century, though the Ottomans went to war less often, the general pattern was of defeat rather than victory.

The Ottomans, after defeating the Russians in 1738, signed a peace treaty on the banks of the River Prut, in modern-day Bulgaria. After recapturing Belgrade from the Austrians in 1739, the Ottomans also signed terms of peace with them. This gave the Ottomans the breathing space necessary to reform and reinvigorate its administration and military structure. For over twenty years the Ottomans did not engage in any military campaign against any adversary. This was ample time to undertake the kind of radical reform necessary to rebuild the military and the administration, however, this opportunity was not utilised. In an earlier era, the Ottomans would analyse every military campaign in detail; every possible strategic or tactical lesson would be noted and incorporated into the next campaign. The Ottomans would also eagerly follow any developments in tactics or technology among the other powers and adopt them. As far as they were concerned in technical matters, war, tactics, science and technology there was no conflict in adopting from others. By the 18th century, the Ottomans had lost the incentive that drove such a way of thinking – carrying Islam to the world. It had also lost the capable thinkers who could undertake such analysis in order for any adoption to take place.

In 1768, the Ottomans re-opened hostilities with the Russians but quickly found that it had learnt or gained nothing through those twenty years of rest. After six years of war, the Russians had pushed them right back from north of the Black Sea to less than 100 miles from Istanbul. At one pass at Sumla, the Grand *wazeer* found that he had only 8000 troops between the advancing Russian troops and the road to the capital. The Ottomans were forced to accept peace negotiations on Russian terms. After negotiations were finished, the Russians delayed signing the treaty for four days so that it would fall on the anniversary of the treaty of 1711, erasing their historic humiliation.

In the Treaty of Küçük Kaynarca, signed on 21 July 1774, there were four main concessions yielded by the Ottomans to the Russians:

- The Crimean Tartars were given independence from the Caliphate, an independence that they, as Muslims loyal to the Ottomans, did not want. Ten years later, the Russians absorbed the Crimea into their empire.

- The principalities of Moldavia and Wallachia were returned to the Caliphate, but the Russians were given the right to make representations on behalf of their populations with the Ottomans.

- Russian ships were given the right to access the waters of the Caliphate, which meant that for the first time since Muhammad al-Fatih had opened Istanbul, foreign ships could enter the Bosporus.

- The Russians were given the right to make representations on behalf of a church, which would be built in Istanbul. A right, which they later claimed gave them the right to represent all Christians in the state.

This treaty had far-reaching implications for the Ottomans. It became clear to all that reform was an urgent issue if the Ottomans were going to survive in the face of the Russian threat. For the western powers, they viewed the treaty with alarm, because to them it meant the effective annexation of the Ottoman Caliphate by the Russians. It gave the Russians access to the Mediterranean and they feared it could render her a superpower. For this reason, the other European powers were eager to increase their influence over the affairs of the Ottoman Caliphate, so as to stand as a block to any strengthening of the Russian position, even at times rivalling each other.

The Ottomans military dominance declined because changes in European military tactics and weaponry in the military revolution caused the once-feared Sipahi cavalry to lose military relevance. The development of pike and shot and later linear tactics with increased use of firearms by Europeans proved deadly against the massed infantry in close formation used by the Ottomans. While European armies were constantly upgrading their artillery and firearms, the Ottomans let theirs stagnate, thus putting them at a disadvantage against their enemies. At the same time, Europeans were reviving the Roman concept of strict drill and discipline to create much more efficient and reliable armies. However, the Ottomans failed to adopt these techniques and as a result found themselves increasingly at a disadvantage when fighting against European armies.

The Ottomans had not really developed a clear conception of the relationship between their new position in the world, Islam and the particular administrative systems that they had developed in their rise to dominance. When times, methods and techniques changed, with the rise of Europe, the Ottomans needed to let go of such policies and adopt new ones for the new era but the Ottomans stuck to them rigidly.

The Ottomans humbled by military defeats and the accumulation of huge debts opened the doors to military and scientific experts from the west. It decided that one of the ways to reform was to start building modern infrastructure, for this it turned to those with capital such as France, England, Russia, Germany, and Austria, all of whom were vying for the spoils once the Ottomans collapsed. From this time onwards, the continued existence of the Ottomans was dependent on the sole assistance of different foreign powers. The introduction of military and scientific schools throughout the Caliphate increasingly led to the creation of Western-oriented elite, who held greater reverence for the works of Voltaire and Rousseau than At-Tabari and Ibn Katheer. A historian confirmed:

> *"Each loan granted was on condition of guarantees and security. Each province under the Ottomans became a country and each had its own banks, monopolies and controllers. Banks, railways, mining companies and forestry, gas and water works were all foreign built, run and owned. France had seen to it that the tobacco monopoly had been turned over to her in 1883 as well as the docks at Beirut and Constantinople (1890), Smyrna (1892), and Salonica (1896). In 1890 followed the rights to exploit natural resources at Heraklion and Salonica as well as running the Jaffa-to-Jerusalem Railway; in 1891 the Damascus-Homs and Mudanya-Bursa railway rights; in 1892 the rights to the Salonica-Constantinople Railway and in 1893 to the Smyrna-Kasaba Railway. The English had a healthy share in the "Ottoman Bank." Through the mediation of an Armenian, Calouste Gulbenkian, they obtained sole oil rights in Mosul in 1905. The Russians enjoyed various privileges, had secured the rights to all customs duties in Constantinople and in Black Sea ports. The Germans had secured the rights to free port docks at Haider Pasha (1899), railway shares and a municipal transport monopoly, and the docks at Alexandretta (1905). Through the operations of diverse companies the foreign powers sucked the wealth out of what remained of a much declined Ottoman empire. The share of the*

national income did not even flow directly into the Sultan's coffers but went to London, Paris, Viennese or Berlin banks, European capitalism were at its zenith and drank the blood of its victim.'[ix]

From these circumstances unfolded a ferocious struggle between the western powers over the Ottomans territories. Through their companies and outright occupation links were made with officials in the Ottoman hierarchy who were more loyal to London, Paris and Berlin than to the Sultan. These individuals and the western oriented elite saw reform as only through the wholesale adoption of western culture. Islam had been undermined as a system of society as the Muslims of the Ottoman Caliphate lost confidence in its applicability in the face of an emerging Europe and advances in technology and science.

If we really evaluate what happened to the Ottomans in terms of defeats and setbacks, the vast majority of its problems lay in the area of administrative reform and adoption of technology, matters which the Ottomans had been so proficient in learning before. What affected them was that they became complacent due to their strength in relation to the Europeans. For any people to be successful, its ideology must provide the constant impetus for improvement, even when it has reached the pinnacle of excellence. In the case of the Ottomans, a strange paradox occurred, in an empire built and based on a specific ideology i.e. Islam, which the people embraced as their creed. Accordingly, they would be considered to be a revived nation with the ability to face any issue. However, these people lost the capability to take this ideology as the basis for their solutions, thus, they fell into backwardness and decline. Decline was evident in its political and economic policies as well as its unfolding military impotence.

What made the decline of the Ottomans even more stranger was the fact that Islam, which it took as a basis for its legislation, foreign policy and its basic purpose, gave the Ottomans a clear position on science and technology. Islam which is based upon the Qur'an and Sunnah (the authoritative sayings, actions and consent of the prophet Muhammed (saw), primarily addressed human actions and categorised them into permissibility and prohibition amongst others. When it came to objects, technology, science and administration these are viewed as universal and thus are all permitted. These are seen in Islam as material objects that are permissible to be used in undertaking actions. Consequently, from an Islamic perspective the sword is an object that can be used to murder an innocent person, something expressly prohibited in Islam, or in the defence of Muslim land under an invasion, something permissible. How it may and may not be used is the realm Islam came to address; when it comes to objects, they are all permissible in origin. This is why there is no conflict between Islam and science and both have coexisted side by side, with Muslims throughout the ages taking advantage and excelling in this area. The Ottomans however, failed to unlock this position from the Islamic text after the era of Sulayman the Magnificent. The Ottomans viewed having a large cavalry when going to war as an Islamic obligation when the Europeans were developing large cannons, better artillery and more mobile forces. So the Ottoman forces were constantly obliterated at war with these new developments. They should have adopted these new developments as they were merely styles and means, which naturally change over time. Spreading Islam, defending the Islamic territories and creating an image of strength is what Islam obliged and this remains fixed and does not change according to time and place. How this is achieved is a matter of tactics, technology and strategy that inherently change over the course of time. Not delineating between the two, led to losses militarily, led to incompetent leaders and a faltering economy and in the end the questioning of Islam itself and eventually its abandonment.

By the turn of the 20th century, Europe was considered the centre of the world, a far cry from its position in 1600. Europe had been at peace for around 85 years since Napoleon attempted to conquer Europe. The enlightenment values of science, doubt, individualism, representative rule and secularism had spread far and wide. Economic growth was spectacular and technological progress at this point was astonishing. The Europeans had intellectually, ideologically and from an industrial perspective defeated the Muslims, the Ottomans, and the Mughals of India had also been removed from power. Europe had colonies totalling 25 million square miles. Britain, the global superpower at the time, ruled 15 million of those. Belgium controlled the Congo. Holland governed millions of people in Indonesia and France had its own empire in Africa and Indochina. The Europeans also informally controlled Egypt and China too.

Despite this, an extremely weak Ottoman state still remained within Anatolia and much of the Middle East. European powers had armed and funded many a nationalist movement and independent movements in the Balkans which had all but left the Ottoman Empire. The biggest challenge Britain, France and Russia faced in completely destroying the Caliphate was not the military capabilities of the Ottomans but the competition and differences on dividing the spoils amongst each other. Britain had for some time propped up the Ottomans from completely collapsing as much of it would have likely ended up in Russian hands. However, WW1 presented Britain with the opportunity to finally occupy Istanbul and destroy the Ottoman Caliphate.

German reunification in 1871 led to the rapid development of the nation both industrially and militarily. Germany literally emerged on the international scene overnight and created a shock to the global order at the time. Very quickly the newly unified Germany became larger, wealthier and more populous and set its sights on challenging the global balance of power. Overrun by France in the Napoleonic wars (1800 – 1815), these competing states were transformed by Prussia into a unified military power by the iron will of its chancellor, Otto von Bismarck. After unifying these states into a united Germany by 1871, Germany turned its army on Europe's traditional powers. Germany calculated that its economic, political and military ascent will make its rivals choose war – mainly Russia and France. The solution for Germany was rather than wait for its neighbours to invade, Germany would pre-empt war by initiating one at a time and place of its own choosing, rapidly destroying France and dealing with Russia at its own leisure. The war the Germans envisioned was developed by Field Marshall Von Schlieffen and came to be known as the Schlieffen plan. Though the actual hostilities of WW1 began in September 1914, this plan was formally adopted in 1905.

THE OTTOMAN EMPIRE, 1798-1923

AUSTRO-HUNGARIAN
EMPIRE
Autonomous-1817,
independent-1878

ITALY

BESSARABIA
To Russia-1878

BOSNIA -HERZEGOVINA
Annexed by Hungary-1908

ROMANIA *Autonomous-1859,*
independent-1878

MONTENEGRO
Independent-1878

SERBIA

BULGARIA *Autonomous-1878,*
independent-1908

ALBANIA
Independent-1912

GREECE
Independent-1830

TURKEY

ARMENIA
Independent 1918-20

TUNIS
French protectorate-1881

CRETE
To Greece-1898

SYRIA

Mediterranean Sea

PALESTINE
British occupation-1917,
British mandate-1920

IRAQ

TRIPOLITANIA
To Italy-1911

ALGERIA
French

NEJD
Under Saudi family
from 1746, subdued
by Egypt-1812-1820,
Saudi control over
most of Arab
peninsula
established by 1926

FEZZAN
To Italy-1911

EGYPT
Independent dynasty under
Muhammad Ali-1805, occupied
by Britain-1882, British
protectorate-1914

FRENCH WEST
AFRICA

——	Ottoman Empire, 1798
▨	Lost by 1886
▨	Lost by 1914
⌁	Frontiers, 1914
▢	Lost by 1920
▢	Ottoman Empire under the Treaty of Sevres, 1920
▬▬	Turkey under the Treaty of Lausanne, 1923

Red Sea

ANGLO-EGYPTIAN SUDAN
Ruled from Egypt-1820,
indigenous rule under Mahdist
regime-1882, Anglo-Egyptian
condominium-1898

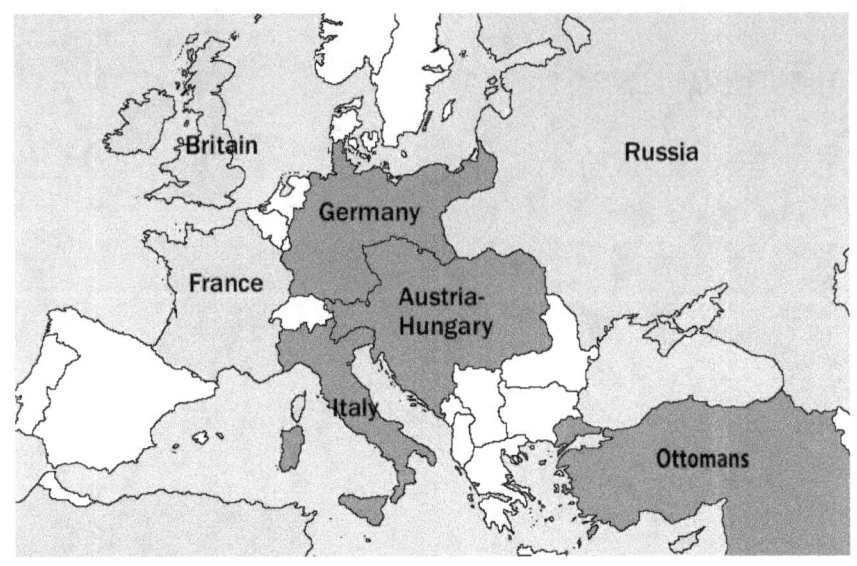

When Austria-Hungary declared war on Serbia in 1914, it was effectively a German satellite state. Germany then mobilised its huge army to invade Belgium and Luxembourg before moving towards France. WW1 had begun. The Ottomans realised they could not remain on the side-lines and would eventually be swallowed up by the victors. Sensing the emergence of a powerful Germany, the Ottomans had cordial relations with Germany ever since it unified in 1871 and believed siding with it would allow it to maintain its territories and possibly regain some lost ones. Whilst WW1 in origin was not the Ottomans war it, nevertheless, entered the war on the side of Germany. Ottoman support was critical for Germany because as the western front settled into a battle of attrition, Russia on the Eastern front had been annihilated and desperately needed weapons, ammunitions and war material from Britain. The Ottomans were able to cut the Mediterranean off for these supplies as it sat in between Russia and Britain. These actions by the Ottomans led to the Gallipoli and Mesopotamia campaigns by Britain. By 1918 Britain and France occupied Istanbul and a variety of treaties were imposed upon the Ottomans which required the dismembering of all its territories. The dismembering of the Muslim world had been a British strategy well before WW1.

The British strategy had been to make numerous agreements with anyone and everyone in order to weaken the Ottomans and justify taking its territory as spoils of war. British officials had made promises to the Zionists in creating a homeland for them. The establishment of a Jewish homeland had been proposed by British Prime Minister Henry Bannerman in 1906:

> *"There are people (the Muslims) who control spacious territories teeming with manifest and hidden resources. They dominate the intersections of world routes. Their lands were the cradles of human civilisations and religions. These people have one faith, one language, one history and the same aspirations. No natural barriers can isolate these people from one another ... if, per chance, this nation were to be unified into one state; it would then take the fate of the world into its hands and would separate Europe from the rest of the world. Taking these considerations seriously, a foreign body should be planted in the heart of this nation to prevent the convergence of its wings in such a way that it could exhaust its powers in never-ending wars. It could also serve as a springboard for the West to gain its coveted objects."[ix]*

In 1917, British foreign secretary Arthur Balfour merely made public the British position to Walter Rothschild, 2nd Baron Rothschild, a leader of the British Jewish community, in what came to be known as the Balfour Declaration:

> *"His Majesty's government view with favour the establishment in Palestine of a national home for the Jewish people, and will use their best endeavours to facilitate the achievement of this object."*

So the creation of a Jewish homeland and the purpose it would fulfil for the British Empire should be clear.

The second agreement Britain made was with Sharif Hussain, who was the Sharif of Makkah and Madinah, effectively in charge of the

Holy sites. His influence was virtually zero in the Muslim world and politically he had no clout with the Ottoman leadership in Istanbul. Britain needed the Arabs to revolt against the Ottomans in order to separate the Arab lands from the Ottomans. The McMahon–Hussain correspondence was an exchange of letters from July 1915 to January 1916 during WW1 between Sharif Hussain and Sir Henry McMahon, the British High Commissioner in Egypt, concerning the political status of lands under the Ottoman Empire. Sharif Hussain was looking to revolt against the Ottomans, an act of treason by all definitions, and the British would support this simply because it had its eyes on the Arab lands and in return Britain would make Hussain the leader over a new Arabia. The Arab Revolt began in June 1916, when an army of 70,000 men moved against Ottoman forces. They captured Aqabah and severed the Hijaz railway, a vital strategic link through the Arab peninsula which ran from Damascus to Medina. This enabled the Egyptian Expeditionary Force under the command of General Allenby to advance into the Ottoman territories of Palestine and Syria.

The third agreement was with Muhammad ibn Saud and later with his son, Abdul-Aziz. The relationship between the British and the Saudis are contained in official documents drafted by the British political officer in Bahrain in the early 20th century by Colonel Harold Richard Patrick Dickson (H.R.P. Dickson), which he dispatched to the British Foreign Office in London on October 26th, 1922. Four decades later, Dickson wrote his memoirs about the years in which he served as his government's envoy in Arabian Gulf countries, published in London in the 1951 book *Kuwait and Her Neighbours*. He highlighted Captain William Shakespeare, a British civil servant and explorer who mapped uncharted areas of Northern Arabia and made the first official British contact with Ibn Sa'ud. He was the military adviser to Ibn Saud from 1910 to 1915, and agreed the Treaty of Darin, of 1915 on behalf of the British government. But a series of correspondence that began in 1902 between Abdul-Aziz al-Saud and his father Abdel-Rahman, and the British political officer in Bahrain and the British political officer in Bushire, showed the goal of the letters was to woo the British and offer services to them. Britain's real goal was for Ibn Saud to harass its Ottoman enemy and their allies, the House of Rashid in Ha'il, and for his forces to be a proxy army through which Britain would fight the Ottomans in southern Iraq until British forces arrive from India. The British also had another demand, which was for Wahhabi clerics to issue a fatwa prohibiting Arab soldiers from serving in the Ottoman army and calling on them to defect. Dickson recalls that the Arabs were a majority in the Ottoman army in Iraq and the Levant.[xi] And indeed, the Wahhabi mufti found a pretext for such a fatwa, saying that Turkey had forged an alliance with the German infidels in the war, which is prohibited in the Quran. The fatwa helped immensely in Britain's propaganda. Accordingly, Sir Percy Cox offered knighthood to Emir Abdul-Aziz bin Saud on behalf of the British king, making him "Sir Abdul-Aziz bin Saud," a title used in British official documents for a few years thereafter. However, Abdul-Aziz himself never used the title, and wore the medal for one day so that the British may take a picture, and never wore it again after that. Though the British promised rule and supported two competing clans, this ensured Britain would end up on the winning side but as both clans received similar promises, one was going to lose out.

The fourth agreement and the one that was implemented was the Sykes-Picot agreement, named after French diplomat Francois Georges-Picot and his British counterpart, Sir Mark Sykes. The French and British diplomats negotiated on behalf of their governments a secret treaty that divided the possessions of the Ottoman Empire into zones of British, French and Russian influence. This secret understanding between Britain and France was to carve up the region after WW1, despite the other promises made. So in 1916, in the middle of the First World War, two men secretly agreed to divide the Middle East between them. The deal they struck, which was designed to relieve tensions that threatened to engulf the Entente Cordiale, drew a line in the sand from the Mediterranean to the Persian frontier. Territory north of that stark line would go to France; land south of it, to Britain. This pact formed the basis for the post-war division of the region into five new countries Britain and France would rule. One historian outlined the situation at the time, recounting the role European powers played between 1914 and 1922 in creating the modern Middle East:

> *"Massive amounts of the wealth of the old Ottoman Empire were now claimed by the victors. But one must remember that the Islamic empire had tried for centuries to conquer Christian Europe and the power brokers deciding the fate of those defeated people were naturally determined that these countries should never be able to organize and threaten Western interests again. With centuries of mercantilist experience, Britain and France created small, unstable states whose rulers needed their support to stay in power. The development and trade of these states were controlled and they were meant never again to be a threat to the West. These external powers then made contracts with their puppets to buy Arab resources cheaply, making the feudal elite enormously wealthy while leaving most citizens in poverty."*[xii]

The borders that were drawn were done so without regard for the wishes of the people living in the region. The borders were not based on any ethnicity, geographic points or religious boundaries – they were truly arbitrary. It is important to note that even today political borders in the Middle East do not indicate different groups of people. The differences between Iraqis, Syrians, Jordanians, etc. were entirely created by the French and British as a method of dividing the Arabs against each other. The European model of individual rights expressed to the nation states did not fit their cultural model. For the Arabs, the family — not the individual — was the fundamental unit of society, with loyalty to the Caliph. Families belonged to clans and clans to tribes, not to nations. The Europeans used the concept of the nation-state to express divisions between "us" and "them". To the Arabs, this was an alien framework which to this day still competes with religious and tribal identities. The states the

Europeans created were arbitrary, the inhabitants did not give their primary loyalty to them and the tensions within states always went over the border to neighbouring states. The British and French imposed ruling structures before the war and then a wave of coups overthrew them after World War II. 100 years ago lines were drawn in the sand and called borders. Kings were shipped in from outside the region and called governments. 100 years ago there was no such thing as a Jordanian or an Iraqi and there was no such place called Lebanon. What we have in the Middle East today was literally an invention from thin air. After negotiating the Treaty of Lausanne on July 24, 1923 allied forces started evacuating Constantinople on 23rd August 1923 and completed the task on 23rd September 1923. In response to this, protests were made in the House of Commons to the British Foreign Secretary Lord Curzon, for recognising Turkey's independence. Lord Curzon reportedly remarked,

"The situation now is that Turkey is dead and will never rise again, because we have destroyed its moral strength, the Caliphate and Islam."

During WW1, Mesopotamia became important as oil came to be seen as the strategic resource of the future. Sir Maurice Hankey, the powerful Secretary of the British War Cabinet, wrote to Foreign Secretary Arthur Balfour during the war's final stage, to argue that oil had become absolutely vital to Britain and that oil resources in Mesopotamia would be crucial in the future.

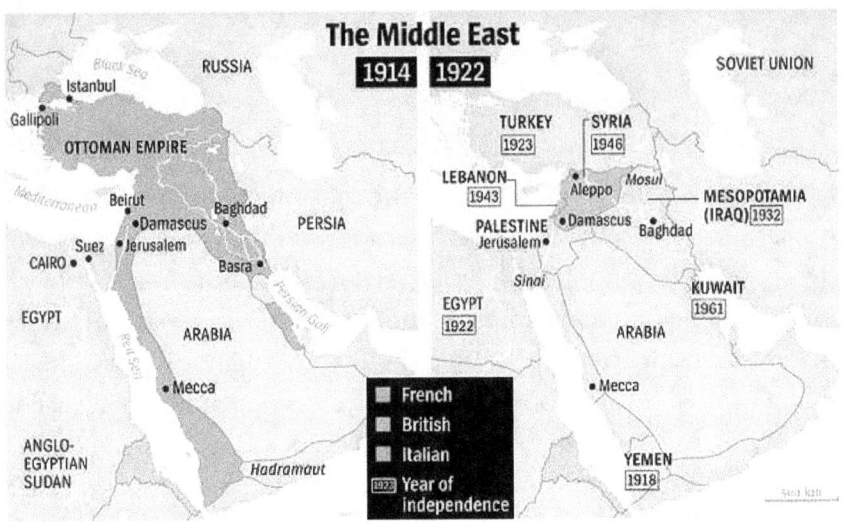

The Middle East 1914 1922

"Control of these oil supplies becomes a first-class war aim," Hankey said enthusiastically, as British troops closed in on Baghdad.[xiii] The British had ceded much of the oil-producing area in northern Iraq to their French ally in the secret Sykes-Picot agreement as a result British diplomacy and military plans changed course to recoup what had already been given away. British forces raced to capture the key northern city of Mosul several days after the armistice was signed. Britain thus, outmanoeuvred the French, establishing a military fait accompli in the oil zone of Northern Mesopotamia. The republic of Iraq only came into existence in 1920. There was no such thing as the Iraqi people or nation prior to this. Britain created a new monarchy out of thin air, as reward for Sharif Hussain for his treason against the Ottomans. Sharif Ali's son, Faisal, was made the King of Iraq. Prior to this, the Ottoman provinces of Baghdad, Mosul and Basra, were what existed. Britain effectively left a minority Sunni king to rule over the majority Shia, who himself was a foreigner to the newly invented country.

The Hashemite Kingdom was created out of thin air also, purely as a reward to Sharif Hussain. The country was constructed around a narrow strip of arable ground to the east of the Jordan River. For

56

lack of a better name, it was called Trans-Jordan, or the other side of the Jordan. In due course the "trans" was dropped and it became Jordan. Prior to this period some Bedouin tribes existed there but its proximity to Ash-Sham is how this area was known, otherwise it was considered desert wasteland with very little resources. Jordan has never existed in history and the region it today occupies was under the Syrian – al- sham administration. After WW1 Britain literally drew some lines on a map and put Sharif Hussain's son Abdullah as King. Today's King Abdullah II is the great, great grandson of the first king. As an artificial country, Jordan today has very limited resources and as a result its economy has always been fuelled by the Gulf States. The 1967 six day war with Israel resulted in an influx of Palestinians being expelled, who today remain in Jordan and constitute over 50% of the nation's population.[xiv] Like Iraq, Britain brought a foreigner, from outside the region and created a monarchy. King Abdullah was not even from this artificially created country.

The British named the area to the west of the Jordan River after the Ottoman administrative district of Filastina, which turned into Palestine on the English tongue. However, the British had promised the Zionists a homeland in Palestine and viewed a Zionist state with both Jews and Muslims living together i.e. one state with the Zionists ruling over the subjects. Britain paved the way for Jewish migration to the region and eventually created a state for the Jews called Israel. The indigenous people of Palestine had no say over the land they had resided on for hundreds of years. The United Nations General Assembly decided in 1947 on the partition of Palestine, giving 55% to the Jews, although they represented only 30% of the population. 70% of the Muslim population were only given 40% of the geography. Following its founding war of 1947-49, Israel came into existence but chose not to define its borders and today it remains with undeclared borders. But it took 78% of Palestine, a percentage it has steadily increased in subsequent years, which has seen the expulsion of the indigenous population.

During World War I, while the British were fighting the Ottomans, they had allied with a number of Arabian tribes seeking to expel the Ottomans. The first tribe was the Hashemites; the second was the Sauds. Two major tribes, hostile to each other, were the major British allies. The British had promised post-war power to both. It gave the victorious Sauds most of the Hijaz, much less than what it promised for their rebellion against the Ottomans. Iraq and Jordan were created from thin air for Sharif Hussain, who had for all intents and purposes been defeated by the Sauds in the Hijaz. He lived his days out in his son's monarchy in Jordan.

The French took everything north from the Mediterranean to Mount Hermon. Prior to this this was the Ash-Sham region. The wilayah of Damascus, wilayah of Aleppo and wilayah of Der ar-Zour were what existed previously. A wilayah was the equivalent of a modern day province. Between 1920 and 1946, the French mandate provided a critical boost to Syria's Alawites. In 1920, the French, who had spent years trying to legitimise and support the Alawites against an Ottoman-backed Sunni majority, had the Nusayris change their name to Allawi's to emphasise the sect's connection to the Prophet's cousin and son-in-law Ali and to Shia Islam. Along with the Druze and Christians, the Alawites enabled France to build a more effective counterweight to the Sunnis in managing the French colonial asset.

Lebanon was an invention carved out of Syria. The French, who had been involved in the Levant since the 19th century, had allies among the region's Maronite Christians. They carved out part of Syria and created a country for them. Lacking a better name, they called it Lebanon, after the nearby mountain of the same name. The country would not have been viable without the Sunni and Shia coastal cities. But after World War II, the demographics changed, and the Shia population increased. Compounding this was the movement of Palestinians into Lebanon in 1948. This shows why the country's politics, even today, are highly sectarian.

Britain declared a protectorate over Egypt and set up the last Khedive's uncle as Sultan Hussein Kamil from 1914 to1917. Succeeding his elder brother, Fuad I who took the western title King in 1917 to 1936 when Egypt nominally became independent in 1922. However, as in Iraq, Britain retained military bases and a strong influence on ministerial appointments. Fuad I worked with the Egyptian parliament and promoted education, establishing a secular university in Cairo. His son King Farouk came to the throne in 1936 to 1952, as a popular, intelligent and handsome young man. Egypt's prestige soured – being the centre of Arab cultural output in film, newspapers and education. When the Arab League was formed in 1945, Cairo was the natural choice for its headquarters. But Farouk's power was curtailed when the British, wary of his antagonism during the Second World War, imposed a new government in 1942. Farouk's rule lasted another decade until he was deposed by the Free Officers movement in 1952.

The British were also behind Libya's brief monarchy. The Italians seized the North African coast adjacent to Sicily from the Ottomans in 1912, taking advantage of their defeat in the First Balkan War. In 1920, to aid their control, the leader of the Sufi Senussi religious-tribal order, Sidi Mohammed Idris al-Senussi had become their vassal as Emir of Cyrenaica in the east around Benghazi, but he soon went into exile in British-occupied Egypt. He got his reward for ardently supporting the British against the Italians and Germans in the Western Desert during the Second World War when, at the end of Allied military occupation, the British installed him as King Idris (1951-1969). Idris consolidated his power with the help of the old elite Ottoman-Libyan families and multinational oil companies. Into the 1960s Idris allowed his nephew and heir Hassan al-Senuusi, to exercise increasing power. In 1969 Idris announced that he would formally abdicate in favour of his nephew. However, Idris was deposed by Colonel Gaddafi while on an overseas medical trip.

Britain also decided the fate of Persia, as Iran was known at the start of the 20th century. The huge oil deposits along the Persian Gulf had been discovered in 1908 and as a result Britain occupied Persia in 1918. Britain put the head of the Cossack Brigade of the Iranian army, a certain Reza Khan, as ruler of the country. Very quickly Iran became the most important source of fuel for the British army before the start of World War II.[xv] Britain was forced to send its armies into Iran in 1941 so the nation's oil would remain a stable and secure supply line in order it fully supported the allied war effort. Shah Reza Pahlavi was also replaced by his son as he came to be seen as an obstacle to achieving this aim, due to him being despised by his people.

When WW2 broke out in 1939, Britain was in no position to face-off against Nazi Germany. In fact, through shrewd political manoeuvring Britain was able to conceal its weakness and stay in the global game of nations. The United States economy became the world's largest economy in 1888 and has remained so ever since. When WW2 ended in 1945, the US economy was 10 times the size of British in GDP. Fareed Zakaria, the Newsweek international columnist in his book The Post American World, encapsulated British policy:

> *"The photographs of Roosevelt, Stalin and Churchill at the Yalta Conference in February 1945 are somewhat misleading. There was no 'big three' at Yalta. There was a 'big two' plus one brilliant political entrepreneur who was able to keep himself and his country in the game, so that Britain maintained many elements of great powerdom well into the late 20th century.'*[xvi]

During WW1 Britain was able to bring the US out of its self-imposed political isolation and continue the war effort when it desperately needed it. At the end of the war the US went back into isolation. The US entered WW2 when Britain once again needed it but on this occasion the US did not go back into isolation, rather the US and the Soviet Union replaced Britain as the world's powers.

The US took an interest in the Middle East before WW2, but during WW2, after tasting the benefits of Gulf oil it decided that it could no longer remain isolated and began manoeuvring in the region. In 1944, the US State Department described the Arabian Peninsula:

> *"the oil resources constitute a stupendous source of strategic power, and one of the greatest material prizes in world history."* [xvii]

The US was aware that control of the region's oil supply was a lever to control the world. As George Kennan, the influential planner of the containment of the Soviet Union put it in 1949:

> *"If the US controlled the oil, it would have veto power over the potential actions in the future of rivals like Germany and Japan."*

Adolf Berle, one of Franklin Roosevelt's closest advisors, remarked years later that controlling Middle East oil reserves meant obtaining *"substantial control of the world."* With the decline of Britain after WW2, the US inherited this system of client and puppet rulers. The US, like Britain and France, funded and armed them as long as they protected US interests in their respective countries. This started the Anglo-American struggle in the Middle East of coups, counter coups, revolutions, dictator rulers and ruling families changing loyalties. The first major change was the British-sponsored monarchies in Iraq and Egypt, which did not last very long.

The architecture Britain and France created 100 years ago, was inherited by the US after WW2. Through persistent struggle in the second half of the 20th century, Britain continues to maintain some of its influence in the Middle East. Whilst the US replaced Britain as the world's dominant power, both countries are in agreement that anything which brings about any Islamic unity between the sons of the Muslims needs to be contained. Whilst the Caliphate was the body that maintained global Islamic unity and Europe was successful in finishing off the Caliphate, being Muslims there is always the prospect that they would unite upon an Islamic basis and re-establish the Caliphate. To ensure this never materialises the politics, economics, military and culture of the Middle East and beyond needed to be controlled. Former British Foreign Secretary Jack Straw described Britain's role in carving up the Muslim world:

> "A lot of the problems we have to deal with now, I have to deal with now, are a consequence of our colonial past. ... The Balfour Declaration and the contradictory assurances which were being given to Palestinians in private at the same time as they were being given to the Israelis—again, an interesting history for us but not an entirely honourable one.'[xviii]

ARTIFICIAL NATIONS

Numerous nations have been created via the Sykes-Picot agreement between France, Russia and Britain during WW1. Egypt historically has been the most important country in the Middle East and it remains so today and this is why it make sense we begin with the most important nation in the region for this chapter.

EGYPT

As a nation, modern day Egypt occupies over 1 million square kilometres (386,000 square miles). It is twice the size of France, but most of its territory is wasteland desert. Just less than 35% of the 1 million square

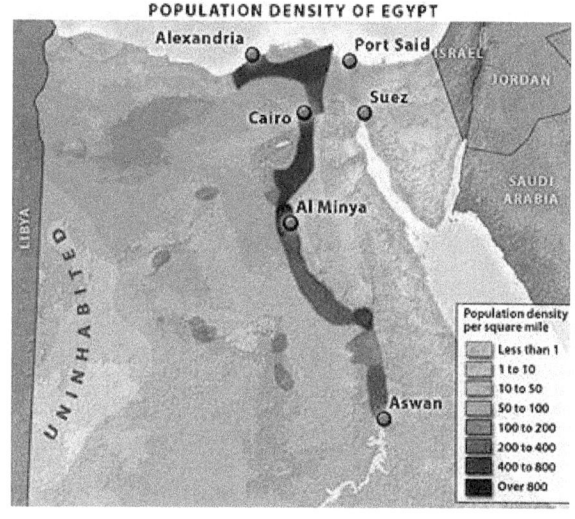

kilometres, a land area roughly the size of Belgium, is actually inhabited. This tiny portion of great Egypt, from the Aswan High Dam to the Mediterranean shore is the Egypt's core and home to 99% of the nation's population of 83 million. Egypt, which has the largest population of any country in Africa or Middle East, is stretched thin, clinging to the banks of the River Nile in a strip that is almost always less than 18 miles wide.

King Farouk 1

Egypt came under Muslim authority in the year 641. Egypt was a colony of the Byzantine Empire at the time and was ruled through a Byzantine civil service and military, both of which were filled by a Greek ruling class to the exclusion of the native Coptic-speaking populace. Egypt was ruled from the capital Alexandria with various fortresses including the bulwark fortress of Babylon on the Eastern Bank of the Nile. Egypt at the time was inhabited by a mixture of people, such as the Copts, Jews and Romans. It took the Muslims the best part of a decade to conquer Egypt beginning from the South and making its way up to Alexandria. The permanent loss of the Egypt left the Byzantine Empire without an irreplaceable source of food and money.

Egypt remained under Islamic rule until the arrival of the European colonialists in the 19th century, save for a period of 200 years, from 750

when the Fatimids ruled over Egypt. The Fatimids are not considered Muslims, due to doctrinal differences with the majority Muslims. Napoleon's forces arrived and conquered Egypt in 1798. He completely defeated the Mamluks who for hundreds of years were undefeatable. Napoleon's army almost wiped out the entire Mamluk army and sealed the French occupation of Egypt, which led to Napoleon setting up an administration in Cairo. This conquest confirmed for all weaknesses of the Ottoman Empire in the face of a changing Europe rocked by the French Revolution. However, Napoleon's administration did not last long as British sea power prevented him from receiving any reinforcements from France, thus bringing his campaign to a halt. The British army finally reconquered the country for the Ottomans in 1801. This left a political vacuum and as a result the Ottomans sent one of its generals, Muhammed Ali Pasha, to Egypt to restore order. During his reign he put down a number of rebellions including the first Wahhabi revolt in the Hijaz in 1811. Nonetheless, his subordination to the Ottoman Empire was merely nominal as the Ottomans were in decline, facing revolts across its empire. Muhammad Ali Pasha began using the title of 'Khedive,' roughly translated as viceroy and established a dynasty that was to rule Egypt, a dynasty that effectively became a British puppet. The Suez Canal, built in partnership with the French was completed in 1869. Its construction led to enormous debt to European banks. By the 1880s Egypt was unable to repay its debts and as a result the British Empire, its largest lender, used this as an excuse to occupy Egypt for the next half century.

BRITAIN'S MONARCHY

When the First World War broke out in 1914, the Khedive 'Abbās Ḥilmī Pasha was visiting the Ottoman capital Constantinople. The British, now at war with the Ottomans, could not accept this and deposed him. Britain maintained a firm grip over Egypt, but Britain's last King – King Farouk was overthrown in the coup of 1952 by the Free Officers movement. King Farouk became more and more licentious as the years progressed and his weight ballooned. He died overweight, choking on his meal at a restaurant table in Rome in 1965, aged 45.

ENTER THE USA

Having abolished the monarchy in 1952, Egypt's new leaders, Muhammad Naguib, who was raised as a child of an Egyptian army officer in Sudan, and Gamal Abdel Nasser, believed the only way to end British domination in Sudan was for Egypt itself to formally abandon its sovereignty over Sudan. Since the British claim to control in Sudan theoretically depended upon Egyptian sovereignty, the revolutionaries calculated that this tactic would leave the UK with no option but to withdraw. Their calculation proved to be correct, and in 1954, the governments of Egypt and the UK signed a treaty guaranteeing Sudanese independence. On 1 January 1956, the date agreed between the Egyptian and British governments, Sudan became an independent state, ending its nearly 136-year union with Egypt and its 56-year occupation by the British. However, the loss of Egypt and Sudan was going to be a far bigger loss for Britain.

Gamal Abdul Nasser and the Free Officers Movement was never an independent movement as many believe when studying this era. The US emerged the world superpower after WW2 and was working to reduce British influence and remove it from the region. The CIA worked on a project in 1951 known in the CIA as "Find a Muslim Billy Graham". Miles Copeland the CIA operative published classified information in his memoirs in 1989 titled "The Game Player: Confessions of the CIA's Original Political Operative", about how the CIA supported the coup that ousted the British puppet King Farouk. Copeland, who activated the project, explained that the CIA needed a charismatic leader who would be able to divert the growing anti-American hostility that was building up in the area. Copeland recollects that in the first secret meeting he had with three army officers one of whom was Major Abdel Moneim Ra'ouf (a member of Gamal Abdel Nasser's inner circle). In March 1952, four months before the coup that ousted King Farouk, Kim Roosevelt head of the CIA Near East Operations and Nasser began a series of meetings that led to the coup. After much discussion it was agreed that no support from the Islamic groups was required and that the army would take control and gain the support of the urban populace. It was also agreed that future relations between the US and Egypt would publicly eschew phrases such as "re-establishing democratic processes" but privately there would be an understanding that the pre-conditions for democratic government did not exist. Both the CIA and Nasser were in agreement on Israel. For Nasser's talk of war with Israel was irrelevant. Much more of a priority was British occupation of the Suez Canal Zone. Nasser's enemy was Britain. The US could assist Nasser by not opposing the coup. Right up to the day of the coup 23 July 1952, the CIA station operatives stayed in very close contact with the members of the Free Officers.

According to Copeland the coup took place without a hitch with General Mohammed Naguib nominally at its head. For the next six months the only contacts with Nasser and the Revolutionary Command Council were maintained by the embassy and not the CIA. After the coup the CIA assisted in the reorganisation of the *mukhabarat* (intelligence service). Key courses were set up designed to acquaint members of the Revolutionary Command Council with what they could reasonably expect from the US. Nasser agreed to all of this. In addition, Zakaria Mohieddin, head of the *mukhabarat*, agreed to send an English-speaking Free Officer, Captain Hassan Touhami, to Washington. There Touhami was shown the whole range of services the CIA, FBI and police agencies could offer the government. The CIA's relationship with the Egyptian government was kept secret and to assist this Copeland's employers, Booz-Allen & Hamilton, and the CIA joined forces advising Egypt's Interior Ministry. This entailed making improvements in the immigration and customs services, tackling the system of identity cards and vehicle registrations. All this was a cover for the CIA's real agenda. Through agents such as Nasser, the US was successfully challenging and undermining Britain's position in the region. At the same time, the US was duping the Muslims and Arabs into thinking that its puppet and Arab nationalism was their saviour. Britain's influence was lost from Egypt and the US continued the style of supporting coups and dictators in order to remove British influence throughout the Middle East. This was despite the fact that all the parties involved were on the same side less than 10 years earlier in WW2

The army from 1952 dominated Egypt's politics, economy, foreign policy and national defence. It has until this very day protected US interests in the Middle East. The army initially set out to consolidate its grip on the country by developing a support base. It did this through agrarian reform and the confiscation of private property. By limiting land ownership to 80 hectares (200 acres) per person — reduced to 20 hectares in 1969 — and redistributing some of the confiscated land to peasants, the military established its populist roots. The nationalisation of the industry and service sector and the creation of a mammoth public sector were other key factors sustaining the military regime. By January 1953, the army disbanded all political parties, abolished the 1923 constitution and declared a three-year period of transitional military rule. Key civilian roles went to army officials or retired army officials. While Nasser and many of his close allies had become civilian leaders, the military remained very much part of the government. It was not until Egypt's defeat at the hands of Israel in the 1967 war that the military truly began moving away from actual governance.

The nationalisation of the Suez Canal, which led to the 1956 war, made Nasser a national hero and enhanced his stature in the wider Arab world. Nasser then began interfering in every country Britain had influence in, such as Syria, Yemen, Iraq, Algeria, Lebanon, Saudi Arabia and Jordan. Nasser was America's biggest foreign policy success as he was a charismatic leader, who for long had the support of the people as they believed he would navigate them through colonialism, the Israeli occupation and independence. In the end, as US intelligence revealed, he was on US payroll for the whole duration.

THE SADAT ERA

Nasser's death due to a heart attack in September 1970 brought Anwar Sadat to power. It was under Sadat's rule that the major moves to separate the government from the military took place. Initially, Sadat ran into a number of challenges, including the fact that he lacked Nasser's stature and was opposed by those loyal to his predecessor both within the military and the ruling party. For the first three years Sadat got rid of two sets of senior regime leaders — first, the Nasser loyalists, and then those he himself had brought to replace the pro-Nasser elements. For example, he replaced his vice president, Sabri, with el-Shafei, whom he eventually replaced with Hosni Mubarak in 1975.

In 1974 Sadat initiated an open-door economic policy, known as "*Infitāh*" which steered the country away from the Nasserite vision of a centralised economy based upon Socialist lines and led to the creation of new economic elites loyal to Sadat. To further weaken the Nasserites and the left wing, he also worked to eliminate the idea of a single-party system by calling for the creation of separate platforms within the ruling party. As a result, the ruling party weakened and was dissolved in 1978 and its members formed the National Democratic Party (NDP). In addition to a new ruling party, Sadat allowed multiparty politics in 1976. Sadat also relaxed curbs on the country's largest Islamist movement, the Muslim Brotherhood, allowing it to publish material and carve out a limited space in society as part of his efforts to counter left-wing forces.

The Sadat era saw the creation of a new civilian elite consisting largely of ex-military officers. Sadat gave the military the freedom to engage in business enterprises. While on one hand he promoted economic liberalisation, allowing for the return of the private sector, he also promulgated Law 32 in 1979, which gave the armed forces financial and economic independence from the state. The military became heavily involved in the industrial and service sectors including weapons, electronics, consumer products, infrastructure development, agribusinesses, aviation, tourism and security. This kept the military from draining state coffers, which it eventually did via subsidies for the military and its businesses. In the 1980s, the military created two key commercial entities: the National Services Projects Organisation and the Egyptian Organisation for Industrial Development. These two entities effectively are the twin engines of Egypt's economy even until today.

During the Sadat era a new generation of US-trained military officer came to dominate the senior positions. It was Anwar Sadat, with US President Jimmy Carter, in 1978 that concluded the peace treaty between Egypt and Israel giving Israel the much needed space from arguably the region's power, at the same time protecting another one of America's regional interests. From this point onwards it has been Egypt that has maintained Israel within the region. The changes that Sadat brought did not alter the reality that the military was embedded throughout the fabric of state and society. Senior serving officers in the presidential staff and at the Defence Ministry, governors in most provinces, and a parallel military judicial system provided a structural mechanism through which the security establishment maintained a say in policymaking.

The Mubarak Era

When Hosni Mubarak took charge in 1981 after Sadat was assassinated he did not alter the reality that the military was embedded throughout the fabric of state and society. Mubarak engaged in limited reforms and expanded on the process of developing institutions in an effort to consolidate the regime. During the 1980s, Egypt began having multiparty parliamentary elections but the army firmly controlled national security issues.

However by 1992, the Algerian experiment with democracy had

scared the Mubarak government about the risks of allowing multiparty polls. The Algerian elections almost saw a relatively new Islamic movement, Front *Islamique du Salut* (The Islamic Salvation Front), secure a two-thirds majority in parliament. An army intervention annulling the polls denied victory to the group which sparked a decade-long insurgency. From the point of view of the Mubarak government, the Muslim Brotherhood (MB) was far more organised than Front *Islamique du Salut*, and Egypt's Jihadi movements were just as well established. This viewpoint received validation from *Al-Jamā'ah al-Islāmīyah* (The Islamic Group) attacks against the government.

Having political opponents operating within constitutional bounds served the military by stabilising the regime and giving it a democratic veneer. However, the move to allow these forces led to the rise in popularity of the Muslim Brotherhood. The NDP could only go so far in rigging the system in favour of the government, which meant the ruling party needed to take steps to enhance its domestic standing. This was achieved through economic liberalisation with the privatisation of state-owned enterprises in the mid-1990s, but with army assets off-limits. The economic liberalisation and the need to bolster the ruling party allowed for the rise of a younger generation of businessmen and politicians. Towards the end of the 1990s, Mubarak's son Gamal was heading the Future Foundation and was brought into the ruling party. The Gamal group included prominent businessmen, Mohammed Abul-Einen, and steel magnate, Ahmed Ezz. This new guard led by Gamal quickly rose through the ranks of the NDP and by February 2000, Gamal, Ezz and another key businessman, Ibrahim Kamel, became members of the NDP's General Secretariat. Their entry immediately created a struggle between the military-backed old guard and the business-supported rising elements within the NDP, given that new voices had begun contributing to the policymaking process.

EGYPT TODAY

On the eve of the Arab spring the army was heavily involved in the national economy. According to some estimates, as much as 40% of the Egyptian economy is controlled by the military and they would for obvious reasons want to maintain such a position.[xix] The Egyptian military has played a central role in protecting US interests in the region. Ever since the military coup in 1952, the US has showered the Egyptian military with aid in excess of $30 billion.[xx] This US aid is in effect bribe money to maintain the regional balance, which Egypt's military leaders have been more than happy to implement. For the small geography Egypt needs to defend, just 35% of the nation's 1 million square kilometres is actually inhabited. The size of Egypt's ground forces is massively disproportionate and puts a huge strain on the nation's finances. Shana Marshall of the Institute of Middle East Studies at George Washington University highlighted: *"There's no conceivable scenario in which they'd need all those tanks short of an alien invasion."*[xxi] More than 500 Egyptian military officers train at American military graduate schools every year. There's even a special guest house in northwest Washington, D.C., where visiting Egyptian military officials stay when in the American capital.[xxii] Every year, the US Congress appropriates more than $1 billion in military aid to Egypt. But that money never gets to Egypt. It goes to the Federal Reserve Bank of New York, then to a trust fund at the Treasury and, finally, out to US military contractors that make the tanks and fighter jets that ultimately get sent to Egypt.[xxiii]

Life for ordinary Egyptians has been nothing but a struggle since the 1950s. The problem with the Egyptian economy is the fact that an elite few control it. When elites control an economy, they use their power to create monopolies and block the entry of new people and firms. This is how Egypt worked for three decades under Hosni Mubarak. The government and military own vast swaths of the economy and even when they did 'liberalise,' they privatised large parts of the economy right into the hands of Mubarak's friends and those of his son, Gamal. Big businessmen close to the regime such as Ahmed Ezz (iron and steel), the Sawiris family (multimedia, beverages, and telecommunications), and Mohamed Nosseir (beverages and telecommunications), received not only protection from the state but also government contracts and large bank loans. Together, these big businessmen and their stranglehold on the economy created astronomical profits for regime insiders but blocked opportunities for the vast mass of Egyptians to move out of poverty. Meanwhile, the Mubarak family accumulated a vast fortune estimated to be as high as $70 billion.[xxiv]

With a small elite controlling most of the nation's wealth and with the army controlling key industries, the 83 million population of Egypt is struggling in between these two factions. Since the Arab spring poverty has worsened as today at least 50% of Egypt's population lives under the internationally recognised poverty line and is bound to become progressively worse.[xxv] Successive governments tried to deal with the population's deteriorating condition in two ways, both of which have only made matters worse. Egypt, like many of its neighbours, long relied on subsidies to ward off social instability. Since the 1920s, Egypt relied on a complex subsidy system that included bread, gasoline, diesel, natural gas and electricity totalling $29 billion in the 2011-2012 fiscal year and accounts for nearly 30% of government expenditures (around 13% of Egypt's GDP). Making foundational changes has proved too difficult for previous governments because poor Egyptians were wary of price hikes, and previous governments favoured short-run social stability to maintain power rather than long-term economic stability. These subsidies were never sustainable and have now indebted the country. The second manner the government attempted to deal with poverty and social cohesion in general is through borrowing its way out of any problem. Egypt's national debt amounts to $46 billion today, in Egyptian pounds (EGP) that is 1.8 trillion. The government in Egypt spends more than 60% of the revenue it collects in debt repayments. This amounts to over 120 billion EGP annually.

There are two relationships that have defined Egypt's position in the region: its relationship with the Soviet Union and the US. Whilst much has been made of Egypt's relationship with the Soviet Union, the relationship never reached the level of political coordination or political influence by the Soviet Union. Nasser was brought to power by the US and aside from commercial, military and economic deals, politically Nasser protected US interests in the region despite the rhetoric to the contrary. For the US, having a Soviet presence in the Middle East was to overstretch it across the world and also to counter the British influence in the Middle East who was the real competitor for the US.

From the US perspective it had turned Egypt into a subordinate state from the time the Free Officers were brought to power in 1952. Egypt's successive rulers executed its foreign policy in line with US interests in the region to the point the US now controls all aspects of Egypt's foreign policy. As one of the most powerful nations in the region, Egypt's normalisation with Israel in the 1979 treaty, normalised Israelis position in the region – another one of America's interests in the region. US foreign aid and military sales to the Egyptian army ensures it controls the posture and disposition of the army. Internally, the US has major influence over many domestic institutions within Egypt such as the judiciary, the parliament, a number of opposition parties and many of Egypt's intellectuals. An example of US influence in Egypt was the electoral victory of the Muslim Brotherhood's Muhammad Morsi in the presidential election in June 2012. The announcement of the result of the election was delayed, until Morsi gave assurances to the US that he would abide by the treaties and agreements concluded by the former regimes, primarily the Camp David treaty, as evidenced by American statements before and after the elections. Morsi was compelled to highlight he would maintain the status quo in spite of running an election campaign to the contrary, due to America's huge influence over the country.

Egypt is a subordinate state to the US since after the removal of the British controlled monarchy in 1952. Throughout the period Egypt has been the lynchpin in projecting and protecting US strategic interests in the region. In return, the US has showered the military leadership with aid in order to control its domestic population as a means to fulfil the role the US has given Egypt. Muhammad Morsi failed to maintain domestic stability which led to impacting the role Egypt would have played in the region, and as a result he was overthrown by the military with the support of the US.

Abdel Fattah el-Sisi, since his coup in July 2013 has worked to consolidate his rule by working to destroy the Muslim Brotherhood (MB), imprisoning others who could be a potential threat, including many revolutionary groups who the army previously supported. Soldiers and police opened fire on hundreds of MB supporters that gathered in Cairo in numerous protests; hundreds of people were killed in what Human Rights Watch described as *"the most serious incident of mass unlawful killings in modern Egyptian history."*[xxvi] A kangaroo court was set up where Morsi and other MB members stood trial for "committing acts of violence and inciting killing and thuggery."[xxvii] On December 25th 2013, Egypt's military-backed government designated the MB a terrorist organisation, criminalising its activities and finances, if that was not enough the court also released Hosni Mubarak from prison. Ahmed Maher, founder the April 6 Youth Movement that received significant media coverage in the overthrow of Hosni Mubarak was thrown into Egypt's infamous Tora prison. Mohamed El-Baradei refuses to return to Egypt, despite supporting the overthrow of Morsi and after playing a central role in the uprisings that brought the army back to power. El Baradei still faces the Egyptian courts for a betrayal of trust. The army used various individuals and groups to regain power under the guise of ridding the country of an incompetent MB. Once Morsi was removed the army threw aside all the liberal and secular groups who brought them to power. Today Egypt is back under military control and nothing has really changed since 1952, when the army undertook its first coup.

After WW1 and with the dissolution of the Caliphate, France had already secretly agreed that it would take the northern portion of the Middle East in its agreement with Britain. The region had lived for centuries under Islamic rule which had served as protection against European rule. Syria or Ash-Sham (Greater Syria) had been under Ottoman authority for more than 400 years. The geography of Ash-Sham consisted of a number of *vilayets* (administrative divisions). The region was comprised of Aqaba and Sinai in the south, the Taurus Mountains in the north, the Syrian Desert in the east, and the Mediterranean Sea in the west; this means Ash-Sham at the time consisted of what is now Jordan, Israel, Palestine, Lebanon and Syria and parts of Southern Turkey. With the defeat of the Ottomans in Syria, British troops under Field Marshal Edmund Allenby entered Damascus in 1918 accompanied by troops of the Arab Revolt led by Faisal, son of Sharif Hussein of Makkah. Faisal established the first Arab government in Damascus in October 1918. Faisal formed local governments in the major Syrian cities and the Pan-Arab flag was raised all over Syria. He hoped earlier British promises would be maintained, regarding a new Arab state that would include all the Arab lands stretching from Aleppo in northern Syria to Aden in southern Yemen.

The French seized Damascus as per the Sykes-Picot agreement on July 26th, 1920, overthrowing Faisal and his nationalist government. Though the French sent him into exile a year later, feeling pity for him he was put on the throne of the British mandate of Iraq. After the occupation of Damascus, Alexandre Millerand, the French prime minister, proclaimed that Syria henceforth would be held by France: *"The whole of it, and forever."*[xxviii] When the French arrived in Damascus resistance came from both the Arab political societies, dominated by Iraqi and Syrian officers of the Arab army, and the wider Sunni population of Damascus and Aleppo. The French strategy after the dismemberment of the Ottoman Caliphate was to artificially create new national identities, citizenship and social class to replace the identities of clan, tribe and Islam. The French divided their mandate into segments to block nationalist sentiment and action. The partition began with *Le Grand Liban*, Greater Lebanon, as well as the state of Damascus, Aleppo, Alawites, Jabal Druze, the autonomous Sanjak of Alexandretta (modern-day Hatay). The carving of these states was based on exploiting the diverse sectarian makeup of Ash-Sham. Most of these were hostile to the French mandate and to the division it created ultimately resulting in numerous revolts until 1940. This was because in 1940, the French were defeated and conquered by Hitler's Nazi forces in just six weeks in WW2.

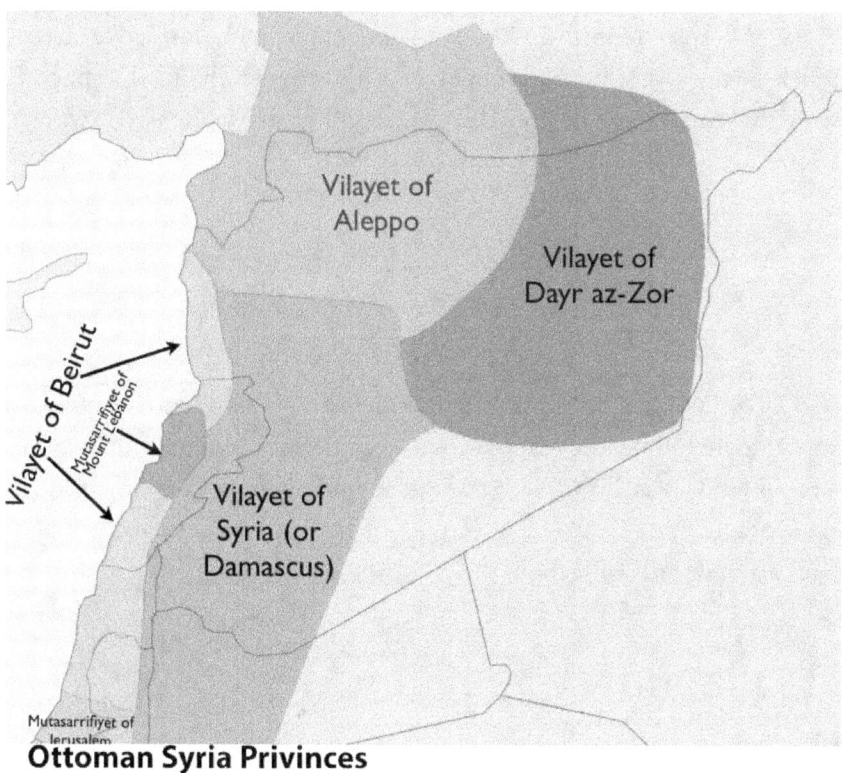

Ottoman Syria Privinces

When the Nazi's established the Vichy government (the term for the German occupation government in France) in June 1940, the French in Syria recognised the new government and declared an immediate cessation of hostilities. By 1941 German aircraft flying to the war zone in the Persian Gulf were allowed to refuel in Syria. To combat this, British and *Françaises Libres* (Free French) army troops invaded Syria and stayed until 1946. WW2 ended French influence across much of the world as the global balance of power changed, especially with the emergence of the US. The last French troops left Syria in 1946.

ALAWI'S

Hafiz al-Assad's coup in 1970 ushered in a new era for Syria. It was the first time the Alawi's had complete dominance over Syria. This is why it is important to understand their history in order to understand Syria today. The origins of the Alawi sect can be traced back to the ninth century.

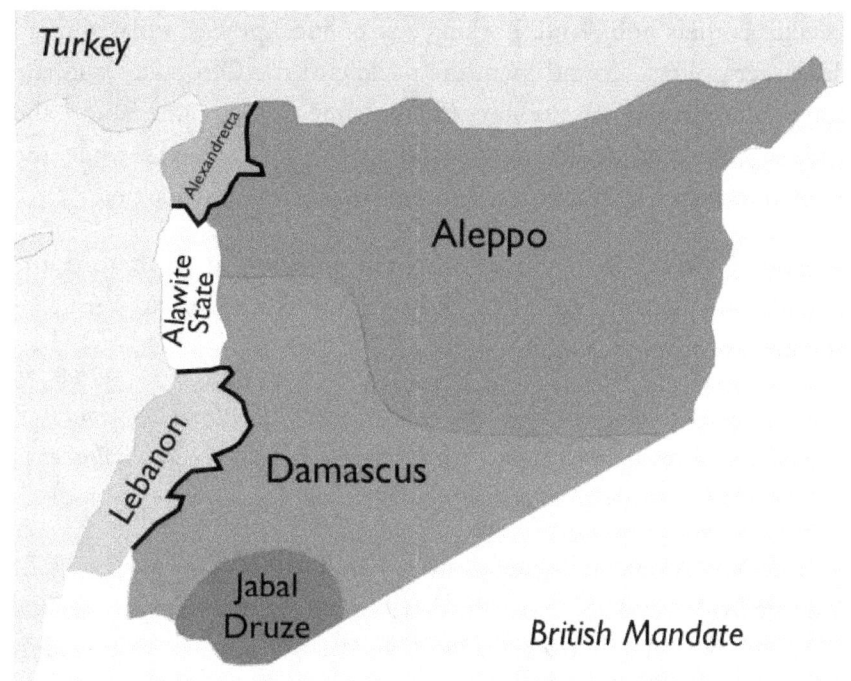

French Syria 1924

In 859, Ibn Nusayr, a follower of the eleventh Shia Imam, Hassan al-'Askari declared himself the *bab* 'gateway to truth.' On the basis of this authority, Ibn Nusayr proclaimed a host of new doctrines, which brought Alawism into existence and rendered him an apostate from Islam. Alawi beliefs include holding Imam Ali (the prophet's cousin and son-in-law and one of the first Muslims) divine as well as holding the Alawite faith in strict secrecy from outsiders. The five pillars of Islam are viewed as symbolic only and therefore not practiced. Alawis are much closer to Christianity as they celebrate most of their festivals, they also believe in reincarnation. Thus, Alawis are not remotely close to the Shia and their beliefs are what led them to being ostracised from Islamic society for most of their history.

Centuries of hostility defined the Alawi psyche. They acquired a reputation as fierce and unruly mountain people who resisted paying taxes they owed the authorities and frequently plundered other villages. Alawis retreated to the mountains and have historically taken

Latakia as their homeland. Lacking any political power, isolated from the larger politics around them the decline of the Ottoman Caliphate could not have come sooner. By the time WW1 came about the Alawis were considered the poorest in the East. It was when the French took hold of Syria in 1920 that Alawi fortunes changed.

The Alawis adopted a pro-French position even before the French conquest of Damascus in July 1920. According to Yusuf al-Hakim, a prominent Syrian politician,

> *"The 'Alawis saw themselves in a state of grace after hell; accordingly, they were dedicated to the French mandate and did not send a delegation to the [General] Syrian Congress."*[xxix]

The Alawis rebelled against Prince Faisal, whom they suspected of wanting to dominate them, in 1919 using French arms. General Gouraud received a telegram in late 1919 from 73 Alawi chiefs representing different tribes, who asked for

> *"the establishment of an independent Nusayri union under our absolute protection."*[xxx]

The French, similar to their colonial strategy in Africa, were looking to consolidate their rule through forging links with minorities. French efforts to cooperate with minorities meant the Alawis gained political autonomy; the state of Latakia was set up on 1 July 1922. They also gained legal autonomy; a 1922 decision to end Sunni control of court cases involving Alawis was transferred to Alawi jurists. The Alawi state enjoyed low taxation and a sizeable French subsidy. Not surprisingly, Alawis accepted all these changes with enthusiasm. At the time when resistance movements were mounted against the French mandate, when Damascus, Aleppo, and the Ḥawrān witnessed continuous rebellions on behalf of independence, the Alawis were blessing the division of the country into tiny statelets.

The French mandate provided the critical boost to the Alawis. The French spent years trying to legitimise and support the Alawis against the Sunni majority. The French even had the Nusayris change their name to "Alawi" to emphasise the sect's connection to Ali (ra) and to the Shia. Along with the Druze and Christians, the Alawis enabled France to build a more effective counterweight to the Sunni Muslims in managing the French colonial asset. The French reversed Ottoman designs of the Syrian security apparatus which allowed for the influx of Alawis into military, police and intelligence posts to suppress challenges to French rule. Consequently, the end of the French mandate in 1946 was a defining moment for the Alawis, who by then had got their first real taste of a privileged life after centuries of poverty.

The Alawis dominated the armed forces upon the French departure. While Muslims occupied the top posts within the military, the lower ranks were filled by Alawis who could not afford the military exemption fees paid by most of the Muslims. The seed was thus planted for an Alawite led military coup. The 1950s 1960s and 1970s were periods of intense struggle between the British and the US which led to numerous coups and counter coups in the region. Husni al-Za'ims coup on April 11th 1949 was the introduction of US interference in Syria. Declassified records and statements by former CIA agents confirmed the coup was sponsored by the United States CIA.[xxxi] The CIA's continued support to several subsequent military coups in Syria throughout the 1950s and 1960s against its European rival is what caused the instability that lasted over two decades.

The birth of the Ba'ath party in Syria in 1947 was a key tool for eventual Alawite domination of Syria. The Ba'athist campaign of secularism, socialism and Arab nationalism provided the ideal platform and political vehicle to organise and unify around. In 1963, Ba'athist power was cemented through a military coup led by President Amin al-Hafiz, who discharged many ranking Muslim officers, thereby providing openings for hundreds of Alawites to fill top-tier military positions. This measure tipped the balance in favour of Alawi officers who staged a coup in 1966 and for the first time placed Damascus in the hands of the Alawites. But the bloodless military coup led by then-air force commander and Defence Minister General Hafez al-Assad against his Alawi rival, Salah Jadid in 1970, Alawi rivalries and Syria's string of coups and counter-coups were also put to rest.

Upon seizing the reins of power, Assad stacked the security apparatus with loyal clansmen while taking care to build patronage networks with Druze and Christian minorities that facilitated the al-Assad rise. Just as important, the al-Assad leadership co-opted key Muslim military and business elites, relying on notables like the Tlass family to contain dissent within the military. The Alawi state took over the administration of religious funding, cracked down on groups deemed as extremist and empowered it to dismiss the leaders of Friday prayers at will. With a minority ruling over the majority and after centuries of being marginalised the Alawite leadership dominated by the al-Assad family ruled with brutal force oppressing the Muslim majority. Hafez Al-Assad and his son Bashar al-Assad proved to be ruthless, preventing any challenge to Alawi rule, banning an open press and political debate. Both strengthened the *mukhabarat* (secret police) and turned them into permanent informants.

Today, Syria's population, based on the country's official census, is 22 million. Up to 85% of this population is Muslim, despite the minority Alawis who dominate the political landscape. This disproportionate situation crafted and maintained with foreign support is due to a number of pillars in Syria, which is currently being challenged with the uprising in the country.

The first pillar is in the Ba'ath party's monopoly on the political system with most of this power in the hands of the al-Assad clan. This dominance has allowed the Ba'ath party and the al-Assad clan to dominate all political life in the country; any opposition has been dealt with ruthlessly. The Ba'ath party controls political life as there is no other political party in the country. This has meant any foreign power would need to deal with the Ba'ath party to gain any influence in the country as there are no other centres of power in the country. This is why until the uprising in 2011, most of the anti-regime activity was by dissidents from abroad. By consolidating the Ba'ath party's power in the al-Assad clan, key positions such as the intelligence head and the elite units within the armed forces are led by al-Assad brothers and cousins. For these reasons, the al-Assad clan has been able sustain the political architecture of the country, even though they, the Alawis, represent a tiny fraction of the country's populace.

The second pillar has always been the Alawite population from whom the al-Assad family are from. As a minority, they consist of at most 2.3 million people, 11% of the population. The Alawites of Syria remain composed of four tribes: *Matawira*, *Khayyatin*, *Haddadin* and *Kalbiyya*. The al-Assads, belonging to the *Numailatiyaa* clan of the *Matawira* tribe, hail from the north-western village of *Qardaha*, near the coastal city of Latakia. For the Alawi regime to subdue a Muslim majority, it has to control every aspect of the state's apparatus. The Alawis permeated every sector of the state's institutions and aligned themselves with other minorities like the Druze, Christians and Shia in a position of unquestioned power. This sectarian base has managed to hold throughout the Arab spring uprising, but discontent is brewing due to the accumulation of deaths within the Alawi officers that fuelled discontent of their families.[xxxii] On September 28th 2012, a fight broke out between Assad family members and other prominent Alawite families in al-Qardāḥah, the heart of the Assad regime, which led to the killing of Mohammed al-Assad, cousin of Bashar al-Assad.[xxxiii] Alawi unity which for long was the support base of the regime is being severely challenged.

The third pillar is the security apparatus. Syria's four main intelligence services are directly under the control of the Syrian president and have overlapping functions so that the regime is not overly dependent on any one of them. Each operates in near total secrecy. The secret service is responsible for internal surveillance of the population in general and detecting signs of organised political activity that run counter to the interests of the regime. Over the past 40 years, the Syrian security apparatus has been successful in clamping down on the entire country. Political dissent was virtually non-existent, whilst any Syrian citizen wishing to travel abroad would have to pass a number of stringent security checks. However, the Syrian security apparatus has seen its grip on the country shaken following the outbreak of the Arab spring.

The fourth pillar has been the patronage networks the regime established with a number of Muslims in order to placate the majority Muslim population. The Tlass family, who Hafez al-Assad established links with soon after he came to power in 1963, was critical to the al-Assad clan's ability to maintain military support among the Muslim elite. The family was also a major link between the Alawi and the Muslim business community. Mustafa Tlass, the patriarch of the Tlass family, was the Muslim pillar of the predominantly Alawi al-Assad regime. He served as defence minister for the al-Assad regime from 1972 to 2004 and played an instrumental role in ensuring that the young Bashar al-Assad would have the support of the old guard in succeeding his father, Hafez al Assad. His son Manaf Tlass was a close friend of Basil al Assad, Hafez al Assad's eldest son and heir apparent until his death in a 1994 car accident. Having attended military college with Bashar al-Assad and after Hafez al-Assad's death in 2000, Manaf Tlass became Bashar al-Assad's right-hand-man. Manaf Tlass helped Bashar al-Assad increase his base of support by introducing him to members of the Sunni business elite. Tlass even held unsuccessful talks with the Syrian opposition during the Syrian uprising in order to dilute their demands for real change.[xxxiv]

The fifth pillar is the army. Before the uprising in 2011 the Syrian military consisted of air, ground, and navy forces. The numbers of active personnel were estimated to be 300,000 with an additional 314,000 in reserve. The majority of the Syrian military were Sunni; however most of the military leadership were Alawi. The Alawis made up 12% of the Syrian population but are estimated to have made up 70% of the career soldiers in the Syrian Army. The army was however stretched to breaking point by the uprising. On paper, the army had 220,000 soldiers, but most of the rank-and-file were Sunnis – and their loyalty to al-Assad was not guaranteed. Consequently, the burden of the fighting fell on two elite units: the 4th armoured division, under the de facto command of Bashar's brother, Maher, and the Republican Guard. Together, these formations had no more than 30,000 men – less than 14% of the army's total strength and they bore the lion's share of the task of combating the uprising.[xxxv] Bashar al-Assad has been forced to utilise only a small fraction of the army as he cannot count on the loyalty of the majority of the Muslims. This also explains why after so many years, despite possessing more capability than the rebels the regime failed to quell the uprising.

Since the emergence of the Alawis Syria has been presented as an axis of evil, state sponsor of terrorism and the chief cause of instability in the Middle East. The constant criticism of Syria by the west has isolated Syria in the Middle East and is a great concern for the existence of Israel. A closer inspection of Syria's actions and policies in the region show much of this is simply empty rhetoric as Syria has permanent record of protecting US interests in the Middle East.

In an Al-Jazeera interview on July 2nd, 2001 ex-senior Ba'ath member, Amin al-Hafiz outlined that Hafez al-Assad, the then Defence Minister, ordered the pull-out out of the 1967 war to secure Israel. He outlined that Hafez al-Assad sent a strict order of withdrawal to the Syrian army from the Golan Heights at the beginning of the war. This was before any sign of defeat or real confrontation against the Israeli military which resulted in the occupation of such a strategic location.[xxxvi] It was through this move, al-Assad gained the trust of the US in defending Israel's northern border and continued to do so for the next three decades. Despite much rhetoric to the contrary, the northern border until today remains Israel's most secure border. After the 1973 surprise war with Israel, the US should have slammed Syria with sanctions, however, in 1974 President Nixon personally paid a visit to Damascus to strengthen relations with the Assad regime.

The US accepted the Syrian occupation of Lebanon when it began in 1976. Syrian troops invaded Lebanon at the beginning of the civil war. The silence on part of the US against such an occupation was a "green light" to Hafez al-Assad to initiate and continue this invasion until 2005, when a French-mandated resolution pushed the Syrians out with American reluctance. One political analyst described the role of the US by saying: *"[The US] seemed tacitly to acquiesce to continued Syrian ascendancy in Lebanon."*[xxxvii] In 1989 both the US and Syria Cooperated in the Tai'f Agreement which was signed in Saudi Arabia between the different Lebanese factions to put an end to the civil war in Lebanon. The US was the power broker besides France, Saudi Arabia, Egypt and Syria that helped form the agreement, "prompting international support for Syrian—guardianship over Lebanon."[xxxviii]

Syria participated in the US led multinational coalition aligned against Saddam Hussein in the first Gulf war (1990-91), which marked a dramatic watershed in Syrian relations with other Arab states. It was one of the only non-monarchical Arab states to have backed the United States against Iraq during the first Gulf War dispatching troops to support Operation Desert Shield (ODS).

By the time George W. Bush came to office in 2001, his administration may have depicted Syria as an international *pariah* state, however, away from public scrutiny the US government viewed Syria as a surrogate that was needed in the region. The US even secretly orchestrated talks between Syria and Israel to settle the matter of Golan Heights. The Israeli paper Ha'aretz said the meetings held in Europe began in September 2004 and were initiated by the Syrians. They involved Dr Alon Liel, a former director general of Israel's foreign ministry, Geoffrey Aronson of the Foundation for Middle East Peace in Washington, and Ibrahim Suleiman, a Syrian businessman living in Washington who is from the same Alawi sect as the Syrian president, Bashar al-Assad. The paper further stated that a document was drawn up, dated August 2005, covering security, water, borders and normalisation of ties. It called for a demilitarised zone on the Golan Heights and an early warning post on Mount Hermon operated by the US with military zones on each country's side. The paper also confirmed that the then US Vice President, Dick Cheney, was kept abreast of the talks. President Assad even tried to convert the secret talks into a formal peace process with Israel but was rebuffed both by Tel Aviv and Washington.[xxxix]

In Iraq, the public perception was that Syria encouraged Islamic fighters to cross over into Iraq to undermine the authority of the Iraqi government. The reality was that Syria played an active role in infiltrating such Islamists and passing on valuable intelligence to the US led coalition. Syria's influence over the Sunni resistance fighters that operated in Iraq was emphasised by the Baker-Hamilton report. In May 2006, the Department of Defence quarterly report, titled "Measuring Stability and Security in Iraq," Syria's influence was outlined:

> "…. Syria continues to provide safe haven, border transit, and limited logistical support to some Iraqi insurgents, especially former Saddam-era Iraqi Ba'ath Party elements. Syria also permits former regime elements to engage in organizational activities, such that Syria has emerged as an important organizational and coordination hub for elements of the former Iraqi regime. Although Syrian security and intelligence services continue to detain and deport Iraq-bound fighters, Syria remains the primary foreign fighter gateway into Iraq…"[xl]

The close cooperation between the CIA and the Syrian regime was so warm that even during the time when Syria was called a rogue state, the Syrian regime offered its services to do the dirty work of the CIA. The regime used its world-renowned intelligence agencies to extract information from detainees and prisoners of war through torture for the CIA. The famous case of Canadian citizen Maher Arar is one example that made international news.[xli]

The Alawite collusion for nearly half a century with the US was confirmed by the WikiLeaks cables in 2011 when a senior Alawi official confirmed, *"about 70% of Syria-US interests are shared interests in the region."*[xlii] Syria's importance is not due to its resources, as is the case with much of the colonised world, but due to its geopolitical importance i.e. its location. Relative to the region Syria possesses few gas and oil fields and even fewer reserves of energy. The country's central location in the Muslim world makes it the heart of the Middle East and this led to the Alawite minority playing a role in the region in order to maintain and protect itself. This is why Britain and America fought over control of the country with multiple coups and counter coups in the past.

As mentioned previously, Syria bordering Israel serves as a top strategic tool for the US in protecting its interests in the region. Syria being at war with Israel would expend considerable Israeli resources so having 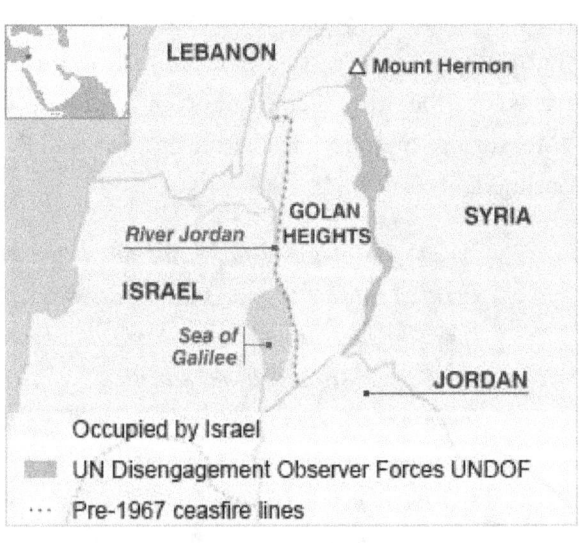 a regime in Damascus, which is friendly with Israel, secures and protects the Zionist state. Since the Arab spring began in Syria, Israeli officials have constantly reiterated they want al-Assad to remain, due to the stability he has brought to the Israeli border.[xliii] The Ha'aretz quoted an Israeli intelligence official in 2013:

> *"Better the devil we know than the demons we can only imagine if Syria falls into chaos and the extremists from across the Arab world gain a foothold there."*[xliv]

The seizure of Lebanon in 1975 for 30 years by Syria shows it can influence the politics of another country that also shares a border with Israel.

Modern Syria was created by France as a colonial asset. The French planned to maintain control by dividing the people and ascribing them new identities from thin air. After WW2, the US was able to gain influence over Syria and till today the US maintains relations with the al-Assad regime in order to protect its interests in the region, this includes securing the protection of Israel. As long as Syria continues with this position in the region, the US will continue to work with the al-Assad clan and the Ba'ath party - a party known to ensure its power through brutal force, death and destruction. The Alawites willingly play this role merely because it is the only way of safeguarding their authority. Hence under such circumstances, it comes as no surprise why the majority of the population took to the streets to bring real change in the country. In Syria today, one is either Sunni Muslim or an Alawi, with another few extremely small ethno-sectarian identities in the country. What can be seen very clearly since the French created Syria is that the national identity of the nation is not an identity anyone in the country subscribes to.

LEBANON

Lebanon today is divided along sectarian lines and was a pure invention carved out of Syria. The Lebanese government has deliberately avoided conducting a census in 77 years (mostly due to Maronite Christians' fears that their votes will be outstripped by the majority Muslim population), so estimates on the ethnic and religious make-up of the country are extremely hard to come by. The country officially recognises 17 religious sects, and the CIA estimated in 1986 that 41% of the country is Shia, 27% Sunni, 16% Maronite, 7% Druze, 5% Greek Orthodox and 3% Greek Catholic. Voting lists from the Lebanese interior ministry for the 2010 general elections showed the number of registered voters split among Sunnis with 27.2%, Shia with 26.7% and Maronite Christians with 20.9%. As part of the Lebanese confessional system, the parliament must be divided equally between Christians and Muslims. Once the parliament is formed, the ruling triumvirate is split by law among a Maronite president, a Sunni prime minister and a Shia speaker of the parliament, while the other main Cabinet positions — the interior, defence, finance and foreign ministries — are divided among a Maronite Christian, a Greek Orthodox, a Shia and a Sunni.

The French created Lebanon for the Maronite Christians and as long as they remained the dominant group, it worked. French-Maronite relations went back to the mid-19th century, whilst Maronite-European relations went back to the Crusades and would play a central role in maintaining French political influence. The French divided Syria and through that carved out Lebanon. The Maronite Christian population was concentrated in Mount Lebanon, but needed the predominantly Sunni and Shia coastal cities and Bekaa Valley to make the country economically viable. Without a dominant group to impose its will over the other factions, Lebanon was a country destined to be engulfed in civil war, politically paralysed and preyed on by outside powers. According to the investigation of the

King-Crane Commission in 1919, the inhabitants of Greater Lebanon were deeply divided over its future. On the Christian side, almost all Maronite, Greek Orthodox and Catholics supported a French mandate and the separation of Syria and Lebanon. On the Muslim side, almost all Sunnis wanted incorporation into an independent Syria, the Druze, led by two powerful families in Lebanon, the *Jamblatts* and the *Arslans*, were strongly against a French-dominated Lebanon; and the Shia of Jabal Amil in the south were afraid of both the Sunnis and the Christians and wanted a loose connection with Syria. The main beneficiaries of the territorial partition were the Maronite Christians. But the French policy increased the possibility of sectarian conflict. With the exception of Beirut, the areas added to Lebanon contained a predominantly Muslim population, whose members objected to being placed within a Christian-dominated political system. Greater Lebanon was brought into existence to provide the Maronites with a distinct political entity in which they were the single largest community. However, they did not make up the majority of the population. By adding several Muslim areas to the new state, the French reduced the Maronites to around 30% of the population.

After World War II, the demographics of Lebanon changed and the Shia population increased. Compounding this was the movement of Palestinians into Lebanon in 1948 with the creation of Israel. Lebanon thus became a container for competing factions and although the factions were of different religions, multiple off-shoots in many of these religious groupings fought each other and allied with other religions as well as external powers for the next 65 years. Domestically, Lebanon became and remains a Pandora's Box of factions whose religious and ethnic fault lines completely overshadow any sense of loyalty to the artificially created nation-state. When the French left after WW2 what they left behind was a sectarian-based political structure, but the Lebanon that emerged upon the demise of the French mandate, which essentially split Syria and Lebanon along a mountain range, has always been invisible to the Syrian eye. The

Syrian political leadership viewed Lebanon as a vital economic outlet to the Mediterranean and as a result its influence extended into Lebanese territory. Lebanon's history from its artificial inception to today has been one of warring clans, factions and sects which have spilled over into the wider region, leading to both regional and international interference.

Following WW2, Lebanon, or more precisely the Lebanese capital, Beirut, became a tourist destination and financial capital. It was eventually given the name "the Paris of the Middle East," due to its French influences and vibrant cultural life that attracted many a westerner. In reality this was just a mirage in the desert and merely concealed the underlying tensions, which would explode into a bloodbath in 1975.

Lebanon was divided into various areas controlled by different factions. The dominant Shia faction was built around Nabi Berri. In 1982, during the civil war Iran created, armed and trained Hezbollah to face-off against Israel and to play the role of proxy for Iran in the country and the region. Each religious faction had multiple offshoots, and within the factions there were multiple competitors for power. From the outside it appeared to be strictly a religious war but that is an incomplete view. It was a competition among factions and offshoots for money, security, revenge and power. Religion played a role but alliances crossed religious lines frequently. The state and central government became far less powerful than the factions. Beirut, the capital, became a battleground for the factions and split apart into mutually hostile cantons.

When the civil war broke out in 1975 it tore the city and country to pieces. More than 100,000 people were killed during a period when Lebanon's population was under 4 million. The civil war was sparked in Beirut by clashes between Palestinian and Christian militias. Christian militias squared off against Palestinian and Sunni ones across a gash known as the Green Line, which ripped through the centre of the city on a northwest-by-southeast axis. To this day, the city remains divided along this line: the eastern half is almost entirely Christian, the western half predominantly Sunni, and the southern suburbs are Shia. The Israelis invaded in 1982 in order to crush the Palestinian Liberation Organisation (PLO). However, the civil war became really destructive when the Syrian army intervened in 1976. By the end of 1976, Syria accepted the proposal of the Arab League summit in Riyadh that gave Syria a mandate to keep 40,000 troops in Lebanon as the bulk of an Arab Deterrent Force (ADF) charged with restoring calm. Other Arab nations were also part of the ADF but they lost interest relatively soon and Syria was left in sole control.

The French had left the Maronite Christians in control of the politics of the country and though this was challenged by both demographic and political trends, they were nevertheless the European hand through which France and Britain maintained influence in Lebanon. The entry of Syria was a direct challenge to European influence in Lebanon. Declassified documents show that the Syrian intervention was due to US orders. Documents and minutes of meetings involving US Secretary of State Henry Kissinger reveal the top US diplomat's open contempt and frustration toward Israeli policymakers for threatening to invade south Lebanon in response to a Syrian intervention. The documents reveal Kissinger saw benefits to a Syrian intervention, in one meeting Kissinger said:

> *"Now if I could design the solution, I would go to Assad and say, If you could move in quickly, and if you could give us an iron clad guarantee that you will get out again quickly and that you will not go south of the [Litani] river, we will keep the Israelis out...We have to go back to Assad ... Ask him what he is up to and if we agree with him, we will do our best to help him... But warn him what he does must be done without the use of Syrian regular forces. I want to make it clear that a Syrian defeat in Lebanon would be a disaster."*[xlv]

The declassified documents also reveal the extremely close

relationship between the US and Assad. The Syrian intervention protected US interests and weakened the European presence in the country.

The Taif agreement in 1989 marked the beginning of the end of the hostilities raging for well over a decade. The agreement made in Taif, Saudi Arabia, put Syria in charge of disarming every militia in Lebanon, a big win for the US as it supported the entry of Syria into Lebanon. The Syrian army oversaw the disarmament and naturally left Hezbollah in place. This post-war occupation of Lebanon by Syria oversaw the political decline of the Maronite population (who were pro-Europe and who the French left in power) as most of their leadership was driven into exile, assassinated or jailed.

In 2005 the insinuation of Syrian officials in the assassination of Rafiq Hariri and the subsequent demands by the EU, Israelis and Lebanese politicians for Syria to withdraw its troops presented fresh challenges to American interests in Lebanon. The EU succeeded in Syria's withdrawal from Lebanon and was able to impose UN resolutions that stipulated the handover of senior Syrian officials—many of them close to Assad—to be tried by a tribunal under the auspices of the UN. The resolutions demanded cessation of support to Hezbollah and for Syria to respect Lebanon's sovereignty. These resolutions and the assassinations of prominent politicians once again deeply divided Lebanon into pro-American and pro-EU camps. The then Lebanese President Emile Lahoud and Speaker of the Parliament Nabih Berry repeatedly thwarted attempts to cast parliamentary votes to legalise the jurisdiction of the UN tribunal, whereas the mass demonstration by Hezbollah sought to embarrass the Pro-EU government internationally.

Lebanon is today a complex of external meddling and faction based ticking time bomb that has made successive Lebanese governments irrelevant. The map may show a nation but it is really a country of microscopic factions engaged in a microscopic political struggle for security and power. Lebanon remains a country in which the warlords have become national politicians. The nation the French created was the first of the Sykes-Picot agreement to come apart. The Maronites who are a Catholic religious group that owes their allegiance to the Pope in Rome have existed in Ash-Sham since before the Muslim conquest in the 600s. They are living proof of the policy of religious tolerance that Islam exercised for the past 1400 years, as they were always given religious freedom without being hassled by the Muslim authorities. The massacres and divisions that have taken place were unheard of in the region until the European colonialists arrived in the region. In the 1840s, conflict between the Druze and the Maronites began to become a problem in the coastal region of Ash-Sham, where the two groups constituted a majority of the population. In order to resolve the problem, the Ottoman authorities divided the region into two administrative districts in 1842. The northern district was governed by the Maronites and the southern one by the Druze.

The French and the British at this time were seeking to increase their influence in the Muslim world, while still competing with each other. As a result, the French supported the Maronites and the British supported the Druze. With international backing, the two groups escalated their violence. In the summer of 1860, over 10,000 Maronite Christians were massacred by the Druze in Damascus. The Ottoman authorities were able to suppress the violence between the two sides within a few months of the outbreak of the war. The Ottomans then re-established direct control over the area to prevent further violence from reoccurring. Regardless of the success of the Ottomans in stopping the violence, the French took the opportunity to intervene. The violence in this part of the Middle East since 1860 was unprecedented and had never been witnessed under Islamic rule. When Lebanon was turned into a nation state it institutionalised the sectarian and faction based population, the heart of the problem in the artificially created nation, called Lebanon. When the Syrian uprising was in full swing in 2012 Walid Jumblatt, the leader of

Lebanon's Druze sect said:

> *"This is the unravelling of the Sykes-Picot agreement, we are seeing the end of what was created 90 years ago. The consequences will be very, very, grave unless they are managed properly."*[xlvi]

JORDAN

Until the defeat of the Ottomans following WW1, Transjordan, today known as the Hashemite Kingdom of Jordan, had been part of the Syrian administrative unit. In March 1921, the British Colonial Secretary, Winston Churchill, convened the Cairo Conference that endorsed an arrangement whereby Transjordan would be added to the Palestine mandate with Abdullah I bin al-Hussein as the Emir under the authority of the British High Commissioner.[xlvii] In 1922, the British modified the mandate over Palestine to include a mandate over the territory east of the Jordan River. Until today, the boundaries of Transjordan relative to Palestine remain undefined. In 1994, the Wadi Araba agreement only defined the borders with Israel and left undefined the boundaries with the Palestinian Authority (West Bank of Jordan). Jordan's Eastern and Southern border with Saudi Arabia was reportedly due to Winston Churchill's 'hiccup,' referring to the abruptly concave section of Jordan's border with Saudi Arabia, causing the border to resemble a zigzag shape.[xlviii] In essence Jordan is an artificial construct. The border with Israel is defined by the Jordan River, but the country itself never existed in history as an entity. The country was created by Britain to satisfy a pledge to their Hashemite allies after the British agreed to give Syria to the French. What was then Transjordan later became Jordan and ultimately served as a buffer with Syria, Iraq and Israel. The Hashemite's themselves were also a foreign import as they were from the Hijaz, so Britain created a precarious situation where the majority indigenous population next to the Jordan River, where being ruled over by a foreign monarchy in the minority!

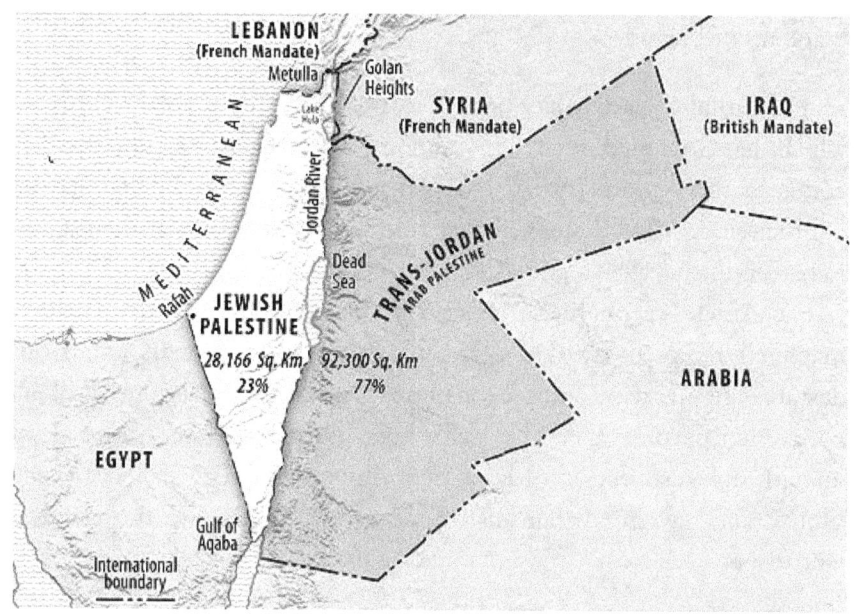

Politically the Hashemite's dominate the political system, which remains firmly in the families grip. Sharif Hussein's son Abdullah was the country's first ruler in 1923. In reality he had very little power and was powerless against the repeated Wahhabi incursions from Najd in modern Saudi Arabia. He relied on British help who maintained a military base with a small air force at Marka, close to Amman. On 20 July 1951, as he was leaving the al-Aqsa Mosque in Jerusalem, King Abdullah was assassinated and his oldest son Talal became King of Jordan. But thirteen months later he was forced to abdicate owing to his mental state, which brought his son to power, King Hussein, who ruled Jordan from 1953 to 1999. A Regency Council was appointed for 10 months for King Hussain to turn 17. King Abdullah II succeeded his father King Hussein following the latter's death in 1999. Abdullah moved quickly to reaffirm Jordan's peace treaty with Israel. Jordan's governance has remained firmly under the authority of the British commissioner. When King Hussein decided to change the heir to the throne from his brother to his son, he made the announcement from London.[xlix] British diplomacy and intelligence has been instrumental in stabilising Jordan since it came under the mandate of Britain.

For Britain, Jordan has been a buffer zone for regional conflicts which has included receiving millions of refugees fleeing conflict zones in the region. Jordan has played this role for the Palestinian conflict since 1948. It played that role when the civil war devastated Lebanon in the 1980's and after 1991 it became a buffer zone for the Iraq conflict. Through the allocation of this role to Jordan, Britain managed to keep rival forces, both local and international, from destabilising Jordan, since a buffer zone serves the interests of all concerned parties. A country with very limited resources, or at best unexplored resources, Jordan's economy had been fuelled by the Gulf States, where Britain also continues to dominate the political landscape.

As an artificial nation, Jordan from its inception faced many domestic challenges which continue today. The Bedouin tribal Jordanians, have traditionally been the core of the Hashemite monarchy, giving it legitimacy and power through the Hashemite domination of the security services, making them a vital source of support for the monarchy. The other important player in Jordan is the Muslim Brotherhood (MB). The MB is composed mainly of Jordanian nationals with Palestinian backgrounds, a segment that constitutes over 50% of the country's population. However in the 1989 parliamentary elections, the MB won 22 of the 80 seats in the lower house, becoming the single largest bloc in Jordan's parliament. The MB then opposed the monarchy on a number of foreign policy issues, including Jordan's 1994 peace treaty with Israel. To contain the MB the monarchy changed the electoral law so that the newly redrawn districts made it increasingly difficult for the MB, which dominates the urban areas of Jordan, to gain large representation in parliament.

As a result, the king successfully maintained the status quo and the Arab spring protests by constantly dissolving the government.

King Abdullah has dismissed various governments on account of challenges to the status quo. Since Jordan's independence in 1946, the palace has appointed more than 60 prime ministers, including three since the Arab unrest broke out in 2011. King Abdullah dissolved the government of Prime Minister Samir Rifai and replaced him with Marouf al-Bakhit, a former army general. Protests still continued, which led King Abdullah to sack Bakhit and his cabinet, naming Awn Shawkat Al-Khasawneh to head the new government and institute new reforms.

As an artificial nation Jordan lacks mineral resources and has an economy which cannot fulfil the basic needs of its people, although this has much to do with the monarchy's incompetency.

75% of Jordan's geography is arid desert. As a result its 6.5 million populous resides in a 150 mile vertical and 80 mile

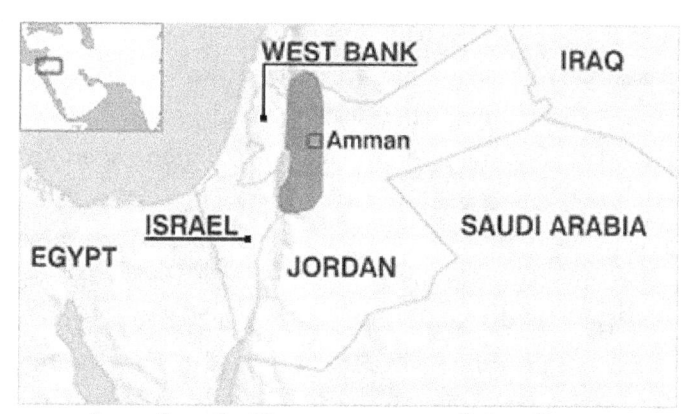

Jordan's Demographic Core

horizontal region straddling the Jordan River. Just over 10% of Jordan's land is arable giving the country limited water supplies. For decades Jordan has received subsidised energy from its Arab neighbours, owing in part to its role as a buffer state with Israel. Before 2003, Saddam Hussein's Ba'athist regime supplied Jordan with discounted crude oil, and shortly after the US invasion of Iraq, Egypt began providing Amman with subsidised natural gas. Due to its small economy, lack of import infrastructure and relative absence of domestic energy reserves, Jordan's heavy reliance on subsidised energy imports from its neighbours has left the kingdom in a precarious position. The only bright spot for Jordan is its oil shale reserves which are the fourth largest in the world, several companies are negotiating with the Jordanian government about exploiting resource.

IRAQ

Iraq has always been the cradle of civilisation. Even before the Muslims came to the region the Assyrians, Babylon's and Nineveh's (Ninawa) had established long and prosperous civilisations. The area around the Euphrates came under Islam during the rule of the second Caliph 'Umar ibn al-Khattab (ra) in 644. This area at the time was part of the Persian Empire, which at the time was ruled by the Sassanid's. Some of the greatest battles of Islam took place in this region and many great cities were built, such as Basra, Kufah, Wasit, Baghdad, Samira and Mosul. This region is an extension of the Arabian Peninsula. The two rivers, Tigris and Euphrates cross this area which historically made it some of the most fertile and productive lands in the world. Iraq's distinctive geographic location at the head of the Gulf made of it one of the most important trade routes connecting Europe with the Indian Ocean. Something the British Empire was to consider strategically important. In 750 the Muslims moved the Caliphate's capital to Baghdad and in turn kick started the Golden Era of Islam. Aside from the period 1258-1261, when the Mongols ransacked Baghdad, the lands that were to become Iraq generally remained under Islamic rule for millennia, up until the British invasion during WW1. Prior to the British invasion the Ottomans established the Wilayah of Baghdad and administered the area around this *wilayah*. Eventually the bustling cities of Basra and Mosul became *wilayat*, Basra had always been a bustling port city. WW1 came to Iraq in the Mesopotamian campaign beginning in November 1914, when the war was in full swing on the western front. Britain never committed its troops to this front despite it being the front line of WW1. This was because the British Empire had more grand aims. The Mesopotamian campaign had no connection to the defeat of Britain's primary strategic rival, Germany, who was busy in France and was about to begin its onslaught of Russia. Whilst British officials maintained they were concerned that a holy war might be ignited in Persia and Afghanistan, thus threatening India, but in reality it was oil that was Britain's main concern in Mesopotamia.

Britain occupied Basra in 1914, soon after the war started. Al-Amara fell, in 1915, but British forces, comprised mainly of personnel from its colonies faced great defeat in Siege of Kut (1915–1916). Facing defeat in Mesopotamia and Gallipoli a new commander was entrusted with reversing this loss. The new commander, General Sir Stanley Frederick Maude, assembled a large force of some 150,000 men, equipped with modern weapons of war and eventually managed to occupy Baghdad in March 1917. But he continued to drive north, eventually occupying Mosul in October 1918. Britain's sudden interest in Mosul was down to, according to the British cabinet secretary Maurice Hankey who had alerted Lloyd George, to the importance of the city eight weeks earlier, after he had read a memorandum written by a senior admiral on Britain's need for oil. The admiral explained that, as oil was four times more efficient than coal, it would eventually take over as the major marine fuel. This would leave Britain vulnerable because whereas it had coal reserves of its own, it depended on the United States for its supply of oil.[1] Against the backdrop of President Wilson's hostility to imperialism, if the British Empire were to remain the dominant maritime power, it was therefore vital to obtain the undisputed control of the greatest amount of Petroleum it could.

Britain once again drew some lines in the desert, which would become the border for a new country, which was to be called Iraq. The Iraq Britain created had never existed in history and was as artificial as its brother next door, Jordon. Both countries were literally brothers as Britain has created a country for Abdullah, the son of Sharif Hussein who served Britain during the Arab revolt. If as though that wasn't enough, Britain created another country for his other son, Faisal, Iraq. Under King Faisal, Britain in reality maintained real power in the newly created country through its three military bases – Ar-Rashid in Baghdad, Al-Habbaniyya, north of Baghdad and Ash-Shiaiba near Basra. The British ambassador in Baghdad had the final word in governing Iraq throughout the Hashemite rule that continued until 1958. King Faisal I died suddenly in 1933 aged 48, while having a health check in Switzerland. His son Ghazi (1933-1939) was something of a playboy and more antipathetic to the continuing British influence and sympathetic to the strong nationalism of Nazi Germany. A lover of fast cars, he died in April 1939 at the wheel of his Buick in a mysterious car accident that many believe was engineered by British intelligence due to the Ghazi's hatred for Britain and close ties to the Nazi's. According to the order of succession to the throne, his young son, Faisal II should have become a king, but Britain appointed his uncle, Abdullah as a prince regent and crown prince, who remained loyal to the British crown until his death in the coup of 1958 along with most of his royal family who were murdered.

After WW2 the US emerged on the international scene and had its eyes on the region's oil. Britain was already forced to concede to the US the oil of Saudi Arabia and many of Iran's large oil fields. Britain naturally did not want to give up the last remaining oil bonanza in the Middle East. What unravelled was an intense Anglo-American struggle over Iraq with numerous coups and counter coups.

In July 1958 Brigadier Abdul Karim Qasim and Colonel Abdul Salam Aarif, led a military coup against the monarchy, which

Brigadier Abdul Karim Qasim (L) and Colonel Abdul Salam Aarif (R), July 1958

effectively cut Britain from the country's leadership. This naturally served US interests as it weakened Britain. Egypt's Gamal Abdul Nasser immediately welcomed the military that led the coup. Britain tried to reverse its loss in Iraq by landing its forces in Jordan, but events had moved beyond its control. The Soviet Union mobilised its forces along its border with Turkey and warned Britain of the consequences if it invaded Iraq. This escalation was too much for Britain and thus a new republican system emerged in Iraq and the country Britain created got out of the British grip after Iraq withdrew from the Baghdad pact. Iraq also dropped the pound sterling as a currency. By 1961, a new Iraqi law reclaimed most of the concessions that were previously given to foreign oil companies, much to the anger of both the US and Britain.

Differences soon emerged between Qasim and Aarif; Qasim got closer to the Ba'athists, whilst Aarif grew close to Nasser and preferred Iraq joining Egypt and Syria in the United Arab Republic, something Qasim was dead against. These tensions led to Qasim removing him from government, a government Aarif was in reality playing second fiddle to Qasim. He was arrested and put on trial. Qasim increasingly worked with the communists in Iraq during the last years of his government, which strengthened their position in Iraq and caused great concern to both the US and Britain in the midst of the Cold war. Multiple coup attempts took place against Qasim, but they all failed. On the 8th February 1963 the Ba'athists and nationalists united around Colonel Abdul Salam Aarif and undertook a bloody violent coup that led to the killing of Qasim and the elimination and torture of the communists in Iraq. Ali Saleh Sa'adi, the then secretary of Ba'ath party said after the coup: *"We came to power on an American train."*[li] King Hussein of Jordan said in an interview with Mohammad Haikal, the editor of Al-Ahram newspaper at the time:

> *"I know for a fact that what happened in Iraq on 8th February was supported by American intelligence ... Many meetings were held between the Ba'ath Party and American intelligence - the most critical ones in Kuwait. Did you know that on 8th February, the day of the coup in Baghdad, there was a secret radio broadcast directed toward Iraq that relayed to those carrying out the coup the names and addresses of Communists there so that they could be seized and executed."*[lii]

The problem with this coup was that it was mixed with officers, individuals and groups with mixed loyalties to both the US and Britain, so instability was going to last unless one faction was able to take complete power, over the other.

The Ba'athists were led by Ali Saleh Sa'di, Mahdi Ammash and Ahmad Hasan al-Bakr who were both close to Britain whilst the nationalists were led by Abdul Salam Aarif, Tahir Yahya and others, who were supported by Nasser and the US. Disputes began almost immediately over government powers. As a result, Abdul Salam Aarif removed the Ba'athists from the authority and simultaneously strengthened his grip on power. But in April 1966, Abdul Salam Aarif died in a plane crash and was replaced by his brother Abdul Rahman Aarif as president of Iraq. But he was a weak leader and was unable to unite his brother's forces around himself and keep the Ba'athists at bay. Events finally settled in Britain's favour in July 1968 when the Ba'athists led by the General al-Bakr and his deputy Saddam Hussein undertook a bloodless coup. The Ba'ath party regime of 1968 was immediately welcomed by Britain when the ambassador in Baghdad wrote:

> *The new regime may look to the United Kingdom for military training and equipment and we should lose no time in appointing a defence attache.*[liii]

The regime's new Defence Minister, General Tikriti, was invited to the Farnborough Air Show and was told by the ambassador that *'it seemed to me we now had an opportunity to restore Anglo-Iraqi relations to something of their former intimacy.'* In reply, General Tikriti said that during the Ba'athist regime of 1963 he had greatly appreciated the cooperative attitude of *'Her Majesty's Government.*[liv]

BA'THISM

Ba'athism attracted some following in the Middle East during the 1950's and 1960's. Many historians when analysing the Arab world view countries such as Syria and Iraq through the prism of Ba'athism as they proclaimed they were and had Ba'athist parties who took power in these countries. Ba'athism was based on Arab nationalism mixed with some Communist ideals and emerged in the Middle East after the collapse of the Ottoman Empire. As the region was primarily Muslims with Islam its ideal and outlook, some Arabs in the confusion surrounding the collapse of the Ottomans viewed pan-Arabism as a way forward. Arab nationalism was seen as a way to remove colonialism and bring dignity to the people of the Middle East. In reality, aside from a handful of ideologues who believed in some vague ideas of Arabism and nationalism based on an Arab identity the masses never adopted it as an identity. The rulers such as Saddam Hussein and the Ba'ath party in Syria used Ba'thism to rally some officers and like-minded people around them, but they were in reality ruthless, pragmatic individuals and groups looking to remain in power. This is why by the 1970's Ba'athism had died as the region had seen it was just a front for power, cloaked in lies.

These lies included the Ba'ath Party's supposed aim of uniting the entire Arab world under Ba'athist rule. The Ba'ath Party in Iraq established an oppressive, totalitarian police state that was rife with informants and fostered intense fear in the population. Iraq in reality became a police state not unlike Communist East Germany or Enver Hoxha's Albania. When Saddam came to power in 1979, he led a *"Stalinesque"* purge to consolidate his control over the Iraqi Ba'ath Party and Iraq. He did not tolerate any dissent and famously killed untold thousands of his own people in his quest to exert total control over the country. Iraq's Ba'athism morphed from a Pan-Arab revolutionary socialist movement to a personality cult centred on Saddam Hussain. The formation of the Fedayeen Saddam — literally *"those who are willing to die for Saddam,"* a force of some 30,000 men who had pledged to lay down their lives for their leader — reflected this cult of personality.

Rather than attempt to unite politically with other countries like Syria to form a Pan-Arab Ba'athist state, Saddam instead opted to expand his Saddamist state by invading first Iran and later Kuwait. Both of these ventures brought disaster upon Iraq and the Iraqi people. Uprisings by Iraq's Shia majority and Kurdish minority were put down with extreme force. Syria's Ba'athist government strongly opposed these expansionist ambitions.

As Communist Party membership was in totalitarian East Germany, Maoist China or the Soviet Union, Ba'ath Party membership in Iraq was important for anyone hoping to hold any type of government office, operate a business or otherwise get ahead. Iraqi Ba'athism was not a winsome nor an attractive ideology. Instead, it was brutally forced upon the Iraqi people. Although there certainly were some true believers, most Ba'ath Party members joined the party for pragmatic purposes.

SADDAM HUSSAIN

During al-Bakr's presidency, Saddam proved himself to be an effective politician but also a ruthless one. He did much to modernise Iraq's infrastructure, industry, and health-care system, and raised social services, education, and farming subsidies to levels unparalleled in the other countries in the region. He also nationalised Iraq's oil industry, just before the energy crisis of 1973, which resulted in massive revenues for the nation. During this time, Saddam helped develop Iraq's first chemical weapons program and to guard against coups, created a powerful security apparatus, which included both Ba'athist paramilitary groups and the People's Army which frequently used torture, rape and assassination to achieve its goals. By 1979, al-Bakr was forced to concede his authority to Saddam Hussein who managed to rally the Ba'ath forces around him. On July 22nd 1979, just days after taking over the presidency Saddam Hussein organised an assembly of Ba'ath leaders and read aloud the names of suspected spies, these people were taken from the room and publicly executed by firing squad. A few years later, in 1982, he ordered the execution of at least three hundred officers who had supposedly questioned his military tactics. Once in control, Saddam surrounded himself with a tightly-knit group of family and friends who assumed high levels of responsibility within the government. These individuals were also not immune to Saddam's paranoia. At one point, Adnan Talfah, Saddam's brother-in-law and childhood friend, was killed in a "mysterious" helicopter crash and in 1996 Saddam had his sons-in-law murdered for being disloyal.

The same year that Saddam ascended to the presidency, 1979, Ayatollah Khomeini led a successful revolution in Iraq's neighbour to the northeast, Iran. This major development presented serious ramifications for both Britain and Saddam Hussain. Britain had brought the Ba'athists to power in Iraq but had lost control of Iran with the emergence of Khomeini. This revolution in Iran presented a series challenge to British interests across the Middle East. For Saddam Hussein, developments in Iran posed a direct threat to him as his powerbase was the minority Sunni population, whilst the Shia population in the South of Iraq represented the majority and Saddam worried that developments in Shia majority Iran could lead to a similar uprising in Iraq. It is important to remember that it was Britain after WW1 that left the minority Sunni in power over the majority Shia in Iraq. On September 22, 1980, Saddam Hussein ordered Iraqi forces to invade the oil-rich region of Khuzestan in Iran. The conflict soon descended into an all-out war, lasting eight years.

The element of surprise seemed to work in support of Iraq as it quickly moved across the border into Iran. Iran seemed destined for defeat. At this point the US began supplying Iran with weapons and desperately needed spare parts for its military equipment. During January of 1981 American supplies worth billions of dollars were sent to Iran through Israel, which enabled Iran to counter the Iraqi offensive.[lv] Within a year thereafter it was Iraq that was close to collapse. During the spring of 1982 Iran threatened to win the war and at this point the US began sending supplies worth billions of dollars through Israel to Iraq.[lvi] Richard Murphy, deputy Foreign Secretary from 1983 to 1989, summarised this American policy in the following manner:

> *"(The) administration's basic position in the war between Iran and Iraq was that a 'victory by either side is neither military achievable nor strategically desirable."*[lvii]

In other words, America was out to weaken both Saddam Hussein and Ayatollah Khomeini, with an ultimate aim of bringing Iraq into the American realm of influence and keeping Iran there. In the end, alongside America's support of both warring sides, the Iran-Iraq war came to an end in 1988 with a ceasefire; over 500,000 people had perished and caused economic losses of £560 billion. During the conflict the international community ignored Iraq's use of chemical weapons, in its genocidal dealing with its Kurdish population.

In 1990, Saddam Hussein waged a new war against Kuwait. The

invasion started on 2nd August 1990, and within two days of combat, most of the Kuwaiti Armed Forces were either overrun by the Iraqi

Republican Guard or escaped to neighbouring Saudi Arabia and Bahrain. The Emirate of Kuwait was annexed, and Saddam Hussein announced a few days later that it was the 19th province of Iraq. Saddam Hussein had failed to deal a blow to Iran, something Britain desperately needed. The invasion of Kuwait would lead to the strengthening of Saddam's position in the region and allow him to propagate British interests throughout the region. The US before the Iraqi invasion of Kuwait gave Saddam its assurance that it would not interfere in its quarrel with Kuwait. US Ambassador April Glaspie conveyed the message to Saddam that the US 'had no opinion' on Iraq's future intentions with regard to Kuwait.[lviii] However, when Saddam invaded Kuwait the US used the incident to expand its influence and effectively seize the Gulf through building military bases, gaining control over its oil reserves and bringing the region's rulers under its influence. Britain had no choice but to join the 'liberation of Kuwait' and salvage whatever it could. It was Britain that ensured the US only liberated Kuwait and did not go all the way to Baghdad, even though it had the capacity and capability to do so. In this way what Britain was able to keep Saddam Hussein in power and the US used the fear of Saddam to interfere in the Gulf for the foreseeable future and an excuse to maintain large forces in the strategic region of the Persian Gulf.

When the US returned to effectively finish the invasion of Iraq in 2003, it overthrew Saddam Hussein and took control of the country's oil, but the plans for this were laid soon after the liberation of Kuwait 1991. The US military, defence establishment, energy companies and the right-wing began planning for Iraqi occupation soon after the fall of the Soviet Union and liberation of Kuwait. This new policy aimed at preserving America as the leading state in the world and maintaining American influence across the world, ensuring no nation in the world could challenge it. Most of the details comprised of unilateral military solutions without the need for UN resolutions i.e. unilateralism. This policy was first called: "peace through strength" in a document issued by the Pentagon in 1992, when Dick Cheney was secretary of defence. Work continued on this strategy until around 1997 when Paul Wolfowitz, Donald Rumsfeld and Dick Cheney became influential members in the US administration and gave it its final name - *"Project for the New American Century."* In 2000 the Project for the New American Century published *"Rebuilding America's Defences: Strategies, Forces, and Resources for a New Century,"* which called for changing unfavourable regimes, distribution of American forces in Europe, South Asia, Central and Middle East. With the aim of controlling the energy resources of the world, militarising space, and beefing up US nuclear capabilities. This document was actually disclosed by the Sunday Herald which pointed out that Bush administration had planned for military control over the gulf for many years, with or without Saddam Hussein in power.[lix] The document mentioned:

> *"The United States has for decades sought to play a more permanent role in Gulf regional security. While the unresolved conflict with Iraq provides the immediate justification for a substantial American force presence in the Gulf."*

All of this shows the US planned to invade Iraq before its invasion of Afghanistan and even before 9/11, these were merely used as justifications.

We should all be familiar with what played out in Iraq; there were no WMDs, the claims of chemical weapons, claims of them being deployable in 45 minutes, democracy promotion and liberating the people were merely lies to justify the occupation. The US divided the country along ethno-sectarian lines which has remained a recipe for disaster to this day, it did this to deal with the insurgency that in 2005 was bleeding it to death. By dividing the country upon ethno-sectarian lines it turned the people against each other, rather than

110

fighting US forces. The US constructed a political system in Iraq which was to protect and maintain its interests. America merely replaced a brutal system with a corrupt system that recognised the ethnic and sectarian breakdown of Iraq that once again led it to intervene in the country in 2014. The US worked with the various Shia groups in the South of Iraq to construct its political architecture. All these groups were close to Iran and both, the US and Iran, have no problem working together on this. After 2003 Iraq firmly came under US control, a country which Britain had created, defended and maintained for a long time.

THE KURDS

The Kurdish question – a term used in reference to the fact that Kurdish people did not have a homeland has dominated Kurdish history as well as Iraq. Historically, the Kurdish people straddled the areas of South Turkey, North Syria and Northern Iraq. Foreign interference is the primary reason why a Kurdish state doesn't exist. But despite the fall of Saddam Hussein in Iraq and the current developments in Syria a viable Kurdish state will continue to avail them. The historical promises made to the Kurds of a truly independent Kurdish state by the US and the British Empire before them, over the last century, were never serious. Both powers exploited the demands of statehood by the Kurds in order to occupy Iraq. The British Empire wanted to instigate a rebellion against the Ottomans in order to colonise the Islamic lands, and for this it supported many nationalistic calls in order to exploit them for its own ends. The British Empire promised a Kurdish state to Mahmood Al-Hafeed in 1919 in exchange for the Kurds to fight against the Ottomans in Sulaimaiyyah. When Al-Hafeed's rebel group expelled the Ottomans, Britain backed away from its promises and exiled al-Hafeed to India. At the Treaty of Sèvres in 1920, in order to frustrate the Caliph Mohammad Waheeduddin, Britain imposed a clause that would establish 'Kurdistan.' However, by 1924 Britain had succeeded in dismantling the Ottoman state and it signed the Treaty of Lausanne with Mustafa Kemal and abandoned the Kurdish state. The US made similar promises to the Kurds in Iraq; the Kurds sided with the US which enabled America to occupy Iraq. Whilst a regional government exists in Northern Iraq today, the Kurdistan Regional Government (KRG) in no way represents an answer to the Kurdish question as it is an artificial state which depends upon Turkish finance and exists to keep Iraq ethnically divided. Both the US and British Empire exploited the Kurds for their own strategic objectives.

The Kurds in origin are an ethnic Iranian group who historically inhabited the mountainous areas to the south of Caucasus, which came to be known as Kurdistan over time. During the 20th and 21st century the British Empire and America used the Kurds demand for statehood to achieve their own strategic objectives and for these reasons an independent Kurdish state never really materialised. The most flourishing period of Kurdish power was during the 12th century when Salahuddin Ayubi united the Muslim lands and recaptured Jerusalem in the Crusades. As part of the Islamic lands, the Kurds embraced Islam and became the leaders amongst the Muslims. This in many ways explains the struggle for independence by the Kurds in the modern era, an ethnic state based on Kurdish nationalism has been a recipe for disaster for them, whilst the Kurds unified with the Muslims around them saw their most glorious period.

Britain created Iraq as an artificial nation in WW1, to divide the people and maintain its dominance of the region. After WW2, the US emerged as the world's superpower and competed with Britain over Iraq, which led to an intense struggle in the Iraq, with coups and counter coups. The emergence of Saddam Hussein, allowed Britain to put an end to US influence in the country, which became a lynchpin for British interests in the region. The US used Saddam's invasion of Kuwait to begin the process of removing him and eventually succeeded in 2003. This competition between the US and Britain is what has caused chaos in the country and both the US and Britain have no problem working with rulers who maintained their positions through brutal methods of torture against the domestic population.

ISRAEL

The state of Israel for all intents and purposes is an artificial state that was created by the colonial powers. From 1900 until its creation in 1947, Jews mainly from Europe migrated in large numbers to Palestine and after confiscating land from the inhabitants and expelling them, the state of Israel was created. The artificial nature of Israel can be seen from numerous perspectives that highlight the nation is not sustainable and will always need foreign patrons, support, aid, finance and cover.

Israel is small in terms of its demography; its population is just over 8 million people. In comparison, there are 22 million people in Syria and 83 million in Egypt. Unable to field a large army compared to others in the region, due to its small population, Israel must rely on its reserves. Israel's small population also increases its sensitivity to civilian and military losses. Losing just one war can mean the end of the country and thus, ever since 1947 Israel faces an existential threat to its survival from the surrounding states as well as non-state actors. The basic challenge of Israel is its national security requirements outstrip its military capabilities, making it dependent on an outside power. The knock-on effect of such a small population is a labour shortage. Israel only has a labour force of 3.3 million. Economic development and industrial development are labour intensive and dependent on knowledge and skills retention. With such a small labour force, Israel is reliant upon foreign knowledge and expertise.

Israel lacks strategic depth. The country has less than 21,000 square kilometres of land, smaller than Wales in the United Kingdom. At its narrowest, Israel is a mere 10 km wide. A hostile fighter could fly across all of Israel (40 nautical miles wide from the Jordan River to the Mediterranean Sea) within four minutes. For these reasons Israel is considered one the most densely populated countries in the world.

Israel is surrounded by Muslim nations. Egypt the largest country in the region and with a population 11 times the size of Israel can field a military that will outnumber the Israeli military. This means Egypt can absorb casualties at a far higher rate than Israel. This would mean the Egyptian military can engage in an extended, high-intensity battle that would break the back of the Israeli military with a rate of attrition that Israel cannot sustain. If Israel was forced to simultaneously engage with the other countries it shares borders with, dividing its forces and supply lines it will run out of troops long before Egypt, even if Egypt were absorbing far more casualties.

Israel faces numerous multifaceted economic challenges due to its artificial nature. Its economy is worth $245 billion, which is just too small to cater for Israel's population. This effects how much tax the government collects as it subsidises the world's Jews to migrate to Israel in order to normalise its occupation. As a result Israel has focused on key industries for its survival. This means many industries such as mining and manufacturing have been neglected. To compensate for this Israel relies on technology, military and foreign aid transfers. It also relies on influential Jews across the world, especially in the US, to influence foreign policies of these states in favour of Israel. Israel has a heavy dependency on the goodwill of other states. If it was to lose favour it is too small for country to be self-sufficient. One effect of such an economy is poverty in Israel. 24% – over 2 million Israeli citizens live below the poverty line. The small budget of the Israeli government has led to many to resort to utilising family links to gain wealth. One report in 2010 highlighted 18 Israeli families controlled 60% of all Israeli companies.[ix] Their wealth is concentrated in four of Israel's largest industries: banking and insurance, chemicals, high tech, and military/homeland security.

Israel has always lacked resources. Because of this, it will never become self-sufficient as it will always have to import energy. Israel relies heavily on external imports for meeting most of its energy needs, spending significant amounts from its domestic budget for its transportation sector that relies on gasoline and diesel fuel while the majority of electricity production is generated using imported coal. It is apparent that the region has an abundance of oil and gas yet none of this is in Israel.

The geography of Israel is not naturally conducive to agriculture. More than half of the land area is desert, and the climate, due to lack of water resources, does not favour farming. Only 20% of Israel's land area is naturally arable. Whilst Israel is now able to produce most of what it consumes it has to also export this as it needs to earn foreign income. Israel's *Achilles heel,* however, is its need to import grain and 80% of its grain is imported, is another strain on government revenues.

Israel also suffers from a chronic water shortage. In recent years it is feared Israel may find it difficult to adequately supply municipal and household water requirements. Israel's water sources are considered to be running out with 95% already consumed. New sources for water are considered to be small and will be unable to replace its main source when it runs out.

Israel's economy is dependent upon foreign markets. Due to

having a very small domestic market (because of its small population) it is forced to search for foreign markets to generate wealth. Industrialised nations generally focus 10% of their economy towards foreign trade both imports and exports. However, 30% of the Israeli economy relies on exports, which is considerably high. Israel's main exports 10 years ago were Jaffa oranges and other agricultural products. Today's exports are increasingly high-tech, an estimated 80% of the products Israel exports are high-tech electronics components. However, Israel has found itself light years behind Japan, China and Germany in this very competitive sector. 40% of Israeli exports end up on US shores even though the US can make the same agricultural goods and computer hardware cheaper and of better quality. A reliance on foreign markets makes an economy reliant on foreigners constantly consuming and links the fortunes of one's economy with others.

ISLAM

Jerusalem is a city holy to the three Abrahamic faiths: Islam, Judaism, and Christianity. It has a history that spans thousands of years, it goes by many names: Jerusalem, al-Quds, Yerushaláyim, Aelia, and more all reflecting its diverse heritage. It is a city that numerous Muslim prophets called home from Sulayman (Solomon) and Dawood (David) to Isa (Jesus), may Allah be pleased with them all. Islamic texts refer to *Masjid al-Aqsa* as blessed and this is why the area holds great importance for Muslims, even today. Jerusalem was part of the wider Ash-Sham area, which itself came under Islamic rule beginning 629. Ash-Sham was a Roman colony where Roman culture and Christianity were predominant. Syrians, Armenians, Jews, Arabs and some Romans resided there. Ash-Sham had been under Roman rule for seven centuries prior to the Islamic conquest and included Palestine and all the desert plains north of the Hijaz to Anatolia. It was during the Caliphate of 'Umar ibn al-Khattab (ra), that Muslims would begin to seriously expand northwards into the Byzantine

116

realm.

By 637, Muslim armies had captured all the areas around Jerusalem. In charge of Jerusalem was Patriarch Sophronius, a representative of the Byzantine government, as well as a leader in the Christian Church. Although besieged, Sophronius refused to surrender the city unless the Caliph, 'Umar (ra), came to accept the surrender himself. Upon hearing this, 'Umar (ra) travelled to accept the surrender of the city and only then Sophronius surrendered it. As was the case with all other cities they conquered, the Muslims drafted a treaty detailing the rights and privileges regarding the conquered people and the Muslims in Jerusalem. This treaty was signed by 'Umar (ra) and Patriarch Sophronius along with some of the generals of the Muslim armies. It was an unprecedented treaty at the time, as usually the inhabitants would be massacred after a conquest. And it was also unprecedented because the city would be ruled by Muslims with religious freedom for minorities protected according to the Treaty of 'Umar (ra). Jerusalem remained under Islamic rule for 462 years until the Crusades; the crusader occupation lasted only 88 years. From Salahuddin's recapture in 1187, Islamic rule remained in the region until British forces arrived in 1917.

ZIONISM

Theodor Herzl is credited with founding political Zionism, a movement which sought to establish a Jewish state, by elevating the Jewish question onto the international scene. In 1896, Herzl published *Der Judenstaat* (*The Jewish State*), offering his vision of a future state and the following year he presided over the first World Zionist Congress. Ever since the establishment of the Zionist movement, the Jews have aimed to achieve economic and political dominion over the Middle East.

The establishment of a Jewish homeland was proposed by British Prime Minister Henry Bannerman in 1906:

117

"There are people (the Muslims) who control spacious territories teeming with manifest and hidden resources. They dominate the intersections of world routes. Their lands were the cradles of human civilisations and religions. These people have one faith, one language, one history and the same aspirations. No natural barriers can isolate these people from one another ... if, per chance, this nation were to be unified into one state; it would then take the fate of the world into its hands and would separate Europe from the rest of the world. Taking these considerations seriously, a foreign body should be planted in the heart of this nation to prevent the convergence of its wings in such a way that it could exhaust its powers in never-ending wars. It could also serve as a springboard for the West to gain its coveted objects."[lxi]

Britain declared its support for a Jewish homeland in the infamous Balfour Declaration in 1917. This was the same year British General Allenby entered Jerusalem and conquered it from the Ottomans. As far as Britain was concerned, creating a homeland for the Jews at the heart of the Muslim world would aid its aim of dividing the Muslims and maintain British hegemony for the foreseeable future. After WW1 and the collapse of the Ottoman Empire, Britain received the mandate for Palestine and from this period until Israel's creation in 1948 Jews from Europe migrated to Palestine. The result was an exponential rise in the number of Jews living in Palestine. According to British census data of 1922, there were 83,790 Jews in Palestine. By 1931, it was 175,138. And by 1945, the number had jumped to 553,600 people. In 25 years, Jews had gone from 11% of the total population to 31%.[lxii] Naturally, the reaction from the Palestinian Muslims was less than enthusiastic. Tension between new Jewish settlers and native Palestinians erupted on numerous occasions. Whilst it appeared Britain was losing control the British were the ones that granted the Jews the opportunity to move to Palestine.

Britain envisaged a secular state over Palestine, dominated and ruled by the Jews, with the indigenous Muslims living amongst the newly migrated peoples. But the emergence of the US as the new global power and looking to remove Britain from the region, it came up with the two-state solution when Britain had been pushing one state with Palestinians and Jews living side by side. The US looked towards Israel, within defined and secure boundaries, even though it was established with dreams of *Eretz Israel* (a greater Israel). This was the first difference between the US and Israel – the position of Israel has always been to never define its borders. The US was able to impose the two-state solution i.e. permanent borders for both the Jews and Muslim Palestinians with Jerusalem under an international force, due to its sensitivity. The peace process for the US has always been where these final boundaries will be.

Seeing the coming end of the British Mandate over Palestine, and the inevitable conflict between the Muslims and Jews, the newly-created United Nations took up the issue in 1947 and came up with a plan known as the United Nations Partition Plan for Palestine. The plan advocated the creation of two states in what has historically been known as Palestine. One state for Jews known as Israel and one state for the Arabs called Palestine. The indigenous people of the region were expected to give up their homeland for the newly arriving Jews. Britain declared an end to the Mandate of Palestine and withdrew from the country on May 14th, 1948. That day, the Zionist movement in Palestine declared the establishment of a new country, Israel. The following day, the neighbouring Arab countries declared their rejection of the declaration and invaded Israel. After the war there was an enormous increase in the size of Israel. The resulting state was much larger than the state proposed by the United Nations, capturing approximately 50% of the proposed Arab state.

The largest impact of the 1948 War was the expulsion of much of the Muslim-Palestinian population. Within the borders of the new State of Israel there had been close to 1 million Palestinian Muslims before the war. By the end of the war in 1949 between 700,000 and 750,000 of them had been expelled.[lxiii] Only 150,000 remained in Israel. In 1947 the Jews constituted 32% of the population and owned 5.6% of the land. By 1949, largely as a result of paramilitary-terrorist organisations such as the Hagenah, Irgun and Stern gangs, Israel controlled 80% of Palestine. The plight of the Muslim Palestinians was well understood from the very beginning by Israeli leaders like David Ben-Gurion, who told Nahum Goldman, then-president of the World Jewish Congress:

> *"If I were an Arab leader I would never make terms with Israel. That is natural: we have taken their country ... We come from Israel, but two thousand years ago, and what is that to them? There has been anti-Semitism, the Nazis, Hitler, Auschwitz, but was that their fault? They only see one thing: we have come here and stolen their country. Why should they accept that?"[lxiv]*

ZIONIST STATE

The Zionist state faced numerous challenges due to its artificial reality. Despite support from the world's powers Israeli politicians needed to navigate the interests of the US and Britain in the wider region, it had to take account of the Muslims in the region who completely outnumbered the Jews, establishing the Israeli state and consolidating it in the region.

Due to Israel's small population it has relied on migration from across the world. The reality of secular Israel is that it practices racism on a state level, even upon the Jews. The close correlation between ethnicity and socio-economic class in Israel remains the main axis along which the Ashkenazi and Middle Eastern Jews fracture is drawn. The consolidation of ethnicity into social class, what some analysts have referred to as the formation of Israeli ethno class, represents a serious cleavage that divides Israel from within like the orthodox-secular division. This apartheid has been entrenched into a system of laws, regulations and practices which govern the operation of state institutions.

Israeli politics is also as split along two lines, the Labour party has pursued a 'land for peace' position which effectively sees a population separation between the 2 million plus residents of the West Bank and Gaza strip and the State of Israel, adjustments in the pre-1967 borders to accommodate Israel's security requirements, including giving up some land if it secures Israel and the requirement for no foreign army west of the Jordan River.

The Likud party represents the opposite of the Labour party. The Likud Party opposes land for peace and sees this as treason to the Zionist cause. Likud's position has been that land for peace undermines the security and integrity of the state of Israel. This voice is based on the belief that the security which Israel seeks can only be achieved by controlling land. Abandoning territories would signal the loss of Israeli expansionism, through which it seeks security, and is hence a dangerous step in the wrong direction. Peace for peace is the Likud position that calls for a cessation of hostilities to be reciprocated by both sides. Israel would continue to hold those lands she felt were vital to her security until she is convinced that the threat against her is no longer evident, thereupon removing the need for land. Thus far, these contradictory political positions have divided Israel as to what is the best course for action. Is a peace agreement with the surrounding Arab states worth the sacrifice of occupied land? Or will compromising the possession of occupied land compromise Israel's security. This division is manifest on the international arena as contradictory policies. This has seriously compromised Israel's ability to forge a consistent course within the international arena. Yitzhak Rabin steered Israel on one course, only for it to be changed when Netanyahu came to the helm, leading to the stop-start nature of the 'peace' process, and all its consequent complications.

Israel historically has pursued a number of policies in order to influence a final outcome. Israel has worked to protect US interests in the region in order to make itself relevant to the US. It has taken an aggressive posture and ensured it remained unpredictable in order to deal a fatal blow by any of the majority Muslim regimes in the region. It has also never defined its borders and used this as a pretext to expand settlements and thus Israel and influence in any future settlement. Israel has continued to alter the facts on the ground. In Al-Quds she has carried out extensive changes by building large Jewish settlements in East Jerusalem, a Palestinian populated area. Israel has always worked to define the final borders by altering the facts on the ground. As the West Bank is large compared to the Gaza Strip, expanding settlements is a policy to expand Israel. However, Israel still needs the US for any final settlement and for these reasons it has organised lobbying in the US and the world's media in order to achieve a favourable outcome.

PEACE PROCESS

The original peace process the US envisaged was based upon the borders of the 1947 UN partition plan, which saw the partition of Palestine, giving 55% to the Jews, all though they represented only 30% of the population. 70% of the Muslim population were only given 40% of the geography. Following its founding war of 1947-49, Israel came into existence but chose not to define its borders and today it remains with undeclared borders. But it took 78% of Palestine, a percentage it has steadily increased in subsequent years, which has seen the expulsion of the indigenous population.

The US plan defined Israeli borders alongside a Palestinian state. The Likud party attempted to unilaterally define the borders by building settlements and expelling Muslims. The endeavour to achieve *Eretz Israel* is complicated by the fact that the Labour party in Israel believes in giving up land for permanent defined borders, it believes this is a price worth paying for the security it needs. America rejects the idea of substituting European influence with Jewish influence, and she also rejects the idea of sharing power with any other country. America is committed to securing Israel, guaranteeing her security and ensuring a prosperous standard of living for the Jews living there. However, she refuses to allow Israel to share the influence with her. It was the late Republican Senator Jesse Helms who called Israel *"America's aircraft carrier in the Middle East"* when explaining why the United States viewed Israel as such a strategic ally, saying that the military foothold in the region offered by the Jewish State alone justified the military aid that the US grants Israel every year.[lxv]

Despite its dependency on western powers Israel from its inception attempted to assert itself and oppose US regional policy in the pursuit of its own interests. Yitzhak Shamir alluded to this point when he said

> *"Much as we want to coordinate our activities with the United States, the interests (of the United States and Israel) are not identical. We have to, from time to time, worry about our own interests."*[lxvi]

Despite numerous attempts at the peace process the US has been forced to balance between utilising Israel in the region, containing Israel in the region, its domestic political cycle and more pressing issues elsewhere in the world. Israel has taken advantage of US preoccupation elsewhere to unilaterally expand illegal settlements in order to influence where the final borders will be. As a result Israel has been able to influence the geography on the ground which will work in its favour. However, Israel has failed to normalise its position in the region and this is where it will always be reliant upon the US.

Israel was the creation of Britain in order to divide the region, through the creation of a foreign entity at the heart of the Muslim world. This conspiracy included offering Zionists something the British had no right to negotiate with. Israel has been protected ever since by western powers, despite expanding and expelling the indigenous people.

PALESTINE

In the turbulent history of the Muslim world, perhaps no struggle has captivated the people more than Palestine. Despite numerous conspiracies to normalise Israeli existence Palestine remains an issue for over 1.6 billion Muslims as well as the wider world. Israel's continued expansion and continued support and financial aid from the US and other Western countries has allowed Israel the necessary cover to legitimise its presence in the Middle East. The Muslims of Palestine and the wider region have been let down time and time again by the Muslim rulers in the region and the international community.

On December 11, 1917, British General Edmund Allenby entered Jerusalem triumphantly through the Jaffa gate, and the city became an occupied territory. On this historic occasion, Allenby reportedly declared that "the wars of the Crusades are now complete."[lxvii] Allenby's statement was a powerful reminder that the British entry into Jerusalem was a continuation of and a "successful" conclusion to the Crusades. From this occupation until Israel was created in 1948 Jews from across the world migrated to Palestine, eventually leading to the creation of Israel and the expulsion of the indigenous people.

An estimated 700,000 Muslim Palestinians fled or were expelled, and hundreds of Muslim towns and villages were depopulated and destroyed. These refugees and their descendant's number several million people today, divided between Jordan (2 million), Lebanon (427,057), Syria (477,700), the West Bank (788,108) and the Gaza Strip (1.1 million), with at least another quarter of a million internally displaced in Israel.

CREATING ISRAEL

The war of 1948 that led to the establishment of the State of Israel, on the surface it is difficult to understand how 40 million Arabs could not match the fighting strength of just 600,000 Zionists. It was only possible due to the complicity and neglect of the region's Muslim rulers. The primary representatives of the Palestinian cause were King Abdullah of Transjordan, King Farook of Egypt and The Mufti of Palestine. Their unity was weak and they were subject to constant manipulation by the British. In particular, King Abdullah's portrayal of himself as a defender of the Palestinian cause was a façade. It was no secret that his father Sheriff Hussein collaborated with the British against the Ottoman Caliphate. His brother Faisal (who became Iraq's first ruler) had sought relations with leading Zionists such as Chaim Weizmann and in 1919 signed the Faisal-Weizmann Agreement, where he conditionally accepted the Balfour Declaration based on the fulfilment of British wartime promises of independence to the Arabs. King Abdullah of the then British created Transjordan studied with David Ben Gurion (Israel's first prime minister) in Istanbul in the 1930's. Abdullah had offered to accept the establishment of Israel in return for Jordanian control of the Arab populated parts of Palestine. In 1946 Abdullah expressed interest in ruling over the Arab parts of Palestine, and had no intention to resist or impede the partition of Palestine and creation of a Jewish state. King Abdullah had the Arab Legion at his disposal, a highly trained unit of 4,500 men, with General John Glubb (Glubb Pasha) an Englishman as its commanding officer. Glubb in his memoirs recounted that he was under strict orders from the British, not to enter areas under Jewish control.[lxviii] Egypt further weakened the attack against Israel when Nukrashi Pasha, the Prime Minister initially did not use existing military units but sent an army of volunteers that had only been organised a few months before the war began. Jordan had also delayed the passage of Iraqi troops across its territory thus thwarting any attack against Israel

Although the combined Muslim forces were 40,000 only 10,000 were trained soldiers. The Zionists had 30,000 armed personnel, 10,000 men for local defence and another 25,000 for home guard. Furthermore, there were nearly 3,000 specially trained Irgun and Stern Gang terrorists. They were armed with the latest weaponry smuggled from Czechoslovakia and funded heavily through Zionist agencies in America and Britain. Despite the preparedness of the Jews, the treachery of the Muslim rulers played a central role in securing a foothold for the Jews in Palestine.

NASSER

As Gamal Abdul Nasser came to the leadership of the Young officer's regime in Egypt in 1952, he proceeded to seize the moral leadership of the Arab world and capture its sentiments. The Israeli occupation of Palestine, sanctioned by the United Nations, had led to the dispersion of the Muslims of Palestine throughout the surrounding region, in particular to Jordan Lebanon and Gaza in Egyptian held territory. Nasser's support amongst the Palestinians in particular was bolstered by the fact that he provided funding and a certain amount of training to the Palestinians in Gaza, which led the Palestinians to regard Nasser as an ally.

Nasser being independent was a façade. Miles Copeland the CIA operative published classified information in his memoirs in 1989, 'The Game Player,' about the CIA backed coup d'état that ousted the British puppet King Farook. Copeland, who activated the project, explained that

> 'the CIA needed a charismatic leader who would be able to divert the growing anti-American hostility that was building up in the area.'

He explains both the CIA and Nasser were in agreement on Israel. For Nasser talk of war with Israel was irrelevant. Much more of a priority was British occupation of the Suez Canal. Nasser's enemy was Britain.

In 1956 Nasser nationalised the Suez Canal. In one stroke this strengthened Nasser's position over this strategic territory, but it impacted Britain the most as it removed control of the vital waterway from the influence of the British. The response of Britain was to lure France and Israel into the struggle. This was outlined by historian Corelli Barnett, who wrote about the Suez in his book, 'The Collapse of British Power':

> *'France was hostile to Nasser because Egypt was helping the Algerian rebels, and attached to the canal for historical reasons. After all, a Frenchman built it. Israel was longing to have a go at Nasser anyway because of Palestinian fedayeen attacks and the Egyptian blockade of the Straits of Tiran. So Sir Anthony Eden (British Prime Minister) concocted a secret tripartite plot with France and Israel.'* He further explained *'that Israel would invade Egypt across the Sinai Peninsula. Britain and France would then give an ultimatum to the parties to stop fighting or they would intervene to 'protect' the canal.'*[lxix]

And so it played out. The Israelis even had to moderate their attack in case they won before the 'intervention' forces could arrive

For Israel, the acquisition of Russian armaments by Nasser lead to alarm amongst the Israeli leadership. An opportunity arose for Israel to escalate tensions when Nasser nationalised the Suez Canal, creating the pretext for Israel to engage in a strike against Egypt. This conflict however was never a war for the liberation of Palestine but rather a struggle between America and Britain for control over the strategically important Suez Canal. Acting with Britain and France, Israel attempted to deal a significant blow to Egypt's military, but the intervention of the US and the USSR, and the subsequent threats against Europe and Israel by the respective superpowers forced Israel to back down.

THE 1967 SIX DAY WAR

Britain had been surpassed as the region's dominant force 11 years earlier, but still retained some influence through its influence in Jordan, Syria and Israel. In an attempt to weaken Nasser, Britain sought to lure Israel into dragging Egypt into a war whereby Israel would seize territory and use it as a bargaining tool in any future peace settlement; a means through which to achieve the security which the Israelis so desperately sought. On 5th June 1967 Israel launched a pre-emptive strike destroying 60% of Egypt's grounded air force and 66% of Syrian and Jordanian combat aircraft.

The Israelis seized the West Bank and east Jerusalem from Jordanian control. King Hussein, prior to the battle, had positioned his troops in different areas from where the main battle was taking place. In a matter of 48 hours the Israelis seized the major West Bank towns. In a similar manner the Israelis seized the strategically important Golan Heights on the 6th day of the war. The Syrian troops occupying the Golan Heights heard news of Israel's capture of the heights through their own State radio despite the Israeli troops clearly occupying them. Israel also dealt America's Nasser a blow by capturing *Sharm al-Sheikh* and securing the waterway of the Straits of Tiran. The objective of weakening the regime of Nasser was achieved, thus indirectly aiding British interests within the region. Israel was able to seize more land and use it as a bargaining asset in any land for peace negotiations, which today is still used as a basis for negotiations rather than the status of 1948. The United Nations established the UN Partition plan in 1947, which gave 57% of territory to Israel with Palestine becoming 42% of its former self. In the 1967 war Israeli occupation increased further with its territorial gains of up to 78% of historic Palestine.

The difficulties experienced by Egypt during the Suez crisis and the six days war contributed to a waning of support for the Palestinian cause. Nasser then opened a channel of communication with the Israelis through the respective delegates of Egypt and Israel to the United Nations to explore the possibility of a permanent peace settlement.

THE PALESTINIAN LIBERATION ORGANISATION (PLO)

It was under this air of frustration with a lack of progress in the Palestinian struggle, at a time when the Arab regimes had all but abandoned the Palestinian cause, that the movement for the National Liberation of Palestine was formed. It used the acronym HATF, which was rearranged to FATH meaning victory. Amongst the founders of FATH was Yasser Arafat, a graduate of the Cairo University working in Kuwait as an engineer. FATH carried out numerous raids against Israel directly, but soon realised that these raids were ineffective in achieving anything without the support of the armies from at least one of the major Arab countries. This led FATH to pursue a path of political dialogue with the other Arab countries.

During the Cairo conference of 1964, the Arab League instructed its Palestinian representative Ahmed Shukeiri to form a Palestinian political body. Shukeiri then organised a meeting of the first Palestinian National Council, attended by 350 delegates who met in East Jerusalem. At this meeting, the delegates formed the Palestinian Liberation Organisation (Agency), which was comprised of various groups including FATH. Ahmed Shukeiri became the chairman of the PLO but stepped down in favour of Yasser Arafat in 1969.

The establishment of the PLO detached the Arab states from being directly involved in the Palestinian issue, placing further emphasis on the Palestinian nature of the issue. The PLO very quickly became the sole representatives of the Palestinians, even though it was in effect a non-state actor. It initially entered into armed struggle but unable to face-off with Israel's large military (relatively) very quickly turned to negotiations. Unable to impose any type of settlement on the Palestinian issue, the PLO compromised and gave up more and more land in the hope of getting a Palestinian state. In 1993 in a Letter from Arafat to Yitzhak Rabin, the Prime Minister of Israel, Arafat said:

> "The PLO recognises the right of the State of Israel to exist in peace and security. The PLO commits itself to the Middle East peace process, and to a peaceful resolution of the conflict through negotiations. The PLO considers that the signing of the Declaration of Principles constitutes a historic event, inaugurating a new epoch of peaceful coexistence, free from violence and all other acts which endanger peace and stability."

The PLO in reality strengthened Israel by entering into negotiations and compromising with everything that it stood for. By recognising Israel it accepted the two-state solution from the beginning of its creation, which was the US plan for this area of the Middle East.

By the time Arafat died in 2004 the PLO in the form of the Palestinian Authority conceded Palestine of 1948 and only demanded the borders of 1967. Then it demanded of the majority rather than all of Palestine of 1967. In 2003 the PA, signed the Geneva document and gave up the right of return for all those who lost their homes when Israel was created. In the end rather than liberating the people of Palestine it sold them out.

1973 WAR

The war launched against Israel in October 1973 by Egypt and Syria had limited aims, which never included the liberation of

130

Palestine. The aims never even included the liberation of the Golan Heights which were to be restored as part of a peace treaty between Syria and Israel. The aims were to solidify the positions of Anwar Sadat and Hafez al-Assad who were relatively new leaders in countries prone to military coups. Sadat in particular was vulnerable given the fact that he had succeeded the charismatic Nasser.

Mohammed Heikal, the respected editor of Al-Ahram from 1957–1974, who witnessed the war, explained the extent of Anwar Sadat's underlying motives. He cites Sadat's mood in the run up to the war. Heikal quotes one of Sadat's generals, Mohammed Fouwzi who gave the analogy of a samurai drawing two swords – a long one and short one in preparation for battle. Fouwzi said that this battle would be a case of the short sword, signifying a limited battle for certain motives.[lxx]

Anwar Sadat had no intention of having a protracted war of liberation with Israel. This is why he sought peace with Israel whilst commanding a winning position in the war. In the first 24 hours of the war Egypt smashed through Israel's much heralded Bar-Lev fortifications east of the Suez Canal with only 68 casualties. Meanwhile 2 Syrian divisions and 500 tanks swept into the Golan Heights and retook some of the land captured in 1967. In two days of fighting Israel had lost 49 aircraft and 500 tanks. In the midst of this Sadat sent a message to US Secretary of State Henry Kissinger in which he said that the objective of the war was 'the achievement of peace in the Middle East and not partial settlements.' The message went on to state that if Israel withdrew from all occupied territories Egypt would be prepared to participate in a Peace conference under UN or neutral auspices.

Thus despite having an immense strategic advantage from which Egyptian forces could seize the Mitla and Giddi Passes – the strategic keys to the Sinai and hence launch an attack on Israel itself, Sadat was in the mood for negotiation in this early stage. Sadat's refusal to press home his initial advantage and his delay in launching the second Sinai offensive allowed Israel to mobilise with aid from the US and she began to seize back lost territory. Hostilities formally came to an end on 25 October 1974.

TWO STATES

Prior to the 1991 Gulf war the US attempted to impose and push ahead with the peace process due to Israel's expansion into the West bank through its settlements. FATAH, individually and through the PLO failed in containing Israel and thus after the first Gulf war the US gathered all the countries involved in the Middle East issue to the Madrid Peace Conference in order to impose the two state solution to them. It was also the first time both Israel and the PLO negotiated directly. The Israelis wanted Arafat to give up areas of the West Bank where settlements had been constructed, which Arafat refused to agree to, leading to long negotiations which effectively never went anywhere.

Britain had been pushed out of the region earlier, but still attempted to complicate America's plan for the region. Britain managed to conclude the Oslo accords in 1993 between the PLO and Israel. This accord was Britain's attempt to bypass the resolutions of the Madrid conference. The US however, managed to change this accord into time-consuming negotiations, which eventually fell apart. By 1994 the US concluded negotiations between, king Hussein of Jordan and Rabin, the prime minister of Israel under the auspices of Clinton that terminated the state of war between Israel and Jordan. Later on, the Wadi Arabah agreement was signed, which officially finished the state of war between the two states.

From this period until today Israel has pursued a tit-for-tat policy, termed "reciprocity," whereby Israel would not engage in the peace process if the PLO continued with what it defined as the Palestinian revolving door policy, i.e., incitement and direct or indirect support

132

of terrorism.

When George W. Bush became US president the events of 9/11 created priorities other than the Israeli-Palestinian struggle. This struggle was low priority in the sight of the Bush administration, as they prepared to invade the Middle East. Israel used this opportunity to reoccupy the areas, which were put under the PA (Palestinian Authority) administrative authority, such as Jericho, Jenin, city of Gaza and Arrabah (Jenin). Israel used excessive violence against the Palestinians. Bush's need for Israeli support in the wars, and Jewish support to get re-elected meant the resolutions of the peace process could not be imposed upon Israel, especially with the Neo-cons dominating the administration.

Under Obama's first term no progress was made on the peace process, as the drawdowns in Iraq and Afghanistan and the financial crisis dominated the administration. All of this allowed Israel to increase and expand settlements. But over a period of 50 years the US policy on the Israeli-Palestinian issue has become clear. America rejects the idea of substituting European influence with Jewish influence, and she also rejects the idea of sharing power with any other country in the region. This is where an independent Palestinian state comes into the equation.

In order to prevent Israeli expansion and the spread of Israeli influence in the region, American policy has been based on isolating Israel from the rest of the region in an attempt to curtail her and minimise her role in the quest to solve the Palestinian issue and the Middle Eastern issue. US policy is centred around establishing a Palestinian state to act as an instrument of containment; by establishing a host of international guarantees and by bringing multinational forces to be deployed along the borders between Israel and the neighbouring Arab countries - Jordan, Syria, Egypt and the future Palestinian State. The American policy has also been based on working towards the internationalisation of Jerusalem, as America sees this internationalisation as a solution to the sensitive crisis of Jerusalem that would guarantee a strong American presence through the presence of the United Nations. The US plans defined Israeli borders alongside a Palestinian state. In order to achieve this the US will need to impose this upon the Israelis and balance this with arming Israel to counter balance the other powers in the region such as Egypt, Saudi Arabia and Iran.

HAMAS

Like the PLO, Hamas has also played a key role in the history of Palestine and very quickly became the competitor to the PLO. Hamas was formally created in 1987, largely due to the public dissatisfaction with the secularist and corrupt Fatah-led PLO and also due to an effort by the MB to respond to the first intifada. The creation of a separate Gaza group that could engage in armed resistance answered the MB's dilemma.

HAMAS, an acronym for *Harakat al-Muqawama al-Islamiya* (Islamic Resistance Movement), was founded by Sheikh Ahmed Yassin, a Palestinian cleric who became an activist in local branches of the Muslim Brotherhood after dedicating his early life to Islamic scholarship in Cairo. Beginning in the late 1960s, Yassin preached and performed charitable work in the West Bank and Gaza Strip, both of which were occupied by Israeli forces following the 1967 Six Day War. Yassin established Hamas as the Brotherhood's local political arm in December 1987, following the outbreak of the first intifada, a Palestinian uprising against Israeli control of the West Bank, Gaza, and East Jerusalem. The following year, Hamas published its charter, calling for the destruction of Israel and the establishment of an Islamic society in historic Palestine. Hamas' original leadership viewed militancy as a means to a political end. Sheikh Ahmed Yassin argued that Hamas was a political movement and it would fight for the rights of Palestinians, with the objective of

134

eliminating Israel. The violent means Hamas has used make it highly controversial as a political player, but it is important to note that Hamas has held political ambitions since its inception.

Hamas' core struggle has always been how to proceed along its political path while presiding over a stateless entity, especially when its reputation has been primarily built on militant resistance, not on political credentials. Whilst Hamas has attempted to keep its finances secret, it is no secret that it received arms, training and finance from Iran, due to Iran's aim of curtailing and competing with Israel in the region. It has been widely rumoured that Iran began curtailing its monthly payments to Hamas after the group's refusal to demonstrate on behalf of the Syrian regime. According to multiple sources, Iran had directed $25 million per month to Hamas; to put that in perspective, Hamas' stated annual budget for administering the Gaza Strip is about $700 million.

Hamas has since its inception tried to demonstrate that it is a political movement that has political aims of establishing an entity in Palestine, but its use of violence against a much larger and resourceful Israel has led its leaders and senior members to in effect compromise with Israel for political recognition. These numerous compromises has in effect diluted Hamas to a mere pragmatic actor in the region and also justified the state of Israel. In an interview in 2011 Hamas' Deputy Foreign Minister Ghazi Hamad told NPR's Robert Siegel that the Islamic political party has accepted a two-state solution that respects the 1967 borders. When asked:

> *"If Israel were to accept a two-state solution in which Palestine would be in Gaza and the West Bank and have its capital in Jerusalem, is that an acceptable aim that Hamas is striving for or is that in and of itself insufficient because there would still be a state of Israel?"*

The deputy foreign minister replied: *"Look, we said, frankly, we accept the state and '67 borders. This was mentioned many times and we repeated many times."* Khaled Mashal, who has been Hamas' leader since the

135

assassination of Sheikh Khaled Yassin in 2004 on numerous occasions has stated he accepts the 1967 borders and two states.

Hamas and the PLO have become two sides of the same coin. Both, despite their claims to the contrary have accepted the right of Israel to exist; their differences are really on how far they are prepared to give up their positions to remain players in the negotiations for statehood.

In conclusion, the West created the problem in the Middle East in order to protect its interests; they have then rushed to solve it by putting forward policies that will enshrine their presence. Israel continues to work within the two-state solutions but by influencing where the final boundaries will be. Syria, Egypt and Jordan gave up the people of Palestine a long time ago. As a result the PLO dominated by FATAH emerged as well as Hamas, The PLO never stuck to any principles, whilst FATAH is just too small to impose anything on the issue, aside from altering some small facts. Hamas has suffered a similar fate.

SAUDI ARABIA

The Arabian Peninsula is today dominated by Saudi Arabia, a country that did not exist 100 years ago. The peninsula today is surrounded by vast deserts; the central Najd plateau is the core of Saudi Arabia and is home to the country's capital, Riyadh. Mecca and Medina, Islam's two holiest cities, are protected by mountains in the west and flanked by the Red Sea. Islam's origins are from this peninsula, the Muslims prophet – Muhammed (ﷺ) united the various tribes of the peninsula and established the first Islamic state in Madinah in 622, within 13 years the whole peninsula was under Islamic authority and became the springboard for Islam's global expansion. As the capital of the Caliphate moved away from Madinah its importance remained for its historical importance, but governance and administration moved to various cities throughout Islamic history. By the time the British Empire arrived in the region the Arabian Peninsula had lost its strategic importance as the Ottomans ruled the Islamic world from Constantinople, but the relationship between the Ottomans, Sharif Hussain of Makkah and Madinah and the Saud Clan – complete unknowns in the 19th century, would leave a lasting effect for the next century.

In the 16th century, the Ottomans added the Red Sea and Persian Gulf Coast (the Hijaz, Asir and Al-Ahsa) and everything in-between to its rule. The degree of control over these lands varied over the next four centuries with the fluctuating strength or weakness of the Ottomans central authority. In many cases the Ottomans appointed governors and gave them significant autonomy on the running of their region, but Constantinople controlled the foreign policy situation. The emergence of what was to become the Saudi royal family, known as the Al Saud, began in Nejd in central Arabia in 1744, when Muhammad bin Saud, founder of the dynasty, joined forces with the Wahabi leader, Muhammad ibn Abd al-Wahhab.

THE SAUD-WAHABI AXIS

Muhammad ibn Abdul-Wahhab established his own school of thought and deemed those who did not follow him as misguided. He set about calling for his opinions, working towards implementing them and attacking the other opinions fiercely. He faced a barrage of opposition and rejection from the various scholars, governors and prominent figures, who considered that his opinions differed from what they had understood from mainstream Islam. The followers of mainstream Islam deemed his opinions as being wrong and contradictory to what they had understood from the Islamic texts. This soon led to violence and soon Muhammad ibn Abdul-Wahhab, was banished from the region. Abdul-Aziz ibn Muhammad ibn Saud, the Sheikh of the tribe of Anzah, had ambitions to rule Arabia and took up arms against the Ottoman Caliphate and fought the Islamic armed forces. These arms came from Britain, who was looking to drive a wedge between the Arabs and the Ottomans. The relationship between the Saud family and Britain has never been given much attention throughout history, but without British help the Saud's would never have their own state. Whilst the US is criticised for working with the Saudi monarchy during the Soviet Union's invasion of Afghanistan which created Osama bin Laden and allowed the Wahhabis to spread – all of which back-fired in the 21st century when the same freedom fighters became the enemy. It was the British Empire that sent arms and finance from British India to the original al-Saud and his Wahhabi compatriots. Ibn Saud gave refuge to Muhammad ibn Abdul-Wahhab, which allowed him to spread his narrow school of thought from a secure sanctuary and give the Saud's religious justification. The Saudi leaders from this point onwards all proceeded in adopting the Wahhabi school of thought as a political tool to strike the Ottoman caliphate in the Arabian lands through the incitement of a sectarian war.

This alliance formed in the 18th century provided the ideological impetus to Saudi expansion and remains the basis of Saudi Arabian dynastic rule today. The first 'Saudi state' established in 1744 in the area around Riyadh, rapidly expanded and briefly controlled most of the present-day territory of Saudi Arabia, but was destroyed in 1818 by the Ottoman governor of Egypt, Mohammed Ali Pasha. A much smaller second 'Saudi state' located mainly in Nejd was established in 1824. Throughout the rest of the 19th century, the Al Saud contested control of the interior of what was to become Saudi Arabia with another Arabian ruling family, the Al Rashid. By 1891, the Al Rashid's were victorious and the Al Saud was driven into exile in Kuwait. At the beginning of the 20th century, the Ottoman Empire continued to have some some influence over most of the Arabian Peninsula. Arabia was ruled by a patchwork of tribal rulers with the Sharif of Mecca having pre-eminence and ruling the Hijaz, and who was working with Britain in the Arab revolt against the Ottomans.

In 1901, at the age of 21, Abdul aziz Ibn Saud succeeded his father, Abdul Rahman bin Faisal, to become the leader of the Saud dynasty with the title Sultan of Nejd. It was at this time that he set out to reconquer his family lands from Ibn Rashid in what is now called Saudi Arabia. In 1902, together with a party of relatives and servants, he recaptured Riyadh with only twenty men by assassinating the Rashidi governor of the city. Ibn Saud was considered a "magnetic" leader and many former supporters of the House of Saud once again rallied to its call following the capture of Riyadh. Ibn Saud finally consolidated control over the Nejd in 1912 with the help of an organised and well-trained army. The British Empire never put its eggs into one basket and by WW1 had cultivated links with both Ibn Saud and his rival Sherif Hussein ibn Ali, leader of Hijaz, whom the Sauds were almost constantly at war with.

The relationship between successive al-Saud's and the British Empire was one of master and slave. Britain supported multiple, competing tribes and clans in order to keep them fighting each other in a classic balance of power strategy. The Gazetteer was the successive British government cables classed as secret/official business for around 70 years at the time and they included a series of correspondence that began in 1902, between Abdel Aziz al-Saud and his father Abdel-Rahman, and the British political officer in Bahrain and the British political officer in Bushire. Four decades later, Dickson wrote his memoirs about the years in which he served as his government's envoy in the Arabian Gulf countries, published in London in the 1951 book *Kuwait and Her Neighbours*, Dickson highlighted the relationship:

> *"On the sixth day Sir Percy ... lost all patience over what he called the childish attitude of Ibn Saud in his tribal boundary idea [between Iraq and Najd]. It was astonishing to see the Sultan of Najd being reprimanded like a naughty schoolboy by H. M. High Commissioner, and being told sharply that he, Sir Perry Cox, would himself decide on the type and general line of the frontier. This ended the impasse. Ibn Saud almost broke down and pathetically remarked that Sir Percy was his father and brother, who had made him and raised him from nothing to the position he held, and that he would surrender half his kingdom, nay the whole, if Sir Percy ordered...Sir Percy took a red pencil and very carefully drew in on the map of Arabia a boundary line from the Persian Gulf to Jabal Anaizan, close to the Transjordan frontier."*[lxxi]

Dickson continued:

> *"His [Ibn Saud] voice quavered, and then he started begging with humiliation: "Your grace is my father and you are my mother. I can never forget the debt I owe you. You made me and you held my hand, you elevated me and lifted me. I am prepared, at your beckoning, to give up for you now half of my kingdom...no, by Allah, I will give up my entire kingdom, if your grace commands me!"*[lxxii]

Dickson also confirmed what was long known, in correspondence with the British resident in Bushire on June 24, 1904, the government in India decided that it was not in its interests to bar weapons from

140

Ibn Saud, the rival of Ottoman-backed Ibn Rashid.[lxxiii]

In 1915, Britain entered into a treaty making the lands of the House of Saud a British protectorate. In exchange, Ibn Saud pledged to again make war against Ibn Rashid, who was an ally of the Ottomans. The treaty was signed by 'Abd al-'Aziz ibn Saud and Percy Cox, the British political resident in the Persian Gulf. The treaty recognized 'Abd al-'Aziz's "authority" in the Najd, under British protection. Military protection as well as British superintendence of his foreign policy formally co-opted 'Abd al-'Aziz into the British orbit. Guns and money were now offered to 'Abd al-'Aziz as well — £20,000 annually in cash, later to be increased to £60,000 — for attacking Turkish allies in eastern Arabia. A year later, 'Abd al-'Aziz was the newest satellite at the gathering of British clients in the Kuwait Darbar presided over by Percy Cox. In the Hijaz, Hussain ibn 'Ali's forces with British advisors were busy sabotaging the Hijaz Railway while 'Abd al-'Aziz's Bedouins were attacking Turkish allies in eastern Arabia, all in the service of British imperialism - or the "infidels" as the Wahhabis would called them.

At the end of WW1 Britain told Ibn Saud they were terminating his subsidies, as he had outlived his use. The British had kept him and Sharif Hussain on their payroll to prevent them from fighting each other. This would have resulted in unravelling all the gains Britain had made in the region. By April 1924, Sharif Hussain, then in Transjordan, immediately proclaimed himself Caliph. 'Abd al-'Aziz realized that this was his opportunity, for Hussain's proclamation would not be viewed with favour in the Muslim world. First, Husain ibn 'Ali was known as a British agent who had led the "Arab Revolt" against the Ottomans. This was something the Muslims could not forgive. Second, 'Abd al-'Aziz ibn Saud's own links with the British were less well known since he was still an obscure figure in Central Arabia. Thus, he could claim to get rid of Sharif Hussein on behalf of the Muslims and earn their gratitude. In the name of "purification" the Saudi assault on Makkah began, again, with the massacre of the inhabitants of Tai'f in September 1924. This was a repeat of the Saudi slaughter in 1802. Estimates about the number of people killed in the latest assault ranged from 400 to 900. It was carried out without mercy. All male inhabitants were put to the sword, even those who had sought refuge in mosques. They also destroyed the mosques after beheading their captives there. When the news reached the residents of Makkah, the slaughter shocked the 70,000 or so pilgrims who were assembled for the annual pilgrimage. They condemned "the Wahhabites' savagery". A year earlier, in July 1923, Ibn Saud's forces had attacked and massacred nearly 5,000 pilgrims from Yemen. With such news and the slaughter perpetrated by Ibn Saud's men at Tai'f, the majority of Makkah's residents fled to Jeddah. The remainder barricaded themselves inside their homes as Ibn Saud's hordes continued the pillage, destroying tombs, shrines and masjids. With British arms the Saudis, in the name of "purifying" Islam from idolatrous accretions, themselves violated many of the fundamental commandments of the Qur'an — sanctity of the mosque. When Makkah fell to Ibn Saud, he was quick to issue a disclaimer to any personal designs upon the throne of the Hijaz or the Caliphate. He said,

> *"I have no intentions of extending my territory beyond my possessions in Najd, but it is my duty to rid the Hedjaz [sic] and my people of the cruelty of the Sheriff [sic]."*

'Abd al-'Aziz's pledge to the world's Muslims would prove as hollow as his promise to the Wahhabis who, as his foot-soldiers, fought to establish Ibn Saud's rule in Makkah and, on December 5th, 1925, in Madinah. Hussain ibn 'Ali, already old and thoroughly dejected, fled from Makkah to Jeddah from where he was taken on an old British steamer into exile in Cyprus. This development suited the British well. Sharif Hussain had already become troublesome after the British reneged on their promise to make him the king of the whole of Arabia. His sons had nearly wrecked the Cairo Conference in 1921 by walking out. The British now favoured 'Abd al-'Aziz over

Hussain to become the ruler of the Hijaz. For Britain, it simply meant a change of faces. Thus, 'Abd al-'Aziz was given the green light to attack Makkah. Without British support Hussain ibn 'Ali's forces were no match for those of Ibn Saud's Wahhabis.

NEW STATE AND OIL

Ibn Saud controlled both the areas of Najd and Hijaz, with the help of his Wahhabi brothers and administered them as two separate kingdoms as King. In 1932 the two kingdoms of the Hijaz and Nejd were united as the Kingdom of Saudi Arabia, Ibn Saud, a loyal British servant had already agreed most of the coastal areas of the Arabian peninsula to Britain. The new kingdom was one of the poorest countries in the world, reliant on limited agriculture and pilgrimage revenues. Saudi Arabia has dense dessert geography, which was not viable for a society to function, but this all changed in 1938.

The Germans in 1871 dispatched a team of scientists to the lands that became Iraq, Kuwait and Saudi-Arabia and concluded that oil had to be present there, but that challenges in regards to transporting this oil to the markets of the West and East would make it difficult for this oil to compete with the oil of America and Russia.

At the turn of the century Emperor Wilhelm therefore sent a technical committee to the Muslim lands in the Middle East to investigate the oil potential again. Emperor Wilhelm's team concluded in 1901 that the Muslim Middle East sat on a veritable "lake of petroleum" of almost inexhaustible supply.

The committee advised the German government to begin work on getting access to these resources, to be able to break the American, Russian and British control over the oil industry.

The German defeat in WW1 ended this German endeavour and the Sykes-Picot borders were drawn to ensure the oil fields alongside the Persian-Iraq belt fell into the British constructed nations. In 1938,

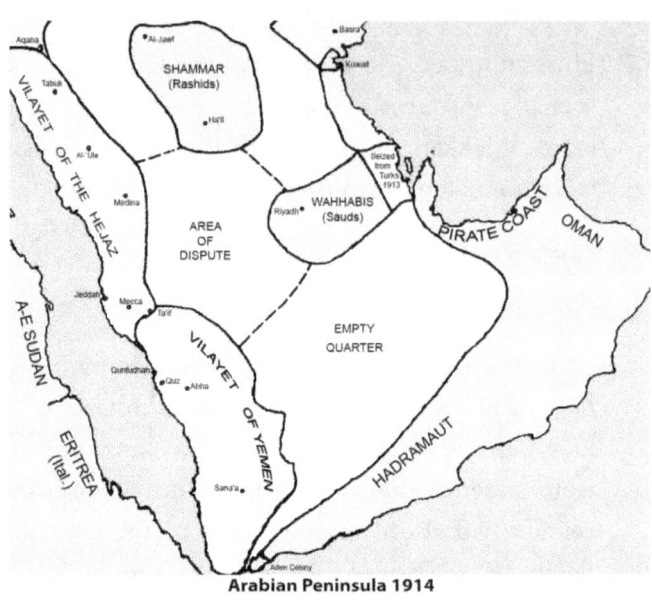

Arabian Peninsula 1914

vast reserves of oil were discovered in the Al-Ahsa region along the coast of the Persian Gulf, and full-scale development of the oil fields began in 1941 under the US-controlled ARAMCO (Arabian American Oil Company). Oil provided Saudi Arabia with economic prosperity, at the same time; the monarchy became increasingly wasteful and extravagant. By the 1950s this had led to large governmental deficits and excessive foreign borrowing. By 1976, Saudi Arabia had become the largest oil producer in the world.

POLITICS

Domestic politics in Saudi Arabia is dominated by the al-Saud family. The Saudi royal family is effectively an oligarchy that has crafted an absolute monarchy, ruled by consensus. As a result the family continues to dominate the political architecture of the country with no other centres of power existing. The throne of Saudi Arabia changes hands through a power transfer that remains firmly within the Saud clan. Ibn Saud is believed to have had at least 70 children from 22 marriages, but power has remained to a select few 37 that shaped and controlled his vast kingdom. They and their offspring form a core of about 200 princes who wield most of the power. Estimates of the number of princes' can range anywhere from 7,000 upwards. The family's vast numbers allow it to control most of the kingdom's important posts and to have an involvement and presence at all levels of government. The key ministries are reserved for the royal family, as are the thirteen regional governorships. Saudi Arabia is a state that, as its name attests, is based on loyalty not to a terrain or an idea but to a family. Abdul-Aziz Ibn Saud, who established the country along with his son Faisal bin Abdul-Aziz (the third monarch), dominated the first generation of Saudi rulers. The second generation has been dominated by the *"Sudeiri Seven"* — the seven sons of Ibn Saud's favourite wife, Hassa bint Ahmad al-Sudeiri — who oversaw political life, often as kings, giving coherence to the family and thus to the ruling power structure. In Saudi Arabia there are no general elections or even a referendum to confirm a King's popularity.

The country's mineral wealth is concentrated in the royal family and the hands of a few other well-positioned families. The royals receive stipends of varying amounts, depending on their position in the bloodline of King Abdul-Aziz. Possessing the world's largest oil field – the Ghawar, has allowed the royal family the means to establish and maintain patronage networks that helped build tribal alliances. Despite debate on the future supply of global oil, the importance of the Middle East will not reduce. In fact, it will become the most crucial area in the world. This is because 61% of the world's oil reserves are in the Middle East. "Proved" oil reserves are those quantities of oil that geological information indicates can be with reasonable certainty recovered in the future from known reservoirs. Of the trillion barrels currently estimated only 39% are outside the Middle East. Today, 61% of global oil reserves are in the hands of Middle Eastern regimes, with Saudi Arabia possessing the world's largest (22%). Saudi Arabia possesses the light sweet type of oil which is the world's cheapest oil to refine. For Saudi Arabia it turned the country into a critical piece of the global economy and gave it immense wealth to play a role in the region and the Muslim world.

ISLAM

The descendants of Muhammad ibn Abd al-Wahhab, the 18th century founder of the Wahhabi school of thought, is only second in prestige to the royal family with whom they formed a mutual support pact and power-sharing arrangement nearly 300 years ago. This pact maintains Wahhabi support for Saudi rule and thus, uses its authority to legitimise the royal family's rule. The most important religious posts are closely linked to the al Saud family by a high degree of intermarriage. The religious scholars have promoted the royal family as defenders of Islam through their international efforts in constructing mosques. In situations in which the public deemed certain policies of the royal family questionable, the scholars would invoke fatwas to deflect any dissent. The Grand Mufti of Saudi Arabia issued a fatwa opposing petitions and demonstrations in the middle of the Arab Spring; his fatwa included a *"severe threat against internal dissent."*[lxxiv]

Saudi Monarchy

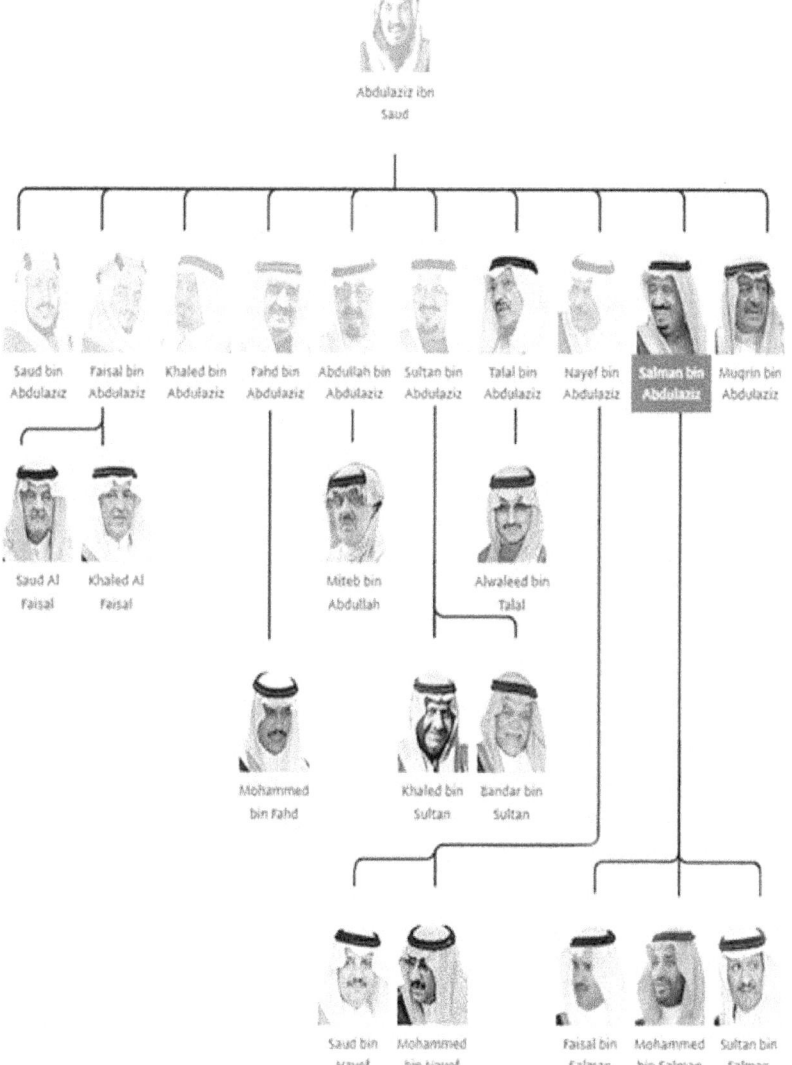

Whilst much of the world views Saudi Arabia as a nation built upon Islam and who implements Islam on its populace, amongst the Muslim world Saudi has very little credibility, whilst the Saudi monarchy is viewed with even more disdain. Saudi Arabia may donate millions of copies of the Qur'an, Islamic books, and a lot of money to build mosques all over the world a monarchy and nation state contradicts the very foundations of Islam. Saudi Arabia rules by a mix of laws, some of which are Islamic and some are man-made. However, to maintain the Islamic perception, it refrains from calling them laws. Saudi uses specific terminologies to differentiate between the Islamic laws and the man-made ones. In a book, written in Arabic, on the constitution of Saudi Arabia the author states,

> *"The words 'law (qanoon)' and 'Legislation (Tashree')' are only used in Saudi to refer to the rules taken from the Islamic Shari'ah ..... As for the man-made such as systems (Anthimah)' or ' instructions (Ta'leemaat)' or ' edicts (Awamir)' ......* '[lxxv]

Aside from this Saudi Arabia is a hereditary monarchy that uses the religious establishment as a tool to control opposition to it's largely monarchy driven pro-West agenda.

SOCIETY

The royal family also controls the nation's information and avenues through which news and information reaches people. The monarchy is able to do this as it directly operates the radio and television companies in the Kingdom and the newspapers are subsidised and regulated by the government. Government censorship continues to plague the press, and legal access to the Internet must be via local servers, which the government controls. The key ministries are reserved for the royal family, as are the thirteen regional governorships. The monarchy controls every aspect of society making it difficult to remove the regime as it will require the elimination of the whole Al Saud clan.

When the Arab spring was in the region the monarchy presented them as small protests in predominantly Shia areas and this caused the bulk of the population to support the crackdown in cities such as Qatif, al-Awamiyah, and Hofuf. The Shia face significant economic discrimination by both, the regime and the religious establishment, because they are viewed as Iranian agents. The government collectively punishes the Shia community by marginalising them in Saudi society. The last line of defence for the Saudi monarchy is the Saudi secret service — the *"Mabahith"*. According to Human Rights Watch, the Mabahith

> *"monitors suspected political opponents and others, targets individuals for arrest, and interrogates detainees. Mabahith agents operate with impunity and have been responsible for a wide range of human rights abuses, including arbitrary arrest, incommunicado detention, and torture."*[lxxvi]

The Mabahith even operates its own prison – the 'Ulaysha Prison in Riyadh.[lxxvii] Anyone who has visited Saudi Arabia or resided in the country will have experienced that public entertainment and street life, let alone protests which scarcely exist, as few people socialise outside their families. This reality is making social media very popular and the launch of twitter will only lead to more questioning of the role of the regime.

Saudi Arabia's foreign policy is dominated by two key themes, Iran and the West. Saudi Arabia views itself as the leader of Islam and with its mineral wealth as someone who should be respected in the region. The monarchy also believes it needs to play a role in the region in order to maintain its position both domestically and internationally. As a result the Saudi monarchy armed and trained Jihadi groups, spreads Islam (which has little credibility amongst the Muslims of the world) and used energy as strategies to maintain this position. The Saudi monarchy actually pursues a nationalist agenda beyond its borders and uses Islam as a cover for this. Saudi Arabia in fact discriminates against non-Saudi citizens domestically, something which is expressly forbidden in Islam. The biggest threat Saudi face is the power across the Persian Gulf, Iran. Despite Iran being Muslim and the Shia being Muslims, Saudi Arabia has viewed Iran as a potential challenger to its position and designated it as enemy number one, even though this is completely contrary to Islam. All of this shows Saudi Arabia is a nation state, built around a monarchy that is driven by nationalism, rather than Islam!

The second theme that has driven Saudi foreign policy is its subordinate role to the West. Saudi Arabia has supported all western initiatives, even against other Muslim countries. Saudi Arabia has accepted Israel's occupation of Palestine and even attempted to normalise this by holding talks between Israel and the surrounding nations, but it immediately sent its forces into Bahrain when the Arab spring reached its shores. Saudi Arabia chooses which oppressed Muslims to defend; despite its avowed claim to be an Islamic state. Israel, the invasion of Iraq and the removal of Saddam Hussain, the Soviet invasion of Afghanistan and maintaining adequate oil production are all areas Saudi Arabia has supported western causes, whilst other directly Muslim related conflicts has seen Saudi sit on the side-lines as it views these issues not from an Islamic lens but a nationalist one. In its foreign policy Saudi is largely a subordinate nation to the west, it has historically shifted from a subordinate to the US and Britain.

There are two institutes that are the pillars of different factions within the Saudi monarchy. The National Guard, also known as the white army has been a critical pillar of some of the kings in the royal family. With numerous coups taking place in the region during the 1950s and 1960s the National Guard was transformed into a force, unquestionably loyal to the king at the time and has until today safeguards the house of Saud. In 2013 the 50th anniversary of the British Military Mission to the Saudi Arabian National Guard took place. King Saud in the 1960s turned to Britain to train and advice this force and as a result the prince in charge of the National Guard has historically been close to Britain and it is through this institution Britain has maintained influence in Saudi Arabia.[lxxviii] The National Guard is a mechanised and mobile force designed to rapidly respond to domestic and internal threats. In the case of an external threat, which is the realm of the parallel conventional army, the National Guard is expected to be an auxiliary force. The National Guard possesses considerable capabilities but its duties have always been internal.

The parallel conventional army is another centre of power and deals with Saudi's regional and external threats. Saudi Arabia's conventional army comes under the Minister of Defence and possesses all of the country's main battle tanks and the vast bulk of the nation's heavy artillery. The Saudi military is largely made up of American weapons, including Boeing F-15 fighters, Lockheed Martin C-130 cargo planes, Boeing Apache attack helicopters and General Dynamics Abrams tanks, supplemented with Europe's Eurofighter Typhoon. The Kingdom of Saudi Arabia is the largest US Foreign Military Sales (FMS) customer, with active and open cases valued at approximately $97 billion. All of this is managed by the United States Military Training Mission (USMTM) to Saudi Arabia. It is a unique Security Assistance (SA) and Security Cooperation (SC) organisation under the authority of the Chief of the US Diplomatic Mission.

In its role it trains, advises, assists and is the provider of defence services. This has allowed the US to play a direct role in the orientation, disposition and capabilities of the Saudi Army and it is through this institution the US has maintained influence in the country.

Almost all of the countries Kings have led or had senior roles in these two intuitions, which allowed them to build their support and credibility and power base. The Saudi National Guard's communications and chain of command maintains a separate network from the regular Saudi Arabian military channels with a senior member of the royal family as its head. King Abdullah commanded the National Guard for three decades, from 1962 and throughout his Kingship until 2010, when he appointed his son, Prince Mutaib bin Abdullah, as the new commander. In addition, three of his sons hold high positions within the National Guard. Through this, King Abdullah attempted to maintain the influence his lineage has, and its relationship with the UK. With a decade long relationship with the UK, King Abdullah protected UK interests throughout the region. Abdullah backed rebel groups with arms and finance, which supported the British position in Syria. In Yemen, King Abdullah maintained the position of Ali Abdullah Saleh and his replacement Abd Rabbuh Mansur Hadi. So close was King Abdullah to the UK, on his death, the union flag was lowered to half-mast on government buildings, something reserved for British monarchs!

The changes the new King, King Salman made secures his lineage within the Kingdom for the next few decades. King Salman was minister of defence from 2011 and in 2012 made an official trip to the US, where he met president Obama. As minister of defence, Salman placed the country's military at the centre of America's military strikes in Syria and Iraq after ISIS declared a caliphate in mid-2014. King Salman's change of succession (something unprecedented in Saudi history) shores up the future of the country with pro-US line of succession with his son with him surrounds the crown prince, who has spent most of his life as the interior minister. The current commander of the National Guard, Prince Mutaib bin Abdullah — a rival of King Salman's son, Defence Minister and Deputy Crown Prince Mohammed bin Salman. To mitigate this threat, there are discussions taking place about the centralisation of the security establishment in the hands of Defence Minister Prince Mohammed bin Salman. This could mean incorporating the National Guard into the Ministry of Defence — effectively ending the National Guard's role as a separate ministry with the ability to counterbalance the conventional army.

Saudi Arabia has constructed its foreign relations to protect and enrich the monarchy and in turn the family of Saud. Put within the context of its immense mineral wealth and military riches, Saudi Arabia's role in the world is largely limited to a mere symbolic leadership due to having the two holy Islamic sites, Makkah and Madinah, within its borders. Saudi Arabia has played a role in a handful of regional issues such as hosting negotiations for the two-state solution and being a hosting ground for US bases. It is dominated by the royal family who have maintained an internal balance, which keeps them in power. Saudi Arabia was a nation created by the Saud family for the Saud family

IRAN

Whilst Iran is not strictly part of the Middle East, its political power and influence has always made it a player in the region and it is for this reason an analysis on its historical role should be considered.

The Persians originated in the Zagros Mountains as a warrior people. They built an empire by conquering the plains in the Tigris and Euphrates basin. They did this slowly, over an extended period at a time when there were no demarcated borders and they faced little resistance to the west. While it was difficult for a lowland people to attack through mountains, it was easier for a mountain-based people to descend to the plains. This combination of population and fertile plains allowed the Persians to expand. The Persian Empire was led throughout its nearly two millennia history by a series of dynasties. The first of these was established by Cyrus the Great in 550 BC, with the Persian conquest of Media, Lydia and Babylonia. Persian dynastic history was interrupted by the Islamic conquest in 651 and later by the Mongol invasion. The main religion in ancient Persia was Zoroastrianism, but after the 7th century this was replaced by Islam. After the Mongol invasion a series of Muslim dynasties ruled Persia independently of the Caliphate.

Persia came under Islamic rule around 640 and was initiated by the second Caliph 'Umar (ra). The Battle of Nihavand was fought in 640 and was the decisive blow to the Persian Empire. The battle came to be known as the victory of victories.

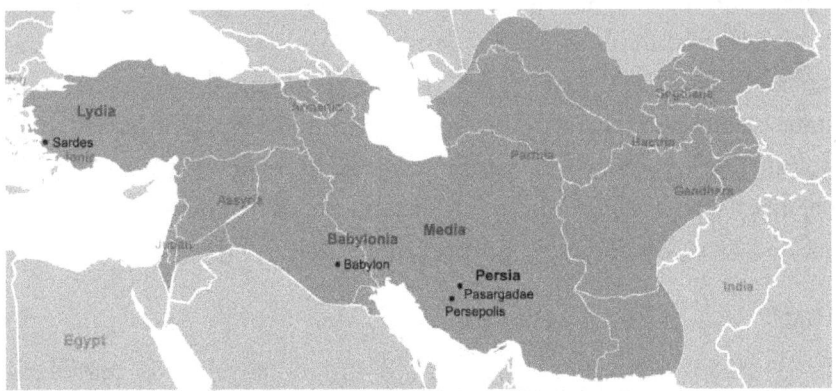

The Persian Empire expanded from the 6th century BC to 7th century AD

Islamic historians mentioned that Firuzan, the officer reporting to the Persian King Yazdgerd III had about 50,000 men, versus a Muslim army about 20,000. The Persians were outmanoeuvred, trapped in a narrow mountain valley, and lost many men in the ensuing rout. Yezdigerd escaped, but was unable to raise another substantial army. It was a decisive victory for Caliphate and the Persians consequently lost the surrounding cities including its Jewel - Isfahan.

THE END OF PERSIA

Persia, as Iran was known at the start of the 20th century, was occupied militarily by the British Empire in 1918. In 1921, Great Britain appointed the head of the Cossack Brigade of the Iranian army, a

Reza Khan Pahlavi (L) and his son Mohammad Reza Shah Pahlavi (R)

certain Reza Khan, as ruler of the country. In 1925 he crowned himself to "Shah Reza Pahlavi of Persia" and he gave the British everything they wanted in Iran, including total control over Iranian oil production, refining and marketing. This is one of the reasons why Iran was the most important source of fuel for the British army before the start of World War II. After Nazi Germany's invasion of Russia in 1941 Iran grew in geopolitical importance. In the face of a common enemy The British Empire and the Soviet Union quickly partnered up and Iran became part of their mutual supply line. On the 25th of August 1941 Britain and Russia therefore sent armies into Iran, to bring the country under their direct control and ensure a stable and secure Iran that could fully support the allied war effort. Shah Reza Pahlavi was seen as an obstacle to achieving this aim, since he was deeply despised by his people because of the tyranny of his rule. The British therefore removed him from his position and replaced him with his son Mohammed Reza Pahlavi. Britain wanted to keep Iranian rule in the Pahlavi family as they feared that otherwise the British hand behind the tyranny of Pahlavi the elder might be exposed.

In 1942 America joined the allied camp. As one of the main suppliers of Russia it too sent troops into Iran. The Americans deeply despised the Pahlavi family because they had kept American oil companies out of Iran for decades despite immense American pressure on them to open up the Iranian oil industry to "international competition." Nevertheless, because the war effort required it, America entered into various agreements with Shah Mohammed Reza Pahlavi to organise American involvement in Iran. The Americans were hopeful, also, that long term these agreements would be helpful in removing the Shah from power, or at least weaken his influence in the country. These treaties put the Iranian army, police, internal security service and public finances under control of American advisors. In a letter addressed to the then American president Franklin D. Roosevelt, Wallace Murray, advisor to the American president for international relations, wrote:

"The obvious fact is that we shall soon be in the position of actually 'running' Iran through an impressive body of American advisers.'[lxxix]

POST WW2

After World War II the British tried hard to maintain their control over the Iranian oil industry through the Anglo-Persian oil company (later British Petroleum). Anglo-Persian controlled the production, refining and marketing of Iranian oil. From 1945 to 1950 this earned it over £250 million. Over the same period Iran made just £90 million on its oil, even less than what the British government made from taxes on Anglo-Persian. Because of the Iranian oil but also because of the influence that could be projected over the Middle East from Iran, both the Soviet Union and America worked to take over the "Persian Prize" from Great-Britain.

The emergence of Mohammed Mossadeq was no accident. Until 1919 Mossadeq had been a very important Iranian politician. Because he was against the British influence in Iran, he was forced to leave the country in that year. In 1921 the British through Reza Khan invited him back to the country, with the aim of utilising his influence to solidify Khan's position. Mossadeq accepted the invitation to return to Iranian politics, but when Khan crowned himself Shah in 1925 he argued so strongly against this move that again he was side-lined. Mossadeq hated Great Britain because of this, which made the Americans interested in him. America saw Mossadeq as a person who could help them remove the British influence in Iran. In 1944 the American consulate in Tehran reported back home that Mossadeq was "a very popular man in Iran, and his words carry a great deal of weight."[lxxx]

Mossadeq won the general election in 1951, with considerable US support. Indeed Mossadeq's first deed after being appointed prime-minister was to nationalise the Iranian oil industry. The British were absolutely furious and developed a plan to have its military invade Iran just as in 1918. When they approached the Americans with this plan to get their endorsement, the Americans refused and flatly told the British they would not tolerate any military moves against Iran. America took Mossadeq's side and forced the British to enter negotiations. This the British refused. Instead, through the United Nations, Great-Britain organised a global embargo on Iranian oil and it instructed its agents on the ground in Iran to organise a military coup against Mossadeq. America was displeased with the British initiatives. The oil embargo upset the global oil markets. There was a concern in Washington also that the Soviet Union might try to make use of the instability caused by a military take-over and launch a counter-coup to establish a communist regime in Iran. America's ability to go against Britain was limited, however, as it needed British support in the Cold War against communism, especially in the Korean Peninsula where America was fighting a war at the time. Therefore, America began to put pressure on Mossadeq. It wanted him to make a deal with Great-Britain. Mossadeq, however, refused to compromise and in discussions with the British refused to give in on critical subjects. Some within the American administration saw this as betrayal and suspected Mossadeq of working with the Iranian communists. The CIA was therefore ordered to organise a coup against Mossadeq. In 1953 the CIA operation "Ajax" was executed and Mossadeq was removed from power.[lxxxi]

BRITAIN, AMERICA AND THE SHAH

Operation Ajax returned Shah Mohammed Reza Pahlavi to power. He knew who he had to thank for his position. It is said that in front of Kermit Roosevelt Jr, head of the CIA in Iran, he remarked that he realised he owned his thrown *"to god, my people, my army – and you.'*[lxxxii] The return of the Shah saw an increase in the American influence in Iran. The CIA organised for the Shah a new internal security organisation named SAVAK. Colonel Schwarzkopf returned to Iran in 1955 to take responsibility for this operation. America also supported the Shah financially. It gave him $68 million following his return to power, approximately one-third of the oil revenues the Iranian state had missed out on due to the British embargo. During the remainder of the 1950s America would lend the Shah a further $300 million for economic development, and $600 million to equip his army.[lxxxiii] All this firmly established the Shah and Iran as a power in the region, but the Shah was widely seen as being too close to the US and promoting America's interests in the region. This gradually began the process of his alienation from the Iranian people.

In 1963 the Shah began major economic reforms, which would end up changing the fabric of Iranian society, more commonly known as the 'White revolution'. The main aims of the programme were land reform and industrialisation of Iran. The Shah once remarked:

> *"In 10-12 years we shall reach the quality of life enjoyed by you Europeans,"* (Arabshahi 2001)

These reforms were to have a dramatic effect. Iran at that time was very much a traditional society with traditional feudal landlords. The rural Iranian economy was mostly a closed world where people traded amongst each other and paid each other in kind, avoiding the main economy. The traditional Iranian village producers co-operated with each other in deciding what to produce and how to produce, with the Shia clergy forming an important integral part of this consultative system. Quite often the Clergy benefited economically from this economic system because of religious endowments of land by ordinary people. Thus the clergy were also landowners. Agriculture formed the backbone of the rural economy with many of the poor working on the land they rented.

The Shah's reforms imposed various measures like higher land taxes all designed in effect to break this traditional system. The aim was to move surplus labour from the traditional rural economy to the newly forming factory based industrialised economy. This in turn was creating a new, small, but wealthy oligarch class of industrial owners who employed many of the rural poor driven off the land because agricultural production, amongst other rural trades, had become unviable. These large scale industrial units specialised in producing goods, which were the mainstay of the rural poor, such as furniture, clothes and the like. The urban areas did not remain unaffected either. Even in urban areas there were traditional areas or zones known as 'Bazaaries' where small traders plied their trade. The Bazaaries again had a close relationship with the Shia clergy, with the clergy again often benefiting economically. The Shah's reforms were again designed to undermine them as well.

Iran's income from oil moved from a few hundred million dollars to around $30 billion a year in the late 1960s and early 1970s. Much of this new found wealth was spent on huge US arms purchases that saw Iran as a pliant client state. However oil prices dipped in the mid-seventies, which resulted in government spending being slashed, tripling taxes on the salaried classes, cancelling public projects and imposing fines on the Bazaaries in a bid to control the price inflation created by the earlier oil boom.

Popular discontent was now brewing in Iran by the mid-seventies, angered by the Anglo-American domination of Iran's oil and the fact that the US was perceived to be benefiting from Iran's wealth. Cronyism, corruption and repression had come to be the hallmark of the Shah regime. The Shah responded by imposing harsh measures, including news censorship. Most of all he used suppression as a tool to deal with discontent, particularly thorough his feared secret security agency, the SAVAK. This alienated people across the political spectrum and led to the beginning of unusual alliances. The academics were unhappy with censorship and dissident academics formed the *National Organisation of University Teachers* to demand greater academic freedom along with the students. Secular Liberals formed their own opposition movement led by Mehdi Bazargan called the *Freedom Movement of Iran*. The Iranian left was also active, with the Tudeh party providing the main communist opposition. The Tudeh party had not forgotten the coup of 1953. In addition to this there were other leftist Iran guerrilla movements such as the Mujahedin-e-Khalq and Fedayeen who had been campaigning for a decade to get rid of the Shah. A popular front of the Bazaaries, the leftists and communists, academics, students, secular liberalists, ordinary workers and of course the Shia clergy was forming, with the clergy providing the ideological drive and backbone. In 1977, then US President Carter was forced to publicly rebuke the Shah by calling for greater freedom, which in turn relaxed censorship laws and released over 300 political prisoners from some 20,000 in his custody.

This ironically began the public dissent and in 1978 culminated in a series of general strikes by workers across the country, including some 30,000 oil workers, which brought the Iranian economy to its knees. The Shah's forces killed ordinary people by firing into crowds in his attempt to cling to power but with millions marching openly he was forced to flee in Jan 1979.

The Shah also began dreaming of a future independent from America by the late 1960s. His policies began focusing on turning Iran into a regional power, willing to compete with America for influence in the greater Middle East, and he began spending large amounts of money to build the strongest army in his region. America did not like this as it threatened to upset the regional balance of power. When the Shah also began threatening America, his fate was sealed. In an interview with US News and World Magazine in 1976 the Shah said about America's power and influence in Iran:

> *"But if you try to take an unfriendly attitude toward my country, we can hurt you as badly if not more so than you can hurt us. Not just through*

oil - we can create trouble for you in the region. If you force us to change our friendly attitude, the repercussions will be immeasurable.'[lxxxiv]

America was furious and decided to remove the Shah from power.

ISLAMIC REVOLUTION

When the Shah was overthrown in 1979 the general perception is an Islamic revolution took place, which was anti-American, all held together by an independent minded Ayatollah Ruhollah Khomeini, with grand ambitions to spread Shia Islam in the region.

From 1978 American diplomats began looking for an alternative to the Shah. William H. Sullivan, the American ambassador to Iran from 1977 to 1979, said about this period:

> *"But in the spring of 1978 (exactly one year before the Islamic revolution) the situations were changed and we seized the opportunity ... our Embassy developed its contact networks within the Iranian dissidents and won their confidence ... Most of them were surprised by our opinions and the fact that how much our opinions were close to them ... he [the Shah] often asked me, 'What are your Mullah friends doing?'*[lxxxv]

When the diplomats and advisors returned to Washington a decision was taken to support the Islamic opposition to the Shah. The national opposition was deemed too weak, while the communist opposition was too closely aligned with the Soviet Union. This Islamic opposition was led by Ayatollah Ruhollah Khomeini. Khomeini had lived in Najaf, Iraq, for many years, from which he organised his opposition to the Shah. In 1978, however, Saddam Hussein expelled him, following which he took up residence in a suburb of Paris, France, called Neauphle-le-Château.

While in Najaf, Khomeini had already been visited by the Americans. Richard Cottam, a member of the CIA that organised the

1953 coup against Mossadeq, had met and discussed with Khomeini in Najaf on behalf of the American government. Cottam had learned at that time that Khomeini was concerned about a communist takeover in Iran, and that he wanted to be careful in his attempt to organise a coup against the Shah so as not to give the communists the chance to make use of the situation. Khomeini asked Cottam to communicate to his masters in Washington that he, Khomeini, would be looking to America for support against a communist coup in Iran.[lxxxvi]

America also sent representatives to Neauphle-le-Château in France to continue discussions and negotiations with Khomeini and his entourage there. In October of 1978 Khomeini and America reached an official agreement under which Khomeini promised to cooperate with America, if America helped him to topple the Shah and following the revolution would not interfere in domestic Iranian affairs. The Americans agreed to this.[lxxxvii] The American president Carter then sent General Robert Huyser to Iran to ensure support for the revolution amongst the Iranian generals in January 1979. President Carter, in his memoires, confirmed that Huyser had indeed been sent with this mission:

> *"Huyser was of the opinion that the army had made sufficient plans to protect its equipment and facilities and that it would not come onto the streets. He had dissuaded some of its leaders from the idea of attempting a coup."*[lxxxviii]

Then on the 26th of January the American diplomat Ramsey Clark met with Khomeini in Neauphle-le-Château. After the meeting Clark told journalists:

> *"I have a great hope that this revolution will bring social justice to the Iranian people."*[lxxxix]

In other words, the revolution had been arranged and was ready to be executed.

Despite the revolution being considered as an Islamic one, the groups involved were mostly non-Islamic and included communists, academics, leftists, unions and many others who were not looking for an Islamic revolution. Once in power Islam was the last thing on Khomeini's mind, despite much hope for change amongst the people. Ayatollah Khomeini came to symbolise 'change'.

What united the people of Iran around the revolution was everyone wanted change, the Shah had not delivered on his promises, and any person could have become the leader, as long as they condemned the Shah.

The revolution marked a change from one extreme to another.

Almost overnight women went from being able to wear the latest western fashion items to being forced to wear the black chador or long dress and head scarf.

As soon as the Islamic revolution was in full swing cracks began to appear with the groups that brought Khomeini to power. What began as an authentic and anti-dictatorial popular revolution based on a broad coalition of all anti-Shah forces was

Ayatollah Ruhollah Khomeini return to Iran, 1 Feb 1979

soon transformed into a power grab. Except for some of Khomeini's

163

core supporters, the members of the coalition thought Khomeini intended to be more a spiritual guide than a ruler. However his core supporters took positions in important offices whilst many of those who had sacrificed to bring Khomeini to power found they were exiled, imprisoned or side-lined.

CLERICAL LEADERSHIP

Today Iran's political class is dominated by the clerics that participated in the Iranian revolution to oust the Shah in 1979. They created a political framework which has allowed them to dominate Iran and its politics ever since. At the apex of this system is the most powerful individual, the supreme leader, a position that has thus far been held by only two individuals. The first was the founder of the Islamic republic, Ayatollah Khomeini, who held the post from 1979 until his death in 1989. He was succeeded by his key aide and a former two-term president, Ayatollah Ali Khamenei, who has been supreme leader for the past two decades and is currently still in authority. The supreme leader is not elected by a public vote but rather by the Assembly of Experts, which is a group of high clerics. He has vast powers and appoints the leadership of the country's most powerful political institutions, including the state broadcasting, the Joint Staff, the Islamic Revolutionary Guards Corps (IRGC) and the Guardians Council.

The potential unravelling of this political system has been evolving ever since Ahmadinejad came to power in 2005. Whilst rifts have always existed in Iran's political system, Ahmadinejad was the first non-cleric to take such an important role. This intense infighting among clerical and political camps resulted in a situation where Iran's leadership is facing a rapidly shrinking body of appropriate political candidates.   Ahmadinejad stood against the old clerical elite, accusing them of corruption, luxurious living and running the state for their own benefit rather than that of the people. Due to his popularity, he was able to undermine many clerics. With the clerics holding vast land, and many involved in big business, the struggling economy has seen much anger vented against the clerical establishment, which Ahmadinejad was able to utilise for his own political ends.

FOREIGN POLICY

Iran is always accused of wanting to dominate the region, a supporter of terrorism and a player that causes instability in the region, but the Middle East from Tehran looks much different. Iran and Persia before it, has played a central role in the region. Persia was a super power in antiquity and in the modern era Iran's energy resources rendered it an influential power in the region. The Persian Gulf and its coastal areas are the world's largest single source of oil and gas. 25% of the world's daily oil production, 66% of the world's oil reserves and 35% of the world's natural gas reserves are in the Persian Gulf. Of these Iran possesses 10% of global oil reserves, produces 5.2% of daily oil production and possesses the world's largest gas field – South Pars. The Persian Gulf also possesses the Strait of Hormuz which is a chokepoint for global energy, 35% of all seaborne traded oil crosses the region.

From Iran's perspective these strategic strengths always need to be protected from the preying eyes in the region and beyond. For Iran this is all best achieved by remaining the dominant power in the region through spreading its influence. Iran has worked to expand its influence

Iran's Political Structure

Iran is ruled from the top by the supreme leader, Ali Khamenei. Khamenei's power extends in all directions.

ELECTED POSITIONS

PRESIDENT
- Four-year term
- Guides domestic policy
- Does not guide foreign and defense policy

ASSEMBLY OF EXPERTS
- 88 members
- Eight-year terms

Appoints supreme leader

Has power to remove supreme leader

PARLIAMENT
- 290 members
- Four-year terms
- Introduces and passes laws

Has power to remove president

Has power to block all laws enacted by Parliament

NON-ELECTED POSITIONS

Commander-in-chief

SUPREME LEADER
- Highest religious and political leader
- In power since 1989

Appoints

REVOLUTIONARY GUARD
- About 120,000 members
- Most powerful organization in Iran

NATIONAL SECURITY COUNCIL
- Advises on nuclear and foreign policy

GUARDIAN COUNCIL
- Six clerics, six jurists
- Controls elections
- Determines who can run

Officialy chaired by president but rarely acts against supreme leader

Source: The New York Times, The Washington Post, Karim Sadjapour, Carnegie Endowment for International Peace, Said A. Arjomand, State University of Stony Brook

throughout the Middle East and developed a whole host of political plans to achieve this. Iran established Hezbollah in Lebanon in the early 1980s and continues to extend its support through training and arms.

Similarly in Palestine the Iranian regime has armed Hamas. Tehran deepened relations with the Alawi regime in Syria and also made itself the official representative of the Shia globally and has used this as a pretext to interfere in countries with significant Shia populations such as Saudi Arabia, Bahrain and Afghanistan and the other Gulf states in the Persian Gulf. Under the guise of a Shia crescent, Tehran has always looked to extend its influence into Afghanistan in the Asian Subcontinent all the way to the Mediterranean coast covering Syria and Lebanon. This was confirmed in January 2016 by Mohammad-Ali Ja'fari, commander of Iran's Islamic Revolutionary Guard Corps (IRGC), in a memorial service for one of its slain soldiers that the IRGC was responsible for training, recruiting and arming 200,000 pro-Iran fighters in Syria, Iraq, Yemen, Pakistan and Afghanistan.[xc] Iran's major challenges in the region include Saudi Arabia and Israel - who are also attempting to spread their influence in the region. Iran also faces challenges from the world's superpower the USA, who does not want to share the region with anyone.

Iran's policy has shifted between not trusting the US and trying to engage with the US, in order that it is taken seriously in the region. The process began during the Muhammad Khatami presidency (1997-2005) to normalise relations between the two countries. In a BBC documentary in 2009 on the 30th anniversary of the Iranian revolution, Khatami outlined the various attempts by his administration to normalise relations with the US. Khatami outlined Iran's sharing of intelligence with the US on targets in Afghanistan after the US led invasion.

SHIITE POPULATIONS IN THE GREATER MIDDLE EAST

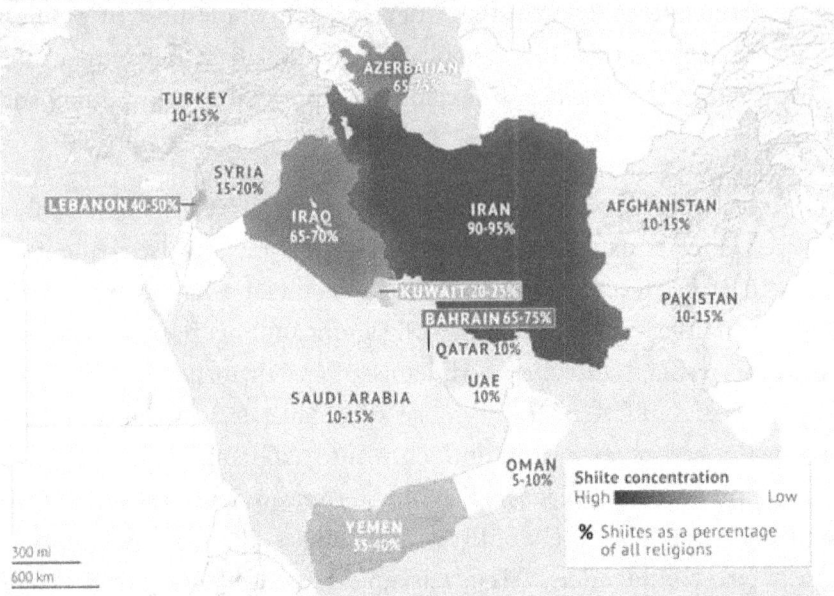

Pew Research Centre; U.S. Department of State; Brandeis University   esri

Khatami highlighted Iran's central role to the Northern alliance taking over Kabul and the help Iran gave the US to create the new government in Kabul. Khatami said that if the US attacked the Taliban this would be in Iran's interests. Another attempt to normalise relations in 2003 was spurned by the US. Richard Haas head of the State department said:

> "but we couldn't get support from the Pentagon office or the Vice President's office, in every case we ran up against the belief in regime change."[xci]

On the issue of Iraq, the BBC documentary included an interview with Khatami and quoted him:

> "Saddam Hussein was our enemy, we wanted him destroyed, let's repeat the Afghanistan experience in Iraq, let's make it 6 plus 6, the six countries bordering Iraq and America and the security council members and Egypt - look at Iran as a power that can solve problems rather than

168

as a problem itself.'[xcii]

The US did not take this offer and Iran watched from the sidelines as America's military machine bombed Iraq back to the Stone Age. Before Khatami's second term finished in 2005 a 'roadmap' emerged from Iran to normalise relations with the US which included accepting the two state solution on Palestine and turning Hezbollah into a peaceful political group. Richard Haas of the State department at the time said

> *"I thought the paper was interesting but I was sceptical, the biggest problem in dealing with Iran at that point was uncertainty, whether the government really spoke for the government, or whether the government spoke for the power centres of the country.'*[xciii]

Iran's development of nuclear weapons is in this light, i.e. to strengthen itself in the region. Whilst Iran has not tested a nuclear device, it continues enriching uranium and has the delivery systems. Once Iran has successfully enriched sufficient uranium and tested a nuclear device this will completely alter the military balance in the region.

America's fundamental challenge has been how to deal with Iran's regional ambitions, and as a result US policy has regularly shifted between containment, engagement and military change. Iran's ambitions to dominate the region, potentially conflicts with US aims in the region and this is America's fundamental problem with Iran. On many occasions the US has been able to use Iran to achieve its aims in the region, however many within the US political class do not trust Iran and as a result attempts to normalise relations with Iran have never been successful until now due to the opposition within the political class. The quagmire in Iraq and Afghanistan forced America to engage with Iran as it needed to save itself in the region, the threats of regime change by the Neoconservative administration very quickly gave way to engagement with Iran on common issues.

Many of Iran's ambitions are not necessarily in conflict with US interests in the region. Without Iran, Iraq and Afghanistan would never have been stabilised. If one looks beyond the rhetoric that comes out of Washington and Tehran it becomes clear both nations have the same interests on most matters, Iran wants a stable Iraq so does the US, Iran wants to secure Afghanistan which it shares a border with and the US wants to solve the Afghan problem which it has failed to do for over a decade. There is no difference between Iran and Israel as US tools in the Middle East, Israel openly protects US interests and is treated as an ally, whilst the differences between both countries is given little media attention. Iran-US differences are given a lot of media coverage and scrutiny, whilst their cooperation is given very little coverage.

For Iran, normalising ties with the US will give it the influence it so craves in the region and for the US it allows it to try and drive a wedge through the Muslim world by pitting Shia against the Sunni. It proves once and for all there is no ideological call or spreading of Islam by Iran, neither is there really any promotion of Shia Islam. Iran's interests are nationalistic, there are merely for Iran as a state to be dominate in the region. The only factor that Iran uses to judge which policies to pursue are those that will give Iran dominance in the region and Iran is prepared to use any means necessary (pragmatism) to achieve this. This is why its Shia crescent policy is a means to an end rather than an end in itself. This is because in reality Iran does not extend support to all Shia globally but only to those that will aid it to achieve it dominance of the region. Iran has not extended support to the Shia in Azerbaijan or Tajikistan even though they are oppressed as they do not achieve its objectives, whilst the Shia in Afghanistan and Saudi Arabia receive considerable support as they are central to Iran's aims of dominating its region.

THE GULF

The Gulf, both the Arabian Gulf and the Persian Gulf, for most of history was the only direct route to the East from the West. Its security has always been perceived to be vital to those seeking to move materials through it. The entire Arabian Peninsula came under Islamic rule at the time of the Prophet of Islam and it remained under direct Islamic rule of the Caliphate despite the capital moving throughout its history. From the 10th century the Gulf for intents and purposes was semi-autonomous, as were much of the Islamic lands due to the Caliphate in Baghdad and Cairo not directly ruling areas further from its centre.

By the 19th century the Arabian Peninsula was one of the world's most resource-poor and underdeveloped regions. Lacking the waters that provided fertility to the Nile Basin and Mesopotamia or a coveted position along the Mediterranean coast, the peninsula remained a bystander on the side-lines of events that developed in Egypt, Turkey, the Levant and Iran.

Economic activity was largely confined to subsistence farming or herding activities before the discovery and export of oil in the early 20th century, although small populations along the coastline of the Persian Gulf participated in pearl diving and limited trade with foreign powers. The discovery of oil on the Arabian side of the Persian Gulf coincided with the consolidation of the multiple tribes and the establishment of the Kingdom of Saudi Arabia in 1932. By the 1950s, Saudi Arabia had started commercial oil sales. Discoveries in neighbouring Bahrain, the United Arab Emirates and Kuwait continued through the 1950s. Development of the Gulf economies progressed rapidly following the semi withdrawal of Britain from the Emirates and because of rising oil output.

British interest in the Persian Gulf originated in the sixteenth century and steadily increased as British India's importance rose in the imperial system of the eighteenth and nineteenth centuries. Realising the region's significance, the British fleet supported the Persian emperor Shāh Abbās in expelling the Portuguese from Hormuz Island in 1622. In return, the British East India Company was permitted to establish a trading post in the coastal city of Bandar 'Abbās, which became their principal port in the Persian Gulf. Empowered by the charter of Charles II in 1661, the Company was responsible for conducting British foreign policy in the Persian Gulf, as well as concluding various treaties, agreements and engagements with Persian Gulf states in its capacity as the Crown's regional agent.

Throughout the 17th and 18th centuries, when the Ottomans were the leaders of the Caliphate, south and east of the Arabian Peninsula was ruled with a mixture of autonomy and complete freedom. Ottoman rule went up to Basra, and this left many tribes from the port of Kuwait, Bahrain, Najd down to the South of the peninsula with self-rule. This led to some clans and tribes to develop ambitions of dominating the other clans and tribes intercept caravans, conduct piracy and invading villages. The worst of these led to the intervention of the Ottomans and the expulsion of some tribes, the Saud family is a good example of one such tribe.

For the British Empire both the Persian and Arabian Gulf crossed the key trade route for British India. This is why Britain was supporting and arming clans and tribes over other clans and tribes to secure the route for the British Empire. In 1853, Britain and the Arab sheikhdoms of the Persian Gulf signed the Perpetual Maritime Truce, formalising the temporary truces of 1820 and 1835. The sheikhs agreed to stop harassing British shipping in the Arabian Sea and to recognise Britain as the dominant power in the gulf. These sheikhdoms thus became known as the Trucial States. An international agreement among the major powers in 1907 placed the Gulf in the British sphere of influence. Britain after WW1 carved up the Middle East and maintained a firm grip on the countries it created, Saudi Arabia, Yemen, Oman, UAE, Qatar, Bahrain and

Kuwait. After WW2 and with Britain's power in decline, Britain struggled to maintain a military presence in the Gulf and by 1971 much of its military presence was reduced in what came to be known as 'East of the Suez.'

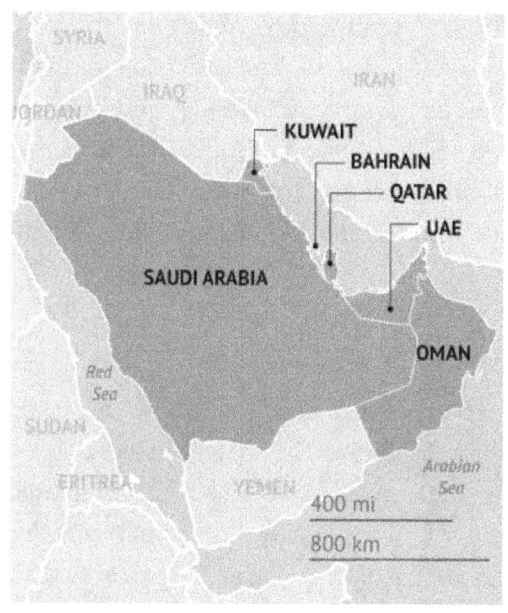

Gulf

Britain may have reduced its military presence but it maintained its political control of the region after working with individual tribes in the Gulf. But even its military presence did not completely disappear. In fact, Britain has never been fully absent from regional affairs, least of all in military terms. The Sovereign Base Areas of Akrotiri and Dhekelia, for example, are enclaves on the island of Cyprus that have remained under British military control since 1960—vital staging posts for air, sea and land forces that maintain a keen eye on security developments in the Levant, around the Suez Canal, and even as far afield as the Persian Gulf.

Britain's political influence was challenged by the US after the 1990 Iraqi invasion of Kuwait. The US used the crisis – the liberation of Kuwait, to effectively seize the Gulf from Britain through building military bases, and thus providing the security for the region and also gaining control of the region's oil reserves. The US had every capability to drive straight into Baghdad and overthrow Saddam Hussein, which it didn't. For the next two decades the US used Saddam Hussein's WMDs and the threat of Iran to consolidate its position in the Gulf. Britain had no choice but to join the US and pick up whatever crumbs it could.

After 9/11 and with the invasion of Iraq in 2003 the US expanded its presence in the region and used the war in terror not just to chase al Qaeda in the Middle East, but to also restructure the political architecture in the region. The US attempted to remove rulers from monarchies and families with which Britain has had relations with going back over 200 years. Despite a large, expanding and growing presence of the US in the Persian and Arabian Gulf it has struggled to remove Britain's political influence in the Gulf Kingdoms as Britain still maintains influence amongst the Monarchs in the region.

KUWAIT

Banu Utub's ancestors were expelled from Umm Qasr in central Arabia by the Ottomans due to their predatory habits of preying on caravans in Basra and trading ships in Shatt al-Arab. They migrated to Kuwait thereafter. Around the 1760s, the Al-Jalahma and Al-Khalifa clans, both belonging to the Banu Utub tribe, migrated to Zubarah in modern-day Qatar, leaving the Al Sabah as the sole proprietors of Kuwait. The Al Sabah's have been ruling the country ever since.

Kuwait prospered and rapidly became the principal commercial centre for the transit of goods between India, Muscat, Baghdad and Arabia. By the early 1900s during the reign of Mubarak, Kuwait was dubbed the "Marseilles of the Gulf" because its economic vitality attracted a large variety of people. But in the Kuwait–Najd War of 1919-1920, Ibn Saud was able to impose a trade blockade against Kuwait, the goal of which was to annex as much of Kuwait's territory as possible. At the Uqair Conference in 1922, the boundaries of Kuwait and Najd were set. Kuwait had no representative at the Uqair conference and as a result Ibn Saud persuaded Sir Percy Cox to give him two-thirds of Kuwait's territory. More than half of Kuwait was lost due to Uqair.

Today Kuwait is a tiny emirate wedged between Saudi Arabia and Iraq, and has essentially functioned in recent decades as a city-state with the world's sixth largest oil reserves. Kuwait has a petroleum-based economy, petroleum and fertilisers are the main export products. The Kuwaiti dinar is the highest-valued currency unit in the world. Petroleum accounts for nearly half of GDP and 94% of export revenues and government income. Kuwait sits on over 100 billion barrels of oil - the world's sixth largest proven oil reserves, making it the world's ninth largest oil producer.

The tiny Kingdom's population is a mere 4.1 million people, which is comprised of 1.1 million Arab expatriates, 1.4 million Asian expatriates, and 76,698 Africans. Indigenous Kuwaitis are a mere 1.2 million of the total population.

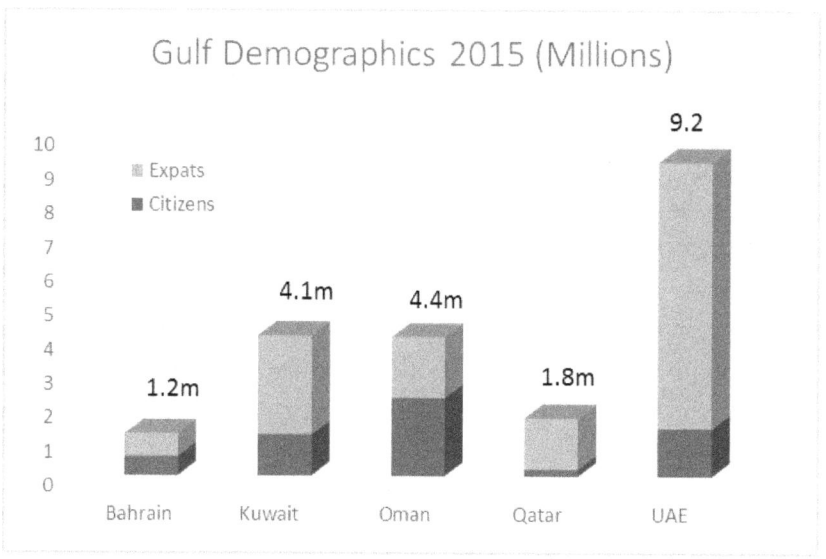

BAHRAIN

Bahrain (from the Arabic word for "two seas") comprises an archipelago of thirty-three islands situated midway in the Persian Gulf close to the shore of the Arabian Peninsula. The islands are about twenty-four km from the east coast of Saudi Arabia and twenty-eight km from Qatar. The total area of the islands is about 691 square km, or about four 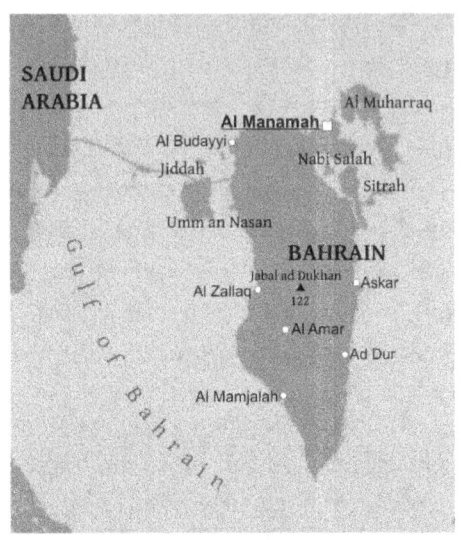 times the size of the District of Columbia. The largest island, accounts for 83% of the country. From north to south, Bahrain is forty-eight km long; at its widest point in the north, it is sixteen km from east to west. Bahrain is an island off the coast of Saudi Arabia; Bahrain and Saudi Arabia are linked by a causeway. For most purposes, Bahrain is part of Saudi Arabia. Unlike Saudi Arabia, it is not a major oil producer, but it is a banking centre. It is also the home of the US 5th Fleet The majority of its population is Shia, but its government is Sunni and heavily linked to Saudi Arabia. The Shiite population has not fared as well economically as Shia in other countries in the region, and tensions between the government and the public have long existed. With a population of only 1.2 million, 70% of which live in the cities of Manama and Al Muharraq, 568,399 of the Kingdom's population are indigenous whilst 666,172 are non-nationals. So foreigners constitute the majority populace.

Bahrain was one of the earliest areas to come under Islamic rule in 628. Bahrain was occupied by the Portuguese in 1521, which in turn were expelled in 1602 by Shah Abbas I of the Safavid Empire. In

1783, the Bani Utbah clan captured Bahrain after being expelled from Najd by the Ottomans. It has ever since been ruled by the Al-Khalifa family. In the late 1800s, following successive treaties with the British, Bahrain came under British patronage and remained so until Britain reduced its military presence in 1971. The Al-Khalifa's developed a divide and rule strategy to maintain their grip on power, it also appropriated land from the indigenous Shia owners and effectively made them into peasants. Even then, the regime operated with the assistance of a number of Shia families who it employed as ministers or tax collectors. Still today, high-ranking government positions are disproportionately awarded to members of the Al-Khalifa family, or other Sunni allies and a few handpicked Shia representatives are given positions of power. Bahrain has a situation where the Shia majority who form around 60% of the population, are ruled over by a minority Sunni Monarchy.

The Arab spring that began in 2011 quickly spread to Bahrain. Protests against the monarchy took place due to the lingering frustration among the Shia majority, leading to many to take to the streets in protest. Protests were largely peaceful, until a raid by police on the night of 17 February 2011 against protesters sleeping at the Pearl Roundabout in Manama, where four protesters were killed. This galvanised the protests and their message was clear – the end of the monarchy, which has ruled Bahrain since the late 18th century. Protesters regularly occupied the Pearl Roundabout which became the symbol of the protests. On 22nd February, an estimated one hundred thousand people, one fifth of all Bahrainis, marched.

On 14 March 2011, worried that Iran would take advantage of the growing protests, Saudi Arabian troops entered the country and opened fire on the protesters, several of whom were killed. Both Bahrain and Saudi Arabia have treated their Shi'a populations with much content. Both countries use sectarianism to remain in power and create a cohesive society by blaming every ill in their country upon the Shia in order to shore up support from their Sunni populace. An uprising by the Shia in the region would have had serious implications as the Shia in Eastern Saudi Arabia – neglected by the Saudi monarchy mainly reside amongst Saudi's coveted oil fields. Any uprising by the Shia could be exploited by Iran and this explains why Saudi very quickly answered Bahrain's plea for help.

QATAR

Substantial development in the pearling industry around the Qatari Peninsula occurred during the Abbasid era. Ships voyaging from Basra to India and China would make stops in Qatar's ports during this period. Chinese porcelain, West African coins and artefacts from Thailand have been discovered in Qatar. Following Ottoman rule, Qatar became a British protectorate in the early 20th century. When Britain reduced its presence in 1971 Qatar had been ruled by the Al-Thani family since the mid-19th century, and it remains in power today. Sons overthrowing their fathers are a common occurrence in Qatar. There is no independent legislature, and political parties are forbidden. Parliamentary elections, which were originally promised for 2005, have been postponed indefinitely.

Qatar's total population is 1.8 million, with a mere 278,000 Qatari citizens and 1.5 million expatriates. Qatari nationals are merely 13% of the population. The country relies heavily on foreign labour, to the extent that migrant workers comprise 86% of the population and 94% of the workforce.

Oil and liquefied natural gas (LNG) are the cornerstones of Qatar's economy and account for more than 70% of total government

178

revenue, more than 60% of gross domestic product, and 85% of export earnings. Since oil was discovered in 1939 the revenue from exports flooded the pockets of the ruling family. But the discovery of the world's largest gas field The South Pars/North Dome field in 1971, shared between Iran and Qatar turned the tiny island into the world's richest country per capita.

Qatar has supported British aims through the region and beyond and is one of Britain's closest partners in the region. Qatar has been aggressive in pursuing regional issues and becoming a hub for global negotiations. Doha hosted and acted as mediator for the peace negotiations that were aimed at brokering an agreement between the government of Sudan and the various Darfur rebel groups. Similarly, it was Qatar which arranged an agreement in April 2011 with Mahmoud Abbas which was to lead an interim unity government to pave the way for new elections in the Palestinian territories. Qatar has also been directly involved in implementing the US-sponsored two-state solution. Similarly, in Yemen, Qatar participated in the negotiations for the transition from Ali Abdallah Saleh to Abd Rabbuh Mansur Al-Hadi. On the Afghan issue negotiations with the Taliban and a Taliban office are in Doha.

Qatar has, however, not proposed any new solutions to the region's problems but has taken part in implementing, hosting, organising and bringing the various parties in the region's conflicts together in Doha. The dominance of Iran in the Persian Gulf has led many of the Gulf States, including Qatar, into seeking alliances with foreign world powers. Qatar has supported the FSA in Syria as well as various groups in Lebanon, Sudan, Yemen and the wider region. All of these groups that it supports and provide sanctuary for are hostile to the US. However, it has protected British interests and has been at the forefront in all the strategies set by Britain. For example, Qatar was central to the *"Friends of Syria"* conference in April 2012, which was a British organized meeting to bring the various groups and factions in Syria together.

UNITED ARAB EMIRATES (UAE)

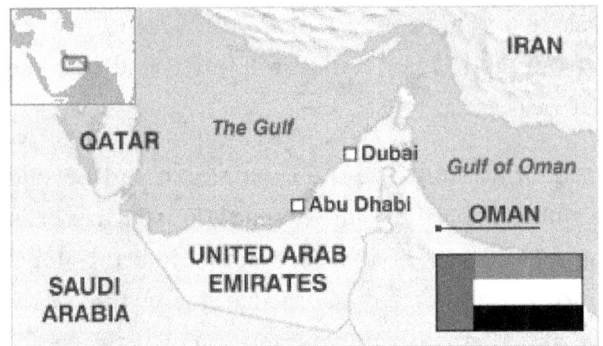

The spread of Islam to the North Eastern tip of the Arabian Peninsula followed directly from a letter sent by the prophet of Islam, to the rulers of Oman in 630. This led to a group of rulers travelling to Madinah, converting to Islam and subsequently driving a successful uprising against the unpopular Sassanid's, who dominated the Northern coasts at the time. By the 17th century, the Bani Yas tribe was the dominant force in most of the area now known as Abu Dhabi.

British expeditions to protect the Indian trade from raiders at Ras al-Khaimah led to military campaigns against the harbours along the Arabian Gulf coast in 1809 and subsequently 1819. The following year, Britain and a number of local rulers signed a treaty to combat piracy along the Persian Gulf coast, giving rise to the term Trucial States, which came to define the status of the coastal emirates. Further treaties were signed in 1843 and 1853.

In order to deal with the ambitions of France and Russia, the British and the Trucial Sheikhdoms established closer ties in a 1892 treaty, similar to treaties entered into by the British with other Persian Gulf kingdoms. The sheikhs agreed not to dispose of any territory except to the British and not to enter into relationships with any foreign government other than the British without its consent. In return, the British promised to protect the Trucial Coast from all aggression by sea and to help in case of land attack. This treaty, the

Exclusive Agreement, was signed by the Rulers of Abu Dhabi, Dubai, Sharjah, Ajman, Ras Al-Khaimah and Umm Al-Quwain. It was subsequently ratified by the Viceroy of India and the British Government in London. In 1922 the British government secured undertakings from the trucial rulers not to sign concessions with foreign companies as they were aware of the potential for the development of natural resources such as oil, following finds in Persia from 1908 and Mesopotamia from 1927. When Britain was reducing its military presence in 1971, the ruler of Abu Dhabi Sheikh Zayed bin Sultan Al Nahyan, tried to persuade the British to remain and honour the protection treaties by offering to pay the full costs of keeping the British Armed Forces in the Emirates. The British Labour government rejected the offer. When the British-Trucial Sheikhdoms treaty expired on 1 December 1971, the rulers of Abu Dhabi and Dubai decided to form a union between their two emirates independently, prepare a constitution, and then call the rulers of the other five emirates to the union. Four other emirates agreed to enter into a union called the United Arab Emirates. Bahrain and Qatar declined their invitations to join the union.

After 1971 UAE became a federation of seven emirates. The constituent emirates are Abu Dhabi (which serves as the capital), Ajman, Dubai, Fujairah, Ras al-Khaimah, Sharjah, and Umm al-Quwain. Each emirate is governed by an

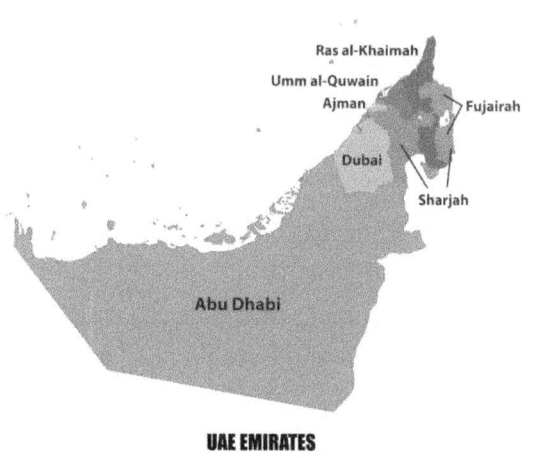

UAE EMIRATES

absolute monarch who jointly forms the Federal Supreme Council. One of the monarchs is selected as the President of the United Arab Emirates.

181

Like the other city states in the region, the UAE's total population is 9.2 million, of which 1.4 million are Emirati citizens and 7.8 million are expatriates. The UAE's oil reserves are the fourth-largest in the world, while its natural gas reserves are the world's seventeenth-largest. UAE has seen significant development as oil revenues have gone into healthcare, education and infrastructure. The city of Dubai emerged into a centre for international trade and transport. However, the country remains extremely reliant on petroleum and natural gas.

OMAN

A decade after Vasco da Gama's successful voyage around the Cape of Good Hope and to India in 1497–98, the Portuguese arrived in Oman and occupied Muscat for a 143-year period, from 1507 to 1650. Their fortress still remains. In 1741, by the leader of a Yemeni tribe, who began the current line of ruling sultans, except for a brief Persian invasion in the late 1740s, Oman has been self-governing ever since. Britain throughout the 20th century built and trained the Sultan's armed forces. Oman's population is just over 4 million, with 2.23 million Omani nationals and 1.76 million expatriates.

Oman's geography has made the country difficult to rule. Uniting the distinct population centres created by the country's mixture of mountains and desert has been a costly enterprise. Oman under Sultan Said bin Taimur, who came to power in 1932, experienced decades of international isolation, a society run along feudal lines and internal rebellion. After deposing his father in 1970, Sultan Qaboos Bin Said opened up the country, embarked on economic reforms and boosted spending on health, education and welfare.

Oman today dominates the south-eastern part of the Arabian Peninsula, equidistant between the emerging and enlarging middle classes of both India and East Africa, lying just outside the Gulf with major ports, Oman is far from the unstable Middle East core. These factors will make Oman an important player going forward.

YEMEN

The country's rugged and mountainous geography led to the development of numerous tribes that constantly compete for limited resources. Modern Yemen has been unified only since 1990. Islam came to Yemen during the time of the prophet of Islam. Several dynasties emerged from the 9th to 16th century, the Rasulid being the strongest and most prosperous. The country was divided between the Ottoman and British empires in the early 20th century. The Zaydi Mutawakkilite Kingdom of Yemen was established after WW1 in North Yemen before the creation of Yemen Arab Republic in 1962. South Yemen remained a British protectorate until 1967. The two Yemeni states united to form the modern republic of Yemen in 1990.

Ali Abdullah Saleh has dominated both North and South Yemen since he emerged in 1978. He is from amongst the Houthis, who are a tribe from amongst the Zaidi's, who follow Shia jurisprudence and comprise 40% of nation's population. Despite being from amongst them, Saleh oppressed the largest segment of society in order to maintain his own grip. Corruption has led Yemen to become one of the world's poorest countries. According to the United Nations, Yemen ranks 151st out of 177 countries on the human development index (HDI), a measure of life expectancy, education, and standard of living. With an economy of only $16 billion, Yemen's population is destitute with half of its 27m population living in poverty. As a result many of Yemen's population were forced to come together on a tribal basis due to the failure of central government to maintain security and meet their most basic needs.

The Arab spring quickly spread to Yemen as the Houthis took to the streets. The Houthis have fought the government on-and-off during the 2000s, due to decades of being marginalised and repressed, but both Saleh and his replacement, Hadi, kept them from real power through dialogues and internationally sponsored talks. Today Yemen is in chaos, the Houthis have entered into a protracted struggle with the government in Sanaa, eventually overthrowing it in September 2014. When President Hadi fled the country Saudi Arabia launched airstrikes against reported Houthi targets in the country's capital.

The basic problem in Yemen today is a large chunk of the population have been neglected and oppressed by the ruler. The Houthis took to the streets when the Arab spring uprisings began in order to overthrow their long standing dictator. It was at this point both regional and international players used the crisis to achieve their own interests. Iran has armed and funded the Houthis in in line with their pro-Shia policy of arming and funding sectarian groups to expand its influence in the region. Iran has provided weapons and training to Houthi rebels for a number of years both directly and through its proxy — Hezbollah.[xciv] This led to Saudi Arabia to interfere in Yemen in order to act against this Iranian influence by acting against the Houthis. It is afraid of the conflict spilling over the Saudi border and parties such as Al-Qaeda within Yemen obtaining more ground. Internationally Britain and the US have taken opposite positions in Yemen. The US position has always been the removal of Saleh, despite the position of Britain in favour of Saleh. Eventually Britain was able to get Saleh a dignified exit, where he left his crony in power.

The US has been undermining this British architecture, senior US intelligence official Michael Vickers made clear that intelligence had been provided to the Houthis for a long time.[xcv]

Yemen has become the official battleground for both regional and international players.

ARAB SPRING

As 2010 was coming to an end, Hosni Mubarak of Egypt had been in power for decades, with the army well entrenched in the country. Muammar Gaddafi of Libya maintained his position with ruthless precision and there was no threat to his rule. In Tunisia, Zine al-Abidine Ben Ali controlled every strata of his nation's society, whilst Ali Abdullah Saleh of Yemen had imprisoned or killed most of his competitors. Then a historical event of global magnitude took place in the Middle East. For the Muslim world, 2011 will remain long in the memory when the history books are finally written. What began with a single man in the markets of Tunisia spread to thousands on the streets in Cairo and evolved to hundreds of thousands demanding political change for the entire region. The self-immolation of Mohamed Bouazizi in Tunisia created a sweeping wave, which crossed the artificial border to Egypt, then to Libya, Yemen and Bahrain until it engulfed most of the Muslim world. The Arab spring saw many brave the streets to protest and change the status quo which has dominated the political, economic and social landscape for so long. The reaction of the Muslim rulers was as predictable as it was brutal with violent clampdowns leaving thousands dead and many more injured.

The Arab spring was unique in the Middle East as many of the rulers maintained their position through brutal methods of torture, which left a psychological impact upon the masses fearing the repercussions of any uprising. This is why many were stunned all around the world when heavyweights such as Zine al-Abidine Ben Ali of Tunisia fell, followed by long-term dictator Hosni Mubarak of Egypt then followed eventually by Muammar Gaddafi of Libya. The Euphoria of 2011, by 2015 had given way to chaos, civil war and disorder. The hopes, wishes and sacrifices of the masses who took to the streets trying to survive the bullets, baton charges, sniper fire and military intervention eventually turned into a disaster and much of this is to do with external causes rather than from purely within the region, this can be seen from analysing the key individual nations that witnessed uprisings.

TUNISIA

When President Zine El-Abidine Ben Ali was forced to flee on 14 January 2011, an interim government replaced him and elections took place in October 2011. The country's Islamic group, the Ennahda Movement won the legislative polls, securing 41% of the seats and proceeded to form a coalition government with the secular parties. Ennahda was founded in the 1980s on the model of the Egyptian Muslim Brotherhood. Over the past two decades Ennahda was effectively banned by Ben Ali, but it maintained its Islamic orientation. But the rivalry between all the different factions created political crisis at every juncture as they all jockeyed for power, including the writing of a new constitution.

The constitution, drafted by six assembly committees, was made public in August 2012. It was then put before another coordinating committee of the assembly that prepared it for presentation to the full assembly for debate and a vote. Ennahda made it clear after running on an Islamic ticket that it will not make the *Shari'ah* the source of legislation in the new constitution and would maintain the secular nature of the state. Ennahda insisted that it will keep the first article of the 1956 constitution in the new basic law. The article enshrined the separation of religion and state, stating that:

> *"Tunisia is a free, independent and sovereign state, its religion is Islam, its language is Arabic and it is a republic. We are not going to use the law to impose religion,"*[xcvi]

Ennahda's leader Rachid Ghannouchi told journalists after the

Islamic parties constituent committee voted to maintain the constitutional article by 52 votes to 12. The article, he added,

> "*is the object of consensus among all sectors of society; preserving Tunisia's Arab-Muslim identity while also guaranteeing the principles of a democratic and secular state.*"[xcvii]

Islam is Tunisia's official religion and while the constitution stipulates the president should be a Muslim, the state remained mostly secular. Some voiced concern that Ennahda would seek to curb women's rights and other liberties in an Arab country known for its progressive laws. However, Ghannouchi said the Islamist party would not

> "*introduce ambiguous definitions into the constitution that risk dividing the people*", adding that "*many Tunisians do not have a clear image of sharia and erroneous practices in certain countries have aroused fear.*"

The people of Tunisia voted in the Islamic party due to their Islamic sentiments. Ennahda once in power made it perfectly clear, that they had no plans to implement Islam. Tunisia thus became the first Arab spring nation that witnessed the ousting of its leader, openly declare that it would maintain the existing system, albeit with some cosmetic changes, but Islam will play virtually no role. Ennahda's leader, Rachid Ghannouchi, explained with regards to establishing the Caliphate after its electoral victory:

> "*Definitely, we are a nation state. We desire a state for Tunisian reforms, for the Tunisian State. As for the issue of the Khilafah, this is an issue that is not one of reality. The issue of today's reality is that we are a Tunisian State that desires reform, so that it becomes a State for the Tunisian People, not against them.*"[xcviii]

The people of Tunisia grew frustrated with the delays in the formation of the new constitution, alongside economic struggles that had persisted since Ben Ali's presidency. Matters reached boiling point when prominent secular opposition leaders and lawmakers were assassinated triggering mass protests and riots across Tunisia. The demonstrations and public criticism by the secular opposition forced Ennahda to step down in October 2013 and allow a technocratic government to draft the new constitution. By January 2014, the new government had created and passed the long-awaited constitution, which effectively maintained the pre-Arab spring system.

Ennahda struggled to rule in any meaningful manner and their strategy of dealing with this was the abandonment of Islam in order to appease the opposition. The elections of October 26 2014 saw the reversal of Ennahda's fortunes and the return of the secular groups, including many cronies from the Ben Ali era. Many in Tunisia united on the post-Ben Ali era, Ali Trabelsi, 38 told Al Jazeera:

> *"I am not going to waste an hour or so queueing for nothing. Last time I voted [for Ennahda] and I haven't seen any tangible changes. I even think it is going to be worse next time. I'd better earn a few dinars instead of going to vote.'*[xcix]

As the months turned into years Ennahda were unable to deal with any of the pressing issues affecting the lives of the people. Broken promises, paired with a struggling economy and violence for long fuelled cynicism of Ennahda. Everyday issues such as poor rubbish collection and widespread joblessness prompted many to say things were better under Ben Ali. Despite receiving the support of the masses only a few years prior, Nidaa Tounes founder, Beji Caid Essebsi, an 87-year-old veteran of both the Bourguiba and Ben Ali regimes, returned to power. Ben Ali's cronies were back in power.

The people of Tunisia took to the streets in one of the most repressed countries in the Middle East to put into the dustbin of history the brutal ruler who for long oppressed them. Many put their faith into Ennahda and its Islamic call as it resonated with their beliefs. Very quickly though Ennahda faced with basic challenges in governance and began to abandon Islam assuming this would preserve their rule. Whilst Ennahda went to great lengths to demonstrate its Islamic credentials to the masses, it went to even greater lengths to demonstrate its moderation to the West. Ennahda's political calculations were all rooted in personal partisan gains. They believed that the Islamic system could only be implemented gradually. Once in power Ennahda lacked much in policy and they went on to argue that Islamic solutions were not ready to deal with problems such as poverty, unemployment and development. They believed implementing Islam would scare minorities, scare investors and scare the international community. Ennahda's officials went to great lengths to explain how Islam must be applied gradually and how it was impractical in Tunisia. Ennahda abandoned Islam and failed utterly even when it attempted to rule with secularism. Ennahda effectively used the peoples Islamic sentiments to come to power, and once in power it presented the impracticality of Islam as a justification for its own incompetency.

EGYPT

The Egyptian army who are the real rulers of Egypt for long maintained US interests in the Middle East by protecting Israel and maintaining cordial relations with it. When protests erupted in Egypt in early 2011, US officials maintained their pro-Hosni Mubarak stance, expecting him to put down any uprising. As the people of Egypt were being mowed down by tanks US Vice President, Joe Biden, highlighted the US position on Egypt:

> *"Look, Mubarak has been an ally of ours in a number of things and he's been very responsible on, relative to geopolitical interests in the region: Middle East peace efforts, the actions Egypt has taken relative to normalizing the relationship with Israel, I would not refer to him as a dictator."*[t]

As far as US officials were concerned, Mubarak was their man in

189

Cairo.

Once it became clear Mubarak could not halt the protests and was being engulfed by them the US decided to turn its back on him. The huge protests against Mubarak in 2011 challenged US influence over Egypt and the architecture the US had constructed. Washington decided to turn its back on Mubarak but the architecture Mubarak and his predecessors constructed remained untouched. Effectively an 82-year-old man, who wanted to have his son appointed as his successor, was booted out by the army. Except for Mubarak, the army remained in charge of Egypt. An army that remained heavily financed and trained by America, whose leaders, Chief of Staff Lt-Gen. Sami Annan and Defence Minister Field Marshal Mohamed Hussein Tantawi, were in constant contact with the US throughout the uprising. On assuming power, the Supreme Council of the Armed Forces (SCAF) suspended the constitution whilst both houses of parliament were dissolved; they also declared the military would rule for six months until elections could be held. The prior cabinet would continue to serve as a caretaker government until a new one was formed. No change occurred in relations with the US and Israel, these remain intact.

The Muslim Brotherhood (MB), long marginalised by successive rulers, dominated post-Mubarak Egypt by initially winning a landslide victory in the parliamentary election in early 2012 and then the presidential election in June 2012. This was a unique moment in the history of Egypt, for a number of reasons. Firstly Mohammed Morsi was elected by the people, something none of his predecessors can claim. He was also the first civilian leader in the country's recent history. His party, the Muslim Brotherhood (MB), had been working for change for over eight decades. Mohammed Morsi took the premier seat in arguably one of the most influential and powerful countries in the region if not the Muslim world. But the MB took the reins of power in an environment, where the powers of the president were not defined and the nation's constitution had also not been written. Both Mohamed Morsi and the MB came face-to-face with the real-world challenges faced by any head of state.

As soon as the MB won the parliamentary elections and the presidential elections, Morsi confirmed he would be respecting all prior treaties. The US set about strengthening his rule as he confirmed he would protect US interests. The US defended Morsi against the growing opposition movement who criticised him for seeking immunity. US State Department spokeswoman Victoria Nuland defended the Egyptian president saying:

> *"President Morsi entered into discussions with the judiciary, with other stakeholders in Egypt. As I said, I think we don't yet know what the outcome of those is going to be, but that's a far cry from an autocrat just saying my way or the highway."*[i]

This was in response to protesters describing President Morsi as a dictator and the new Pharaoh of Egypt.

Very quickly Morsi had inflamed the public by maintaining the pre-revolutionary system. He increasingly became isolated and authoritarian - reminiscent of the Mubarak days. The fragmented opposition capitalised on this groundswell of anti-Morsi feeling, which in a short space of time had captured the hearts and minds of secular Egyptians as well as the vast majority of practicing Muslims. It was the latter segment that had propelled Morsi's Freedom and Justice Party to the fore of Egyptian politics only a year earlier. Now this segment had turned against him and called for his removal. Throughout the rule of Morsi the domestic political scene was never stable and was worsened by the confusion brought about by the Morsi government's decision-making. Morsi constantly retracted his decisions under pressure. Morsi's rule was characterised with anarchy and this instability continued throughout his year in office, which led to the emergence of a growing opposition that challenged his rule. The US needed domestic political stability in Egypt in order for the country to play a role in the region and Morsi failed at this and made matters worse the longer he remained in office.

The Morsi regime was plagued with indecisiveness and the inability to deal with pressing problems as it lacked a grand vision. The MB went to great lengths to demonstrate its moderation to the West. In its rush to placate so-called international opinion, they abandoned all commitment to Islamic governance. When it came to applying Islamic principles they cited constitutional barriers and the need to keep minorities onside. When it came to applying Islamic economics, they cited the need to avoid scaring international investors and tourists. When it came to applying the Islamic foreign policy, they cited the need to show a moderate image and to appease the West – slogans such as 'Islam is the solution,' were very quickly replaced with a call for a civil state. The initial calls for Islam were completely removed from Morsi's statements. Despite compromising on everything, it was never enough for the secular elements, who wished to emerge victorious from their demonstrations. Despite over 80 years touting 'Islam is the solution,' when the opportunity presented itself the MB failed to meet the challenge governance posed. As a result, despite winning the elections, they were always on the back-foot defending their rule.

On 3rd July 2013, after being given 24 hours to sort out the crisis by the head of the army, army commandos came to take Morsi to an undisclosed Defence Ministry facility – effectively a coup. Even his Republican Guards simply stepped away as the Muslim Brotherhood joined the likes of Mubarak, Ben Ali, Saleh and Gaddafi – rulers overthrown due to the euphoria of the Arab spring. The situation in Egypt returned to the eve of Mubarak's overthrow, the army was back in power. With the MB unable to protect US interests due to their inability to bring political stability to the country. Once the coup had taken place Obama said:

> *"The Egyptian armed forces should move quickly and responsibly to restore full power to a civilian government as soon as possible."*[xii]

Obama approved of the coup by not condemning it, he merely demanded the return to power of a civilian government, any government other than the Morsi government. He even refused to call the overthrow of a democratic government, a coup. Secretary of State John Kerry confirmed the return of the military regime as: *"restoring democracy."*[xiii]

The US maintained its influence in Egypt, something the MB did nothing to change. Similarly the Egyptian army never really gave up power. Muhammad Morsi and the MB were powerless as General Abdul Fatah al-Sisi announced the removal of the democratically elected government. Over 300 MB officials were rounded up overnight and placed under arrest. The military had collaborated with the opposition, secular elements, Coptic Christians, as well as the leadership of Al-Azhar on the post MB setup. The army proved, if there were any doubts, that it was the dominant power-broker in the country, despite the elected government's win at the polls. Since Morsi's overthrow in July 2013 General Sisi has worked to consolidate his rule with full blessing from the US. Much of the military government's attention focused on destroying what remained of the MB. Today thousands of MB members have been detained in prison; indeed, the revolutionary youth attend their court hearings in wheelchairs.

At every juncture the Egyptian military ensured that its interests were never harmed and did everything to maintain the status quo. The military formed a coalition of convenience with the MB for much of 2011 and 2012 to manage the post-Mubarak landscape and hold revolutionary aspirations and unfettered popular mobilisations in check. It successfully co-opted the movement against Morsi and, along with the security establishment, emerged as the clearest winner from his overthrow. Today 40% of Egypt's population lives below the poverty line, and it is here that the MB failed and for many and as far as the masses is concerned the army is a better alternative to the failed policies of the MB.

The euphoria that gripped Libya after the fall of Tripoli in August 2011 and the subsequent death of Gaddafi two months later, very quickly became a distant memory. It took around 8 months for the rebels and various other groups in Libya with significant NATO help to bring down the Gaddafi regime. The war had been long and damaging, the wounds deep and what united all the rebel groups was their opposition to Gaddafi. There was never any plan, blueprint or roadmap of what they would do once the Gaddafi regime fell – this is understandable considering the grip Gaddafi maintained for decades. An unelected interim government, the National Transitional Council (NTC) issued a constitutional declaration, otherwise known as the Road Map, which envisaged a lengthy, 18-month transition to something representative of the people. Stage one was the election of a transitional parliament; Stage Two, parliament's supervision of a new constitution. Once that was adopted, by referendum, Libya would successfully have navigated the Arab spring and transitioned to rule that was representative of the people.

Britain's close relationship with Gaddafi has been well documented, especially when British Prime Minister Tony Blair helped engineer Libya's rehabilitation by getting Gaddafi to accept Libya's role in the Lockerbie disaster.[civ] As the Arab spring erupted and forced the removal of Hosni Mubarak and Ben Ali, the British establishment, sensing the end was near for Gaddafi, decided to abandon him. Britain then mobilised a coalition of various tribes and militia groups to overthrow Gaddafi and his regime. After Gaddafi's fall in 2011, these tribes and militia groups came to dominate Libya's largest cities, filling the security vacuum left by the collapse of the old regime. Britain with France created the new political leadership in Tripoli. It established the National Transitional Council (NTC) in February 2011; this temporary government was mainly composed of people from the former Gaddafi regime. Muhammed Jibril, the leader of the NTC, was the head of the Economic board under Gaddafi while the Chairman, Mustafah Abdul Jalil, was a judge under Gaddafi. Then in July 2012 a permanent government was established — the General National Congress (GNC), with Muhammed Jibril as its head. Britain successfully replaced Gaddafi with another set of cronies.

But the Libyan regime struggled with the most basic task of state formation: establishing internal security. The formation of the Libyan National Army – which was meant to be the centrepiece of the government failed at threatening the militias into subservience. The inability of a legitimate central authority to impose its writ on the nation effectively enshrined the diffusion of power to locally elected city governments and the increasing clout of local militias. The nation's security forces failed to prevent renegade militia attacks or to convince regional militia leaders to lay down their arms or join the council's security forces. For instance, the al-Awfea Brigade took over the Tripoli Airport in June 2012 and held it until the next day, when the National Transitional Council negotiated a resolution. In April 2012, the council had to secure the international airport, which Zentan's militia had overtaken, and its inner-city airport, Benita, which had fallen under the control of Souq al-Jomaa, a militia that hails from the central Tripoli suburb of the same name. Former rebel strongholds such as Benghazi and Misurata, continued to work from their hometowns. These regional representatives continued to maintain strong ties to both their communities and local militias, building up their own patronage networks. This also led to a rise in support for locally elected city councils in former rebel bastions, where Tripoli's influence and bureaucratic institutions held little sway. Benghazi's city council even announced in March 2012 that it would take control of the city's day-to-day administrative issues independent of central government and with the support of local militias. Libya, very quickly came to be controlled by a network of armed militias, with many representing powerful tribes. The weakness of central government meant they could operate with impunity.

The US viewed the instability in Libya as an opportunity to gain influence in the country. It made use of Europe's inability to go it alone in removing Gaddafi to steal Libya from Europe and Britain. The US tried to influence affairs in Libya to serve its own interests by making private contacts with various local tribes and certain militias through its consulate in Benghazi. The testimony of Charlene Lamb, Deputy Assistant Secretary of State, before the House Oversight Committee on the security failures in Benghazi on October 10th 2012, revealed the US position. The hearing confirmed there was no real 'consulate' in Benghazi, but a vast intelligence and private contractors web for the CIA and the oil companies. Ms. Lamb gave away the fact that the 'facility' in Benghazi was not a diplomatic facility and confirmed that "there were also three members of the Libyan 17th February [Martyrs] Brigade" in the 'consulate.'[cv] Even the central government in Tripoli was unaware of the level of US presence within the country. The Deputy Prime Minister, Mustafa Abushagour, was quoted in the Wall Street Journal saying that he learned about some of the delicate American operations in Benghazi only after the attack on the mission, in large part because a surprisingly large number of Americans showed up at the Benghazi airport to be evacuated. The Wall street journal article continued

> "among the more than two dozen American personnel evacuated from the city after the assault on the American mission and a nearby annex were about a dozen C.I.A. operatives and contractors, who played a crucial role in conducting surveillance and collecting information on an array of armed militant groups in and around the city."[cvi]

The embassy was in reality a position from which the US was spying on Libya and working to develop links.

With both the US and Britain competing for Libya, it was inevitable the crisis in the country would continue and it came to a full blown fracture in 2014 when the constantly delayed parliamentary elections finally took place. The parliamentary elections which took place in June 2014 only saw an 18% turnout from the eligible 3.4m population. The economist described this as: indicating the 'declining enthusiasm' and 'growing disgust with the authorities' failure to govern.'[cvii] The low turnout led to a complete change in the Libyan parliament, but the old government refused to accept the result. By August 2014 militia groups loyal to the old government seized the airport in the capital, Tripoli and proclaimed their own government. In November 2014 the Supreme Court annulled the election result after an appeal by a group of unnamed MPs on unclear grounds. This forced the new government to flee the capital to Libya's eastern coastal town of Tobruk. They remain holed up in a grey, concrete hotel in a remote port 620 miles from the capital, Tripoli. This government was forced to hire a Greek car ferry which moored in Tobruk Harbour to house officials, activists and their families.

The emergence of former Major General Khalifa Hiftar led to the US having a stake in Libya. Ever since his return to Libya he has worked to weaken the parliament and government, which was constructed by Britain. In 1990 America's CIA negotiated his release from Chad and subsequently Hifter spent the next 20 years in Virginia, USA, where he was trained in guerilla warfare by the CIA. The Business Insider reported:

> "The likelihood that Hifter was brought in to be some kind of asset is pretty high. Just as figures like Ahmed Chalabi were cultivated for a post-Saddam."[cviii]

Dr Guma El-Gamaty who had been campaigning for democracy in Libya for 30 years and after the revolution became coordinator for the British government with the National Transitional Council, highlighted Hiftar's role.

> "Operation Dignity is led by a retired General, (Khalifa) Haftar — he was a comrade of Gaddafi some 45 years ago...he ran away about 20 years ago and now he wants to take over. He is hanging it on the fact that he claims to be fighting terrorists, but he wants to eradicate everyone

197

who opposes him, which is not fighting terrorism but imposing his will by force.'[cix]

The Egyptian entry into the conflict didn't just bolster Hifter, but also US attempts to undermine the old government, that was constructed by Britain. Egypt visibly bolstered its support for forces loyal to Khalifa Hifter, who came to serve as the head of the Libyan National Army's ground forces branch under the mandate of the government in Tobruk. The Egyptian government transferred a number of aircraft to Hifter's troops, including three MiG-21MF aircraft and a few Mi-8 helicopters. Hifter said in August 2014 that:

> *"he agreed with the method chosen by Egypt [to secure the border], even if it reached the point of a military strike within the borders of Egypt's western neighbour."*[cx]

The Egyptian entry was fundamentally to the advantage of Hifter and the US backed Tobruk government who does not control any of the keys towns in Libya – Benghazi, Tripoli and Misrata. They have struggled to weaken Libya Dawn, which is an affiliation of many militias from different cities and towns in the West of Libya.

The people of Libya are still waiting for a transition to a post-Gaddafi era. What they have witnessed is numerous military groups and factions as well as cities and towns backed by Britain and the US fight it out for the country. Despite suffering under the brutal rule of Gaddafi for decades the people of Libya still face immense challenges in the post-Gaddafi landscape. But we can officially say that it is now in the midst of an intense Anglo-American struggle.

YEMEN

Similar to Libya, Yemen has also turned into an intense Anglo-American struggle. The uprising in Yemen erupted simultaneously with Tunisia and Egypt. Ali Abdullah Saleh had been in power for 33 years and had rid himself of all opposition. Even a near-successful assassination attempt in June 2011, when an improvised explosive device (IED) exploded in the presidential compound mosque, couldn't force Saleh from power. However, with intense pressure from the US to step down and transfer power, an agreement was carved out between the EU, US, GCC and Saleh in February 2012 and power was transferred to vice president Abd Rabboh Mansour Hadi. Even though Saleh formally stepped down as President and elections took place, the political transition in Yemen in no way constitutes regime change. The deal between the US, EU, GCC and Saleh merely gave Saleh a dignified exit. Ever since the power-transfer agreement was signed, and despite regular protests demanding that Saleh be stripped of his immunity and that he and his family face trial, Saleh's family continues to hold many high-level positions throughout the government, business community and security forces

Formal elections took place in February 2014 and officially reinstated Saleh's long time right hand man — Abd Rabbuh Mansour Hadi. The elections in fact only had one candidate – Hadi himself. In this way Saleh's party – the Congress party, was able to dilute the demand for real change from the people of Yemen and maintain the status quo.

The Houthis fought the government on-and-off during the 2000s, and were big supporters of the 2011 Arab Spring uprising against then-President Saleh. Towson University's Charles Schmitz highlighted the 2011 American-backed deal that replaced Saleh with Hadi didn't satisfy the Houthis. The Houthis

> *"had no representation in the transitional government,"* Schmitz said, so they *"regard the transitional government as no different from the old regime that conducted wars against them — in other words, a body that cannot be trusted."*[txi]

By mid-2014 the Houthis had enough, as all government promises of more powers and positions of power had still not been met. Constituting 40% of Yemen's population, the Houthis took over the capital city in September 2014.

What made matters worse in Yemen is the interference of the international community. The US used the war on terror to undermine Ali Abdullah Saleh by accusing Yemen of being a hub for Al Qaeda. Ali Abdullah Saleh attempted to appease the US with a host of security guarantees which allowed the US to carry out drone attacks in the country. The uprising gave the US the opportunity to remove Saleh, who however dug in his heels in the face of demands by his own people to leave. He eventually agreed to a transition deal – led by the Gulf Cooperation Council (GCC) – another US tool. However, Saleh was able to transfer power to his own deputy and maintain the position of his party in Yemeni politics. Two days after the rebels took over key state institutions in the capital, Hadi said in a speech at the presidential palace:

"Sanaa is facing a conspiracy that will lead towards civil war,"[cxii]

Hadi meant that there was an outside hand in the crisis. UK Ambassador to Yemen, Jane Marriott visited Hadi on the eve of the Peace and National Partnership Agreement to quell the Houthi takeover of Sana. Marriott reiterated her country's full support to Yemen until completing the remaining tasks of the transitional phase successfully, i.e. she gave Britain's full support to Hadi.[cxiii] The British ambassador also confirmed to Middle East online in September 2014:

"I do not have a direct relationship with Ali Abdullah Saleh, but I communicate with the General People's Congress including parties close to it."

She admitted her communication with the party of Saleh and as he runs the party and has no rival or opponent this would indicate she has been speaking regularly with Saleh. The EU similarly in a statement on 22 September 2014 said:

"Government institutions must return to the control of the legitimate authorities, under the leadership of President Abd Rabbo Mansour Hadi, the Head of State."[cxiv]

Yemen thus became another battleground between the US and Europe.

SYRIA

The Arab Spring officially reached Syria on 15th March 2011 as protests began in Damascus, Aleppo, and the southern city of Daraa. The protests were triggered by the incarceration and torture of several young students, who were arrested for writing anti-government graffiti in the city – *'The people want the fall of the regime.'* The death toll is well in excess of 200,000 people and with half of the country's 22m population been displaced, the demand for real change continues in Syria. What is taking place in Syria has now engulfed much of the world with many from across the world contributing to the demands of the indigenous people for real change. The uprising in Syria has been unique when compared to the other nations that experienced uprisings in that the people have maintained their demand for real change to something in line with their beliefs i.e. Islam and despite the use of chemical weapons, barrel bombs and the siege of towns they continue their struggle.

The people of Syria rose up against the regime of Bashar al-Assad in 2011 in order to bring real change to the nation. They fought the regime across the length and breadth of the country and held the nation's armed forces to a stalemate. The rebel groups organised into battalions and groups of battalions leading a guerrilla war against the regime. Eventually their lack of capability caught up with them, the lack of heavy weaponry and a constant flow of munitions meant they were unable to topple the regime. At this point some of the groups turned to regional players for arms, whilst others turned to international powers. This inadvertently opened the door to foreign interference. Countries such as Turkey, Saudi Arabia and Qatar, as well as the US, Britain and Russia have only provided weapons which create a dependency rather than the heavy weaponry necessary to topple the regime. The Wall Street Journal highlighted:

> *"Some weapons shipments were so small that commanders had to ration ammunition. One of the US.'s favourite trusted commanders got the equivalent of 16 bullets a month per fighter. Rebel leaders were told they had to hand over old antitank missile launchers to get new ones."*[xxv]

All the international powers have maintained support for the al-Assad regime, despite their rhetoric to the contrary. They have provided cover to the al-Assad regime to commit multiple atrocities in order to remain in power. After 5 years, the West has stopped hiding its true intention of maintaining as much of the Syrian regime and is now openly advocating Bashar al-Assad remains in power and the rebel groups should join his regime in some type of coalition government. The anti-regime rhetoric was always a cover for the regime to quell the uprising in Syria. Ryan Crocker, the former US ambassador to Syria, Iraq, and Afghanistan, wrote in 2013, getting rid of Mr. Assad is likely to produce *"a major country at the heart of the Arab world in the hands of Al Qaeda."* As matters stand, ISIS is the enemy and Bashar al-Assad is the moderate who needs to remain in power, otherwise the alternative could be far worse. In the New York Review of Books, Jessica Matthews, outgoing president of the Carnegie Endowment for International Peace, wrote that the U.S. should take advantage of a rare moment of agreement with both Saudi Arabia and Iran and lead an international push for a peace deal that would allow Assad to remain in power but with

> *"most of his power dispersed to regional governors, the prime minister, the parliament, and the military. Though he is a war criminal, Assad's personal fate matters less at this point than his country's."*[xxvi]

These were not new positions though; Hillary Clinton laid out the US position in May 2011:

"There are deep concerns about what is going on inside Syria, and we are pushing hard for the government of Syria to live up to its own stated commitment to reforms. What I do know is that they have an opportunity still to bring about a reform agenda. Nobody believed Qaddafi would do that. People do believe there is a possible path forward with Syria. So we're going to continue joining with all of our allies to keep pressing very hard on that."[txxvii]

Secretary of Defence Leon Panetta, in an interview with the CNN in July 2012, said:

"I think it's important when Assad leaves - and he will leave - to try to preserve stability in that country. And the best way to preserve that kind of stability is to maintain as much of the military, the police, as you can, along with the security forces, and hope that they will transition to a democratic form of government. That's a key."[txxviii]

In order to maintain the status quo the US undertook actions which have been in support of al-Assad. The US quickly began building an opposition of loyal groups and individuals instead of directly intervening to influence the outcome in Syria. Initially the US backed the Syrian National Council (SNC) and viewed them as the legitimate opposition in Syria. The ability of the rebels on the ground to seize Syria's countryside clearly proved the SNC had no influence on the ground. In November 2012 the US worked on replacing the SNC with other elements it could work with and constructed the Syrian National Coalition. Hillary Clinton said:

"We've made it clear that the SNC can no longer be viewed as the visible leader of the opposition. This cannot be an opposition represented by people who have many good attributes but have, in many instances, not been in Syria for 20, 30, 40 years, There has to be a representation of those who are on the front lines fighting and dying today to obtain their freedom."[txxix]

At the beginning of 2015 the rebel groups controlled more

territory than al-Assad; however critical territory still remained in regime hands. Bashar al-Assad had given up regaining the north of Syria; his forces have been weakened after years of fighting the length and breadth of the country. In 2014 the rebel forces were launching attacks in the capital, Damascus itself, until ISIS declared its Caliphate and began taking over areas already under rebel control. By 2015 most of the Iraqi-Syrian border was in ISIS hands and much of the north of the country from Deir ar Zour to al-Raqqa governorate and Aleppo governorate is under ISIS control – although Aleppo was still being contested. At a time when al-Assad's army was overstretched, ISIS caused a division amongst the rebel groups as it began the conquest of the northern areas already under rebel control. This fracture resulted in the rebel groups turning their attention to ISIS giving the al-Assad regime the breathing space it needed. US Secretary of State John Kerry argued in November 2014 that the country's two sworn enemies were propping each other up:

> *"That assumption is actually based on a misreading of the political reality in Syria. In fact the Assad regime and ISIL are dependent on one another, that's why Assad has relentlessly bombed areas held by the moderate opposition while doing almost nothing to hinder ISIL's march."*[xx]

The struggle for Syria became between the indigenous rebel groups and the regime, that has the backing of Iran, US, Russia and Britain, despite their rhetoric to the contrary. The support for the regime is for only one reason and that is because the people of Syria, unlike their brethren in the region want real change with the complete uprooting of the regime. This flies in the face of the West, as despite their rhetoric against al-Assad he has maintained peace with Israel and has ensured the peoples true demands have been held in check. The position of the West was encapsulated in the Washington Times in January 2013:

> *"Sunni rebels appear poised for victory. It's vitally important for the*

Obama administration to discourage a new Syrian government from supplanting the secular dictatorship with a more dangerous regime based on Islamic law. Another Islamic state in the Middle East could threaten regional residents with more religious tyranny, perpetual war with neighbours and another caliphate."

The emergence of ISIS has had a major impact on the direction of the uprising in Syria. ISIS originated as an insurgent group during the US invasion of Iraq, and for the past decade it has been Iraq's pre-eminent group. During that time it has operated under various names, including al-Qaeda in Iraq and the Islamic State of Iraq. When the Syrian uprising started, those fighting in Iraq were sent to take part in the uprising in Syria and stand-off against the regime. Supported by the Islamic State in Iraq (ISI) leader Abu Bakr al-Baghdadi, Abu Muhammad al-Joulani formed *Jabhat al-Nusrah* (Nusra Front) in January 2012.

However, tensions erupted in April 2013 when al-Baghdadi released an audio message in which he announced his organisation had subsumed *Jabhat al-Nusrah*. Al-Baghdadi named the new, expanded organisation the Islamic State in Iraq and Sham (the Levant) – ISIS and reportedly moved to Syria's Aleppo governorate to take charge. The announcement sent shockwaves across Syria and the region, but more so, amongst the leadership and rank-and-file within *Jabhat al-Nusrah*. Within days, Abu Muhammad al-Joulani, the head of *Jabhat al-Nusrah* rejected the proposal and 'reaffirmed' his allegiance to Ayman Al-Zawahiri, who for Joulani, represented the global Jihad, whereas Baghdadi represented the cause in Iraq.

As a result fighters from Iraq moved into the Syrian theatre and began taking over territory *Jabhat al-Nusrah* controlled and was governing. Matters reached boiling point in early January 2014 when Jabhat al-Nusra took over an ISIS position in Atmeh in northern Syria in conjunction with Ahrar Ash-Sham. By 2015 ISIS controlled most of the border towns with Turkey.

As far as the West in concerned, the outcome of Syria will determine the broader Arab spring and for them Islam, which is the demand of the masses, should have no role to play in the future of the country. This is why successive Geneva conferences have been with individuals and groups who have spent most of their lives in Washington, London and Paris rather than in Syria.

In conclusion the following deductions can be made from the Arab spring:

The popular uprising across the Middle East captured the imagination of the global Muslims and has proven that the Middle East is ripe for change. Many have argued that the psychological barrier of fear could never be crossed and some even justified compromise with the corrupt rulers on this basis. If we place the current uprising in the context of the revival of the Middle East there is a clear trajectory. In Central Asia the Muslims have returned to Islam after nearly a century under communist rule, In Turkey the AKP has used its Islamic credentials to remain in power and across Europe there is a clear return to Islam by the Muslims there. These uprisings indicate that the people of the region have realised the rulers are the obstacle that needs to be removed.

In all the countries where rulers were overthrown or have struggled to maintain their grip, be it Tunisia, Egypt, Yemen, Libya or Syria anarchy and chaos came to replace the initial euphoria. In both Tunisia and Egypt Islamic groups replaced previous regimes but have shown themselves to be incompetent when it came to ruling their respective nations. Most of the Middle East, despite possessing abundant energy resources, many have large young populations who remain unemployed and employment opportunities remain scarce. Economic underdevelopment, inflation and maldistribution of wealth continue to be normal in the region. Unable to solve these issues in any way led many to take to the streets again. There were also many elements in Egypt, Tunisia and Libya, who refused to accept the rule of Islamic groups and as a result kept a permanent stand off against the new regime going, in the case of Egypt leading to the collapse of the Muslim Brotherhood regime.

In Egypt and Tunisia, voters in their millions clearly expressed their opposition to secular liberal values and their strong desire for Islamic government. Yet the same parties that went to great lengths to demonstrate their Islamic credentials to the masses in their election campaigns, these parties not only went to greater lengths to demonstrate their moderation to the West, but they abandoned Islamic rule. The political calculations of such groups are rooted in myths. In the case of the Muslim Brotherhood, they undermined Islam by making excuses for their own incompetence.

The uprising in Syria continues to worry the West as most of the rebel groups have maintained their Islamic purity, despite numerous attempts to dilute this. The US invested in the Syrian National Coalition and despite changing its name a few times, its popularity remains in Washington, London and Paris rather than the cities and towns of Syria. The announcement of various groupings based on Islam in Syria and their control over large tracts of the country means Syria remains a work in progress. The Islamic aspect to this uprising continues to worry the West as the masses there are calling for real change rather than cosmetic change.

There can be no doubt that Western governments were caught short by the speed of events. Indeed it was interesting observing shifts in positions on numerous foreign policy issues. What has happened has exposed their relationships to the long standing tyrannical regimes, which belied their repeated claims that they are on the side of people against oppression

Western intervention was only for the protection of their strategic interests rather than for the revolution. The likes of Gaddafi,

Mubarak, Ben Ali etc. all had cordial relations with the West for years. At the eleventh hour when it became clear that such leaders had outlived their use, Britain and the US switched sides. Both nations worked to engineer individuals and groups to ensure a Western friendly opposition developed at the expense of the change the people of the region desire. The West used its NGO's and civic institutions in Egypt and Tunisia to engineer a controlled change.[cxxi]

The competition between the US and Europe for the spoils has been difficult to conceal. In Libya both the US and France and Britain cultivated contacts with the Benghazi rebels to ensure individuals loyal to them came to power. In Syria, the US continues to protect the Assad regime calling for mere reforms as Europe steps up efforts for his removal. Similarly, in Yemen Europe and the US have been at odds on the trajectory of the uprisings.

The Muslim Brotherhood (MB) showed that decades of pragmatism yielded little progress. They failed to present a compelling case that they can rule a nation. The MB has become conscious of the negative connotations of its Islamic branding and tried to focus attention on the idea that it is a well-organised, non-violent, pragmatic and democratic force worthy of a political voice in a post-Mubarak government. The MB started out calling for Islam, even though it was not clear in its details. Over time it mixed Islam with western values and started calling for democracy. They were so pragmatic that today they are openly calling for freedom and democracy and not the *Shari'ah*. However they are still presenting themselves as an Islamic movement even though they have stopped calling for Islam. They feel this pleases the West and is a tactical move to gain power and then maybe implement Islam one day.

There were a number of countries that did not witness uprisings such as Saudi Arabia, Jordan and most of the Gulf States. There are however specific reasons for this. The relationship between the rulers and the people in these countries are different when compared to the relationships between the rulers and the people in Libya, Syria and Egypt. In Libya, Syria and Egypt the rulers ruled with an iron fist, established what were police states and social cohesion was maintained through a large secret service. These factors are absent in the Gulf nations, Saudi and Jordan.

In Jordan, protests were restricted to calls for the removal of the Prime Minister. King Abdullah dismissed various governments on account of the street protests. Since Jordan's independence in 1946, the palace has appointed more than 60 prime ministers, including three since the Arab unrest broke out in 2011. King Abdullah dissolved the government of Prime Minister Samir Rifai and then put Marouf al-Bakhit, a former army general, in charge of forming a new Cabinet and instituting reforms. Protests still continued, which led to King Abdullah to sack Bakhit and his cabinet, naming Awn Shawkat Al-Khasawneh to head the new government and institute new reforms. King Abdullah, for the moment successfully contained the protests by constantly dissolving the government and this has placated the people.

Saudi Arabia has was able to present the protests in its territories as a Shia uprising and this caused the bulk of the population to support the clamp down in cities such as Qatif, al-Awamiyah, and Hofuf. In order to contain the uprising the monarchy announced a series of benefits for citizens amounting to $10.7 billion. These included funding to offset high inflation and to aid young unemployed people and Saudi citizens studying abroad, as well the writing off of some loans. As part of the Saudi scheme, state employees saw a pay increase of 15%, and cash was made available for housing loans. No political reforms were announced as part of the package. The Grand Mufti of Saudi Arabia also issued a fatwa opposing petitions and demonstrations, the fatwa included a *"severe threat against internal dissent."*[txxii]

The Gulf States did not see many protests apart from Bahrain and

Oman. Such city states placated the uprisings through making some reforms, changing cabinets and through economic hand-outs. Although many of them have monarchies they do not rule with an iron fist. Whilst Bahrain continues to clamp down on its Shia majority population Oman was the only other Gulf nation to see significant protests. The Sultan continued with his reform campaign by dissolving some ministries, setting up some new ones, granting student and unemployed benefits, dismissing scores of ministers, and reshuffling his cabinet three times. In addition, nearly 50,000 jobs were created in the public sector, including 10,000 new jobs in the Royal Oman Police. The government's efforts have largely placated protesters, and Oman has not seen significant demonstrations since May 2011, when increasingly violent protests in Salalah were subdued.

Although not strictly in the Middle East, an uprising in Pakistan was notably absent. Pakistan has not been a brutal dictatorship as has been the case with Libya, Syria and Egypt. Since Pervez Musharraf's era Pakistan has moved in such a direction, as can be seen with the disappearance of many people apparently linked to terrorism, this is however a relatively recent phenomena. The rule in Libya, Egypt and Syria was in the hands of brutal dictators and the only way to change this was through an uprising. In Pakistan unlike Libya, Egypt and Syria the political system is not controlled by a single clan, there exist different centres of power, with two families who have historically dominated the political system. Feudal landowners, industrialists, rich families and the army are all centres of power who maintain Pakistan's political architecture. Alongside this, opportunists, factions and many groups have entered the political process for their personal interests. The political process in Pakistan has the involvement of a much wider segment of the population compared to Libya, Egypt and Syria and this has acted as its lifeline. For the moment in Pakistan the call for change is either making the political system more democratic or getting some Islamic laws passed. This is why there has not been an uprising in the country even though the economy continues to teeter on the brink and electricity black-outs have become the norm.

EMERGING TRENDS

The Middle East continues to be subjected to research, analysis, PhD's and critiqued and whilst the century of the region has seen many actors, nations and powers shape it, the next 100 years is set to be very different from the last 100 years. There are numerous trends already taking shape that will present broader, deeper and wider challenges for the status quo. The rulers in the region have little understanding of these and have generally been pragmatic to the trends that have emerged or have used brute force to maintain the status quo. These trends range from economic, social to technological and geopolitical. A closer look at each of these show that whether it's the international powers or the rulers in the region and whether factors outside their control will play a major role in the next 100 years.

DEMOGRAPHICS

22 Nations constitute the Arab region, which is considered the Middle East today. This region begins with Morocco and Mauritania in the Atlantic to Somalia and Sudan, all constituting the North African element of the region. Then on the Arabian Peninsula the region constitutes Iraq and Syria in the North all the way down to Yemen and up to Kuwait in the East.

This region, even before Islam came to the region constituted harsh desert terrain, with much of the population centred on major lakes or coasts. At the turn of the 20th century the population of the Arabian Peninsula was around 4 million. Egypt had a population of 8 million, Sudan 4 million, Algeria 4 million. The Ottomans although in decline ruled over a population of 30 million inhabitants. The Middle

East from Morocco to the Red sea had a demography of somewhere between 20-25 million.

By 1950, the population of the Middle East had grown to 67 million inhabitants. Just 20 years later the

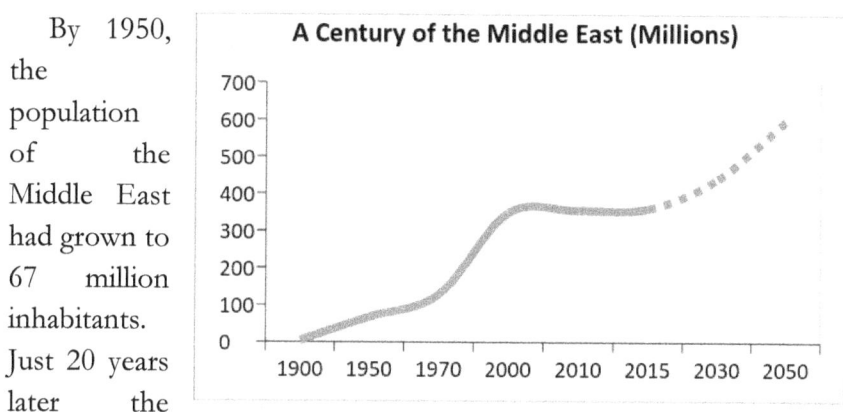

A Century of the Middle East (Millions)

Arab population doubled to 128 million. From 1950 to 2000, the Middle East experienced explosive population growth. The region's population grew from 67 million to 349 million, a five-fold increase, or over 2.7% a year. Just 100 years earlier the population of the region was a mere 10% of this. All of the countries in the region had much the same experience, Israel grew at 3.2% a year, Iran at just over 2.7%, and the Arab countries at just under 2.7%. In 2010, the population of the Middle East had grown to 355 million. The population of the Middle East reached 360 million at the beginning 2016.

To give some perspective to these demographics, one in 20 people in the world live in the 22 countries of the Arab Region. The Middle East is the world's most rapidly growing region in the world after Sub Saharan Africa. Today, about half of the region's population reside in just 3 of those countries – Algeria, Egypt and Sudan. In the 21st century the Middle East has grown faster than both China and India.

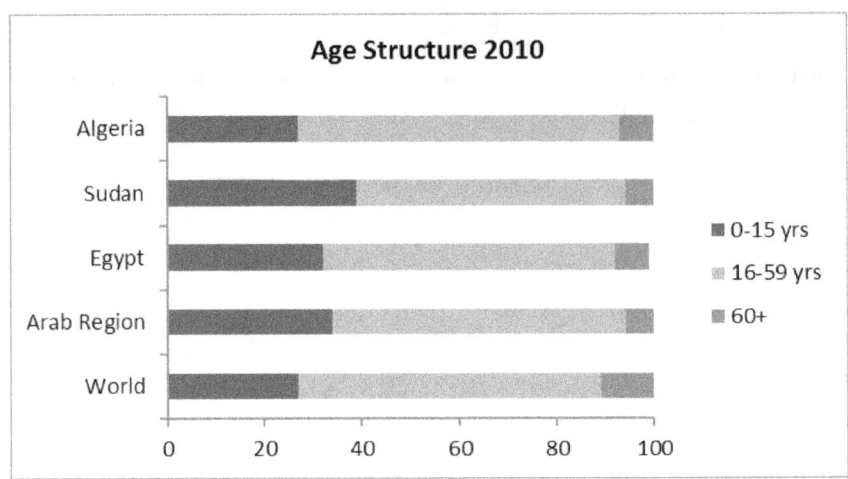

Age Structure 2010

Algeria | Sudan | Egypt | Arab Region | World

Legend: 0-15 yrs | 16-59 yrs | 60+

The age structure of the region is heavily favoured towards the young. Currently, the population of the Arab Region is still young, with children under age 15 accounting for 33% of the population and young persons aged 15 to 24 years account for another 20% of the population. Thus, the majority of the region's population of 54% is under the age of 25. By comparison, 48% of the population of developing countries and 29% of the population of developed countries is under the age of 25. The number of people in the main working ages, 25 to 59 years, is also at an all-time high in the region, totalling 145 million. The size of the working age population is expected to almost double by 2050, to reach 278 million. The large working age population can provide opportunities for economic development if meaningful employment can be generated. Up to 1 million new workers will be looking for employment every year up to 2015, employment that does not exists.

By 2030 the population in the Middle East is expected to grow to 440 million.[cxxiii] According to the UN Arab Human Development Report (AHDR), based on the 2010 projection, the Arab Region will have nearly 600 million inhabitants by 2050. It also expects Iraq, the Occupied Palestinian Territory, Somalia and Yemen to double in population from 2010 – 2050. If the countries of the Arab Region were to maintain current levels of fertility, the population of the region would more than double to reach 781 million by 2050.

The Middle East has a history of a rapidly increasing population. This has been due to the higher fertility rates and, thus, more-rapid rates of population growth. A rate of 2.1 children per women roughly serves to replace the current generation. Fertility rates in Saudi Arabia are 3.4 children per woman, while, in the Czech Republic and South Korea, rates are 1.4 and 1.3 children per woman, respectively. Kuwait, with a per capita GDP comparable to that of Spain, had a fertility rate of 2.9 children per woman in 2007 compared to 1.3 in Spain.

After a century of explosive growth fertility rates have slowed and are projected to slow further from 2020. The population in the Middle East until 2050 is only going in one direction and this is up, although the rate of growth is expected to slow. What this means, going forward, there is few places in the world that will be subject to as much pressure from growing numbers of people as the Arab world. This rising population will need to be watered, housed; they will need new and modern transportation systems and labour markets. Competition for jobs, especially government jobs, and housing and the poor quality and inadequate provision of public services are prime causes of the deep dissatisfaction with the status quo that marks so many of these societies. The stress these demographic pressures exert—and regional governments' ability to mitigate them—will play a major role in determining the future trajectory of the region.

Because of the large increases in population, the number of young people entering the labour markets of these countries has been rising rapidly. The labour supply will continue to expand rapidly for the next decade, adding to the difficulties young people face in finding employment that meets their expectations. For the moment, the rulers in the region have not published or mentioned how they plan to deal with this rapidly growing population.

In the medium to long term, the Middle East will see a larger population, consisting mainly of young persons. They will need jobs, be housed and want a say in the governing of their nations. When the Middle East was rapidly growing during the 1980s and 1990s the rulers used their secret service, army and autocracy to maintain cohesion. Until now, they have not presented any alternative on how they plan to deal with the challenges that a growing demographic brings with it.

ECONOMY

The population of the Middle East has been on an upward trajectory for over 100 years and this will remain the case for the next century. Despite the discovery and development of energy in the region the region's economies have not kept pace with population growth and all of the nations that constitute the Middle East suffer from deep structural issues with their economies.'

The first Arab Human Development Report (AHDR) in 2002 characterised the Arab world as "richer than it is developed." That description highlighted the contradiction between the region's material wealth and its real levels of human development, which pointed to a backlog of policy failures often overlooked by conventional economic analyses at the time. Yet the fabled oil wealth of the Arab countries is itself misleading in that it masks the structural weaknesses of many of the region's nations. Across the region there is a consistent pattern of massive policy failure on very basic matters such as food security, education, development and employment. The World Bank reported in 2011 that over 210 million people (63%) of the region's population live below the $5 dollars-a-day international poverty line.

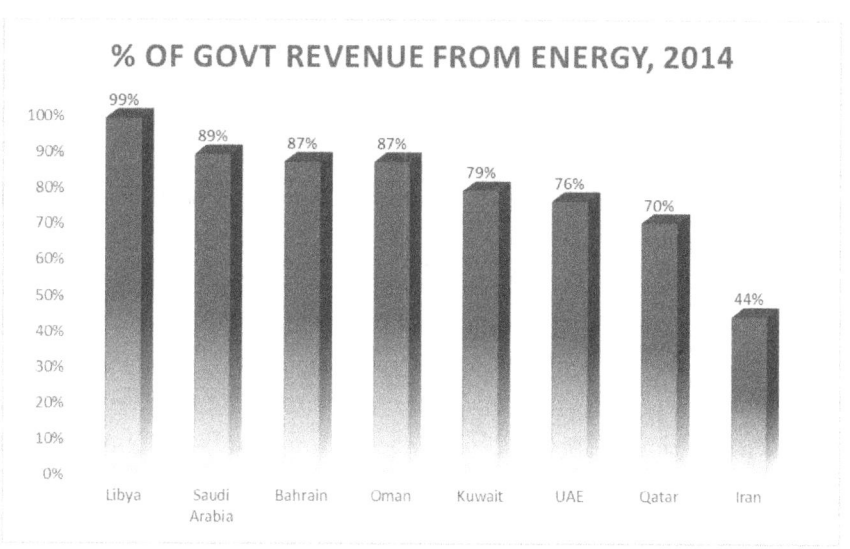

% OF GOVT REVENUE FROM ENERGY, 2014

The story of Arab economies since the 1970s is largely the story of oil. Producer countries gained most, amassing untold wealth, but non-oil Arab countries also benefitted substantially from oil-related services, worker remittances, intra-regional investment flows, regional tourism receipts, and aid. Arab oil revenues fuelled extraordinary wealth and rapid infrastructural and other areas of development in the 12 oil producing states of the region, accounting for almost 90% of their annual public budgets. These revenues also power associated industries, jobs, income and remittances for the citizens of other Arab states. Oil income is thus a major driver in the economic security of the region. But the rulers in the region opted to put much of their energy windfall into foreign investments, external reserves and oil stabilisation funds, foreign military equipment and to repay debts. Very little of this money has been used to construct industry which would have created many jobs, stimulated the economy and brought in taxation for central government.

Oil-led growth has created weak structural foundations in Arab economies. Many Arab countries turned into import oriented and service based economies. The types of services found in Arab countries fell at the low end of the value added chain, contributing little to local knowledge development, and locked countries into inferior positions in global markets. This trend, has been at the expense of Arab agriculture, manufacturing and industrial production. Not surprisingly, most Arab countries have experienced significant deindustrialisation over the last four decades. In fact, the Arab countries were less industrialised in 2007 than in 1970, almost four decades ago. This includes nations with a relatively diversified economic base in the 1960s, such as Algeria, Egypt, Iraq and Syria – although Jordan, Oman, Tunisia, and UAE made noticeable progress in industrial development. Nonetheless, in general, the contribution of manufacturing to GDP is anaemic, even in Arab countries that have witnessed rapid industrial growth.

A number of nations in the region have a heavy reliance on oil exports; this has created a dependency on the oil process and has kept such economies narrowly focused. The energy infrastructure in the region was constructed by foreign companies and today is dominated by foreign companies. Very little technology or knowledge transfer has taken place which could have reduced unemployment significantly. The regional nations have also embarked on major domestic investments in real estate, construction, oil refining, transport and communication and social services. Such huge energy wealth remains in the hands of monarchs, families and business elites with the vast bulk of the population languishing in poverty. In Saudi Arabia the oil wealth remains within the royal family who subsidise the lifestyles of their expanding family or the wealth is spent bailing out Western institutions.

The non-oil economies in the region such as Sudan, Tunisia, Egypt, Algeria, Lebanon, Syria and Jordan, whilst rich in Agriculture and minerals rely upon oil-related services, worker remittances, intra-regional investment flows, regional tourism receipts and aid. This has led to a reliance on food imports that has resulted in more and more of government budgets being spent on food due to the rise in international food prices. The subsequent food riots have led to governments in the region resorting to food and fuel subsidies which have not dealt with any of the underlying problems of food security.

Food security and agriculture in general remain problematic in the region. A third of the agricultural production in the region is exported abroad to earn foreign currency reserves, this is at a time when most of the region is in poverty and with some nations struggling with agricultural production due to the climate.

Unemployment is a major source of economic insecurity in most Arab countries. At the end of 2014 unemployment was at 11%, the highest in the world, with youth unemployment at 30%. This has been mainly caused by the large and unsustainable role public sector plays. The limited size, hobbled performance and weak job-generating capacity of the private sector have also not helped the wider economy.

The inability of many of the region's countries to develop sustainable sectors of the economy has resulted in 14% of regional export earnings going to debt servicing. In Lebanon, debt servicing accounts for 47% of the government's budget. Jordan, Morocco and Tunisia spend more on debt servicing than they do on education; all spend twice as much on debt service than they do on health care. Sudan and Yemen are among the 41 countries identified as Heavily Indebted Poor Countries (HIPCs).

Like much of the world wealth is unevenly distributed across the Middle East. Monarchies and dictators control most of the wealth and they ensure their support base benefit from this only. Wealth is usually used to maintain social cohesion and to keep the masses occupied with day-to-day fulfilment of basic needs rather than the corrupt rulers.

Nearly 50% of the region's wealth is held by just 20% of the population.[cxxiv]

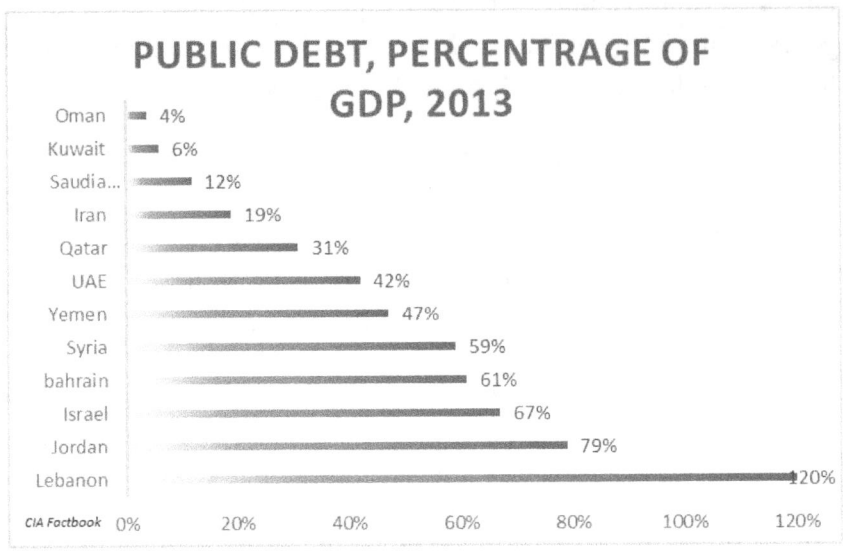

PUBLIC DEBT, PERCENTRAGE OF GDP, 2013

Oman	4%
Kuwait	6%
Saudia...	12%
Iran	19%
Qatar	31%
UAE	42%
Yemen	47%
Syria	59%
bahrain	61%
Israel	67%
Jordan	79%
Lebanon	120%

CIA Factbook

With a growing population and lack of food security, many rulers in the region maintained their grip through subsidies. This ensured the cost of food, fuel, electricity and many other basic necessities being subsidised by the state. In the Middle East, generalised price subsidies have for many years been part of society. But generalised price subsidies have not been well targeted or cost-effective as a social protection tool. Though subsidies may reach the poor and vulnerable to some extent, they benefited mostly the better off, who consume more of subsidised goods, particularly energy products: for example, in Egypt in 2008, the poorest 40% percent of the population received only 3% of gasoline subsidies. Middle East and North African nations are now struggling to maintain their subsidy programmes. Total pretax energy subsidies in 2011 cost $237 billion - equivalent to 48% of world subsidies, 8.6% of regional GDP, or 22% of government revenues. They amounted to $204 billion (8.4% of GDP) in oil exporters and $33 billion in oil importers (6.3% of GDP). Food subsidies are also common in the region, though less costly. In 2011, they amounted to 0.7 percent of GDP for the region. With a growing population in the region and with the advent of Shale energy to keep energy prices low, the energy jackpot will in all likelihood not be able to fund future subsidies. But with poverty still high in the region, any removal of subsidies will lead to price increases which will lead to instability – the very thing the subsidies were created to stop.

The lack of a sustainable driving engine for the region's economies has resulted in unemployment and the lack of direction for the economies of the region has led to weak job-generating capacity. All of this has been plugged by unsustainable subsidies. According to Sundeep Waslekar, a researcher from the Strategic Foresight Group:

> *"Autocratic, oil-rich rulers have been able to control their people by controlling nature and have kept the lid on political turmoil at home by heavily subsidising "virtual" or "embedded" water in the form of staple grains imported from the US and elsewhere,"*[xxxv]

ENERGY

The Middle East today is the carbon region of the world. It possesses the world's largest oil and gas fields and dominates energy production. The region possesses over 60% of the world's oil reserves, more than the rest of the world combined. The region produces 42% of the world's daily oil requirement. The region also possesses 54% of the world's Gas reserves and produces 30% of the world's daily Gas requirements. Oil differs from region to region in its thickness and its chemical composition. The oil pumped from the Middle East is the preferred choice since its extraction is relatively simple and its refining is cheaper due to it being the light 'sweet' type of crude oil. In contrast the heavier crude oils extracted from the Caspian basin are far more costly to extract and refine and are far more polluting. Despite possessing such strengths, much of the region has crumbling energy infrastructure leaving many without electricity.

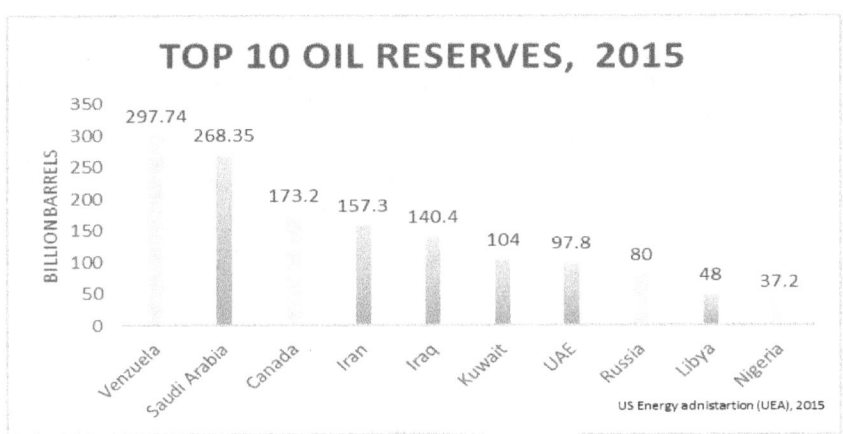

Whilst Saudi Arabia and the Gulf states have advanced energy infrastructures much of their populations live in poverty. Much of the energy infrastructure in the Persian Gulf and the Hijaz was developed by Britain and the US. Whilst the region produces over 40% of the world's daily oil, only 8% of it is refined in the region.

76% of the world's oil is refined in regions with very little oil, but increasing demand for oil. The US refines 20% of the world's oil, whilst Europe refines 22% of the world's oil and the Far East refines 27% of the world's oil. Even though the Middle East has the lion's share of oil, in essence this is useless considering the inability to refine it, for this reason most of the oil is piped to the Far East and Europe to be refined, and then the products are resold to the Muslim world. The region has for the moment not exploited the other renewable options available to it. The dessert geography would give considerable solar prospects, which would lead to the innovation of new technologies, create jobs and reduce the dependency on fossils.

The importance of the Middle East, despite developments in Shale energy is only set to increase rather than decrease. This is because the Middle East will remain the main producer of oil as it is the cheapest to extract and refine. Shale energy requires more energy to extract and will always cost more than oil wells which were discovered less than a mile underground. The challenge going forward is, can this oil bonanza be used to develop and create other industries which will create jobs for the increasing population in the region. For the moment, the rulers in the region have used the oil wealth for subsidies and foreign investment. With a growing population this is no longer sustainable.

WATER

No matter how one looks at it, there is no escaping the fact that the overall picture of the world's supply of freshwater is one of growing scarcity. Global demand already outstrips a sustainable level of supply, and, if business continues as usual, this trend will only get worse.

In the Middle East the water situation has always been problematic and it has long reached crisis point. With its desert terrain the Middle East has always suffered from water shortages.

The region's arid climate makes 80% of the region a desert. The main water resources in this region, which has some 25 rivers, are precipitation, rivers and groundwater. 70% of the Arab countries rely on water flowing from non-Arab territories. According to the 2006 Arab Human Development Report (AHDR) the region basically "ran out of water in the 70s" and depends as much on water from outside the region.[cxxvi] Iran and Turkey are the only countries in and around the region that are self-sufficient in water. Others countries depend on the water of rivers, wells, and springs that flow into their land from neighbour countries. 88% of the stream of the Euphrates River originates from Turkey alongside with the Tigris. The Euphrates River provides the sole reliable water supply to the east of Syria and Iraq. Upon reaching the delta of the Euphrates, Tigris, and the Karun, the Euphrates loses a lot of water and begins to go down direct to its final end, the Persian Gulf.

The Jordan River, which comprises Jordan, Syria, Lebanon, and Israel – delivers 60% of Israel's water and 75% of Jordan's water. Several years from the foundation of Israel, Israel found itself sharing the Jordan River with Syria and Jordan. In the 1967 Israel occupied the Golan Heights as well as the West Bank, which gave it control of the sources of fresh water, in addition to it being a significant strategic military site. Currently, Israel uses water at a high rate around more than 500 cubic meters per person/year. Around 40% of its water is drained from the West Bank.

The Aswan Dam in Egypt effectively dammed one of the largest rivers in the world. The Aswan Dam has helped Egyptian agriculture, but since Egypt's population has been growing the available food per capita had decreased, instead of increasing. The entire reservoir is 2000 square miles in area and 300 miles long. After the treaty between Egypt and Sudan for sharing the Nile waters, 55.5 cubic km/year was allocated for Egypt, 18.5 cubic km/year was allocated for Sudan, leaving only 10 cubic km/year for evaporation from the Aswan Lake, for a total of 84 cubic km/year.

The challenges are monumental with regards to water in the Middle East. Currently, agriculture uses 85% of water in the Middle East. The Gulf region in particular consumes over 60% of the world's desalinated water. The UAE is using over 70% of domestic energy to supply and transport water. The cost of water in Jordan has increased in the last decade, due to shortage of groundwater.

There is evidently no blueprint or solution to the challenges related to water and irrigated agriculture in the region. Most countries in the region face acute problems related to water scarcity that are amalgamated by the highly complex but artificial political map of the region. Many countries in the region are at a crossroads over their future use of water for irrigated agriculture. With the population in the region set to grow social stability and water wars may very well become a reality.

SOCIAL MEDIA

Social media is considered to have played a central role in the Arab spring. Many of the autocrats in the Middle East controlled information through a firm grip on the media, telecommunications, newspapers and magazines. In the monarchies of the region Princes and Princesses operate the main newspapers and magazines. But the Arab spring changed and challenged this old structure. Whilst the regimes controlled traditional forms of media, such as television, Newspapers and magazines, the same cannot be done with the internet. The Internet and social media is challenging the monopoly of information previously enjoyed by authoritarian governments.

The first 15 years of the 21st century has been a time of astonishing advances in communications and information technology, including digitalisation, mass-accessible video platforms, smart phones, social media, billions of people gaining internet access, and much else. These revolutionary changes all imply a profound empowerment of individuals through exponentially greater access to information, tremendous ease of communication and data-sharing and formidable tools for networking.

The Middle East does have some of the lowest access rates when it comes to telecommunications but this is increasing. The Middle East has a mere 8.7% access rate per 100 people when it comes to fixed telephone lines. But with mobile subscriptions its access rate per 100 is the world's highest at 109%. Which means much the public owns more than one mobile phone each. Today, 41% of the world's population is connected to the internet. In the Middle East only 36% of the population is connected to the internet. The rapid growth of Internet and smartphone penetration over the 2000s layered a new dimension onto this rapidly evolving new public sphere. What could once be dismissed as limited to a narrow slice of a largely English speaking, cosmopolitan, and youthful elite is now distributed across wide swaths of the region. In some sectors of society, particularly educated urban youth, Internet access and usage is already for all practical purposes universal. Almost all statistics show that 88% of the regions online population uses social media on a daily basis. In fact there are 58 million Facebook accounts in the Middle East and 6.5 million twitter accounts, more than the estimated total number of newspaper readers in the region.

Going forward repression and authoritarianism are no longer tools that the autocrats in the region can rely upon as these have no impact on the people anymore, as was seen with the Arab spring. People in the Middle East are now exposed to banned news and a variety of opinions, despite attempts by their governments to limit the free flow of information. They can discuss taboo subjects, criticise their leaders, and protest against injustices. Add to this a growing and youthful population the future will be different to the past in the Middle East.

When the artificial borders were created in the Sykes-Picot agreement 100 years ago, new nationalities, or nationalism was hoped would give the region new identities to move forward with. Any deviation from this – the autocratic rulers would bring the people back in line. The assumption was Islamic governance had been undermined and the people of the region would embrace secularism when it came to governance and keep Islam to the mosque, marriages and personal morals. Whilst the Muslim world experimented with socialism, democracy and nationalism in the past 100 years, the next 100 years will see the culminations of three trends that have been gaining speed for decades. These are the increasing use of Islam as a reference by Muslims rather than 'Freedom' or 'secularism,' the failure of nationalism and the illegitimacy of the rulers.

A scrutiny of the created nations through the Sykes-Picot agreement shows that they were artificial constructs with no coherent value system. Muslim societies at the turn of the 20th century were fractured on what values should be the basis of society. In some cases, one would have found some issues amongst the people being settled according to Islamic concepts; in other cases, they were settled upon liberal and even nationalistic ideas. In fact, many of the problems such as poverty, unemployment, development, male and female relations etc were even settled according to local customs and even tribal judgements. Hence, the nations that were artificially created couldn't move forward (progress) since the Muslims were attempting to deal with societal problems in multiple ways rather than a single agreed upon basis, this is what resulted in the myriad of problems at the time. By not having a consistent reference point, the artificially created nations were disjointed and the various nations as a whole failed to move in a unified direction.

Despite the colonial onslaught, Muslims did not adopt or embrace liberal values as a basis for their nations. One example of this is that despite the best efforts of the West in spreading her foreign culture, like the pursuit of individual freedom as a purpose for life in the Muslim lands we find that Muslims did not give up the social system of Islam. So, despite Islam not being completely clear in the minds of the people in the Middle East, the Muslims of the region did not abandon Islam as her identify.

Despite the Muslim world lacking the ability to extract pristine concepts from the Islamic principles, the demand for Islam has only grown during the last 100 years. Turkey was the only country to renounce Islam completely in its constitution. Mustafa Kemal sought to destroy Islam in Turkey and he believed the Turkish people despised their Islamic heritage. However, after just a few decades, pressure on the regime mounted steadily and by the 1950's successive Turkish governments started to play up Islamic sentiments in order to maintain their grip on power. By the 1970's Turkey had its first sign of Islamic resurgence with the incorporation of Necmettin Erbakan in the cabinet. Erbakan like many of the Muslim rulers utilised Islam to gain support from the Masses. In the 21st century, the people of Turkey have only voted for an 'Islamic' government. This is what led to then Secretary of State Madeleine Albright in 1997 to wring her hands about the *'drift of Turkey away from secularism.*[cxxxvii] Such was the heightened sensitivity in the Turkish army that it continues to purge their ranks every year of any Islamic influence. The demonstrations against the AKP party in the early 2000s were another indicator of secularism failure to take hold in Turkey. The huge demonstrations for secularism were not from a position of strength but a position of weakness as after several decades of secularism and the banning of Islam in the nation's constitution, secularists felt the need to take to the streets due to the threat of Islam. Despite secularism dominating Turkish politics, for so long, the people of Turkey have been inclining towards Islam for decades — a far cry from the events post 1924.

The Turkish example is just one of many; Islamic influence in Algeria was so great in 1991 that the Islamic Salvation Front (FIS) managed to win a landslide victory in the country's elections. It took the army, with French support to reverse this. Similarly, the people's love of Islam in Afghanistan, Sudan and Somalia saw the establishment of governments under the pretext of Islam.

For the last few decades Muslims across the world are reacting as one body to the onslaught against their brothers and sisters. Iraq, Afghanistan, Bosnia, Somalia, Palestine and Rohingya Muslim in Thailand have seen Muslims from across the world hold marches and rallies in solidarity with their brothers and sisters. In fact even the Muslims in Palestine, themselves under occupation, have regularly held rallies in support for other Muslims. Muslims feel revulsion when 'freedom of expression' is used to attack Islam, as can be seen with the attacks on the Prophet of Islam (saw) via cartoons in Europe.

Today the Muslims in the Middle East want to live by values that are different to the values that are implemented over them. But we have a dichotomy where the Muslims continue to abide by these values and allow the rulers who implement them to rule over them. This has been possible because the rulers in the Muslim world do not maintain their power by sharing a close affinity with their people, but rather through brutal methods of force and torture in order to subjugate the masses. However, today there is a widening gulf between the Muslim world and their rulers.

The recent history of the Muslim world and the relationship between the people and the rulers shows that this relationship has become tenuous and now the Muslims hold values and sentiments that fundamentally contradict that of the rulers. Furthermore, attempts by Pervez Musharraf to introduce Western culture in Pakistan through his 'enlightened moderation' were discredited. Even in Turkey, on the eve of the second Gulf war was forced to turn down $20 billion in aid by the US as the Muslims in the country considered such cooperation as aiding the killing of Muslims in Iraq. The constant attempts by the Muslim rulers to normalise relations with Israel continually fail.

This gulf was not present for most of the last century. Rulers such as Gamal Abdul Nasser of Egypt enjoyed the strongest relationship with the people. He was seen as the Arab saviour due to his wresting of the Suez Canal from the British in 1957 and his stand against Israel. The Muslims believed that Nasser was reflective of them. The Muslims in the Middle East and beyond hailed Yasser Arafat as one of the lions of Islam, Arafat managed to enlist hundreds of thousands of young Arab men to his rallying call for Jihad against the Israeli occupiers. The Muslims of the Middle East until the late 1980s were oblivious to the actions of the Saudi Monarchy, such as King Fahd and the other Gulf rulers due to their economic prosperity and the influence of the Saudi backed scholars and movements. The relationship between the rulers and the ruled in the Muslim world was always weak; people became oblivious to the Muslim rulers due to a whole host of factors. The chasm was initially masked due to the relative strength of Arab nationalism and other ideas such as Ba'athism and Socialism. In some of the Gulf State's, economic prosperity masked the underlying chasm. This was the case until the fall of Communism.

With the fall of Communism in 1990, there was a direct clash of civilisations between Islam and the Liberal West. The former secretary general of NATO Willie Claes stated;

> *"The Alliance has placed Islam as a target for its hostility in place of the Soviet Union."* [xxxviii]

This open clash between Islam and the Liberal West resulted in the destruction of Western civilisation in the minds of the Muslims not just in the Middle East but across the world.

This destruction and refusal on part of the Muslims, on the whole, to not embrace Western civilisation led to a new, more direct and distinctly more military onslaught against Islam and Muslims. It was as if the US realised that cultural colonialism had not worked against the Muslims in the Middle East and now what was required was the direct military colonisation. Paul Wolfowitz said in a press conference in Singapore in 2002,

> *"It's true that our war against terrorism is a war against evil people, but it is also ultimately a battle for ideals as well as a battle of minds."*[xxxix]

This yearning for an Islamic way of life exposed the gulf between the Muslims and their rulers. The rulers rejected the Islamic culture and have adopted the Western culture and the Western agenda. It took the best part of a century for the Muslim in the Middle East to work out that the rulers are diametrically opposed to the viewpoints of the Muslim masses. What made this all apparent were the number of events that took place in just the last few decades and the intensity of some of these incidents, all of them exposed many of the rulers in the Middle East. These shocks in fact united the Muslims not just in the Middle East but across the Muslim world. Prior to the first Gulf war in 1991, Muslims generally did not sense the western animosity against Muslims. Many thinkers and scholars in the Muslim world could not sense the treachery of the Muslim rulers, and did not even view the West as their enemy. However, after the first Gulf war, which was prosecuted under the pretext of the Iraqi invasion of Kuwait, both the American animosity and the complicity of the Muslim rulers became evident. Not only did the Gulf regimes lose credibility for allowing the American troops bases in the Arabian Peninsula and other places, but the Islamic scholars who justified the war also lost credibility. Muslims could sense the gulf between themselves and the rulers.

A measurement of the Muslims in the Middle East by observing her reaction during the first Gulf war and observing her reaction to the second invasion is very telling. During the first Gulf war, America was not seen as an enemy, and Muslim rulers were able to open up their territories to America virtually unchallenged by the Muslim masses. But in the invasion of Iraq in 2003 the Muslim rulers were in political chains, trapped between subservience to America and the West and fear of removal by their own people. They were unable to send their armies to fight against Iraq because of the sentiments of the masses, their complicity in the war against Iraq is held in contempt and they are living in fear of change. Muslims worldwide are not accepting the American crusade against them, they now view America as an enemy, and they are fighting against her. They also view all their rulers with hatred and do not wish to be ruled by them as was seen during the Arab spring.

The removal of the rulers who allow such a situation to prevail can be clearly seen by their desperate actions for survival. Yasser Arafat regularly ordered the firing on his own people when they held rallies in support of Osama bin Laden and against the American war in Afghanistan. Jordanian troops crossed the border and began killing Israeli soldiers during the second Palestinian 'intifada'. Hamid Karzai insisted on the use of American soldiers for his personal security rather than his own people and as a result managed to live through numerous attempts to assassinate him. Pervez Musharraf and Ashfaq Kayani after him, of Pakistan, insisted on clearing out all the streets when they travelled in fear of being assassinated by their own people. Muslims in Pakistan continued to bomb US targets, which even resulted in the onslaught of the Lal Masjid by Pervez Musharraf to keep his grip on power. King Abdullah of Jordan obliterated the city of Ma'an because of the feelings and sentiments of the people who were undermining his authority. The Egyptian foreign minister was pelted with sandals when he entered the Al Aqsa mosque in 2005 after a meeting with Israel. We also continue to see the charade of the OIC and Arab summits where the rulers are forced to attack the US to keep their host populations happy. There was even an attempted coup in Qatar in October 2002 led by Pakistani and Yemeni army officers which was thwarted by the arrival of American troops — not an example that bodes well for the other Muslim rulers.

Today the artificial nationalities and nations created for the people in the Middle East have failed to placate the masses. The autocrats in the Middle East are no longer invincible and able to do whatever they believe would maintain their grip, the Muslim rulers are now experiencing the reality that unless they execute what the people wish to live by, then they are liable for eventual change. The difference between the rulers and the West on one side and the Muslim masses has never been so stark. Survey after survey in the 21st century confirms and points to the fact that the Muslims in the Middle East view Islam to be a central role in their lives and viewpoints about the world around them and see a central role for Islam in their governance.

Numerous polls and surveys across the Muslim world, many conducted by western institutes confirm such issues. In probably the most comprehensive poll commissioned by the University of Maryland in 2007, conducted across four majority Muslim countries (Egypt, Pakistan, Morocco, and Indonesia) showed overwhelming support for the application of *Shari'ah* law in Muslim countries, unification with other countries in a Pan Islamic state i.e. Caliphate, opposition to occupation and western foreign policy, opposition to the imposition of western values in Muslim lands and opposition to the use of violence against civilians. For some of these issues, the level of consensus is in excess of 75%.

Similarly, in a 2006 Gallup poll titled "Islam and democracy" gathered data from 10 predominantly Muslim countries. In places such as Jordan and Egypt the demand for *Shari'ah* as a source of legislation was in the 80% range. The Pew Research Centre in Washington found in its 2013 survey titled 'The World's Muslims: Religion, Politics and Society', support for *Shari'ah* as the official law of the land was well above 50%, especially in Iraq (91%) and the

Palestinian territories (89%).

The direction the Middle East and the wider Muslim world is heading was confirmed by the US. The US national intelligence council published a report following its 'global 2020' project, entitled 'Mapping the Global Future.' The National Intelligence Council (NIC) is the American Government's Intelligence Community's centre for mid-term and long-term strategic thinking. The report set out the likely scenario the world will face in 2020. The report concluded that the appeal of Islam today revolved around its call to return to earlier roots of Islam where the Islamic civilisation was at the forefront of global change under the Caliphate. The report portrayed a fictional scenario *'of how a global movement fuelled by radical religious identity could emerge.* [xxx] The report revealed unequivocally that at the highest levels of US policy planning, preparation is being made for the emergence of the Caliphate. Other reports from US policy makers and think tanks across the world acknowledged there is a broad based ideological movement seeking for the return of the *Caliphate.*

Nationalism failed due to the artificial nature of the countries created for the Middle East. Its contradiction to Islamic unity also contributed to its failure. The Muslim rulers, as the west's main instrument of defence, has been exposed and undermined as the masses saw them as diametrically opposite to how they viewed the future. Direct western invasion of the Middle East proved how desperate the situation became. Looking forward, the battle between the rulers alongside the West and the Muslim masses is set to only get intense as the Muslim masses want a future which is directly the opposite to the West and the Muslim rulers.

US AGENDA

In the early part of the twentieth century, Britain was at the forefront of Western efforts in moulding the Arab world. Almost a century later, nothing has changed. The West has embarked upon a new campaign to remake the entire Middle East in its image. America is leading a pack of colonial powers in this endeavour and is spearheading efforts in the Middle East.

The US campaign started with the separation of oil rich Southern Sudan in 2011. This model appears to be the strategy the US will pursue for the foreseeable future. The secession of South Sudan under American tutelage spurred Christians in Nigeria and Coptic Christians in Egypt to demand independence. The aspirations of the Coptic leaders were lucidly captured by a Jewish Journalist Oded Yinon in 1982. In his paper, "A strategy for Israel in the nineteen-eighties," he stated:

> *"Egypt is divided and torn apart into many foci of authority. If Egypt falls apart, countries like Libya, Sudan or even the more distant states will not continue to exist in their present form and will join the downfall and dissolution of Egypt. The vision of a Christian Coptic state in Upper Egypt, alongside a number of weak states, with very localized power and without a centralized government as to date, is the key to a historical development which was only setback by the peace agreement, but which seems inevitable in the long run."*

The idea of creating a sacred Coptic state within the contours of Egypt is similar to the one advocated by US Lieutenant-Colonel Ralph Peters concerning Makkah and Madinah. In June 2006, Peters published a map of the "New Middle East" in the June edition of the US Armed Forces Journal. The journal depicted amongst other mutilated Muslim countries the "Islamic Sacred State," which consists of Mecca and Medina segregated from the rest of Saudi Arabia.

Even before, various US officials played upon sectarian and ethnic differences, and called for the creation of a super Shia state that stretches from Lebanon to Pakistan. With US-Iran rapprochement in full swing the creation of such an entity would shift the control of oil away from Sunni domination into Shia hands. The American occupation in Iraq was viewed by some Middle Eastern leaders, as the first step towards Shia domination of the whole region. Jordan's King Abdullah warned:

> "If pro-Iran parties or politicians dominate the new Iraqi government a new "crescent" of dominant Shiite movements or governments stretching from Iran into Iraq, Syria and Lebanon could emerge, alter the traditional balance of power between the two main Islamic sects and pose new challenges to US interests and allies."[xxxi]

He further went to state that Iran was the main beneficiary from the chaos in Iraq. Ever since the Shia's rose to power in Iraq, King Abdullah has oft repeated that America's occupation of Iraq is bolstering Shia power across the region.

American officials have resurrected outdated plans to devour the Arab world once deemed too ambitious to accomplish and too dangerous to talk about in public. In January 2011, US Secretary of State Hillary Clinton could not hide her glee and used the events in Tunisia to fire a salvo at the pro-European Arab leaders. She said:

> "In too many places, in too many ways, the region's foundations are sinking into the sand. The new and dynamic Middle East ... needs firmer ground if it is to take root and grow everywhere. While some countries have made great strides in governance, in many others, people have grown tired of corrupt institutions and a stagnant political order. Those who cling to the status quo may be able to hold back the full impact of their countries' problems for a little while, but not forever. If leaders don't offer a positive vision and give young people meaningful ways to contribute, others will fill the vacuum."[xxxvii]

The term employed by successive American administrations to describe the plight of the Middle East, such as "sinking in the sand," "arc of crisis," "balkanization," or "Greater Middle Eastern Initiative (GMEI)," was done in an attempt to move away from the Sykes–

Picot Agreement, which protected old Europe's supremacy and interests, a colonial legacy which still persist today—albeit in parts. The war in Iraq in 2003 was a desperate bid by Bush and his cabal of neoconservatives to refashion the Middle East through force.

Whilst the US campaigns against the Sykes-Picot borders, it has its own grand plans of further dividing the region and creating newer, artificial and unviable states, which will also require external help for their survival, something the US is more than willing to provide.

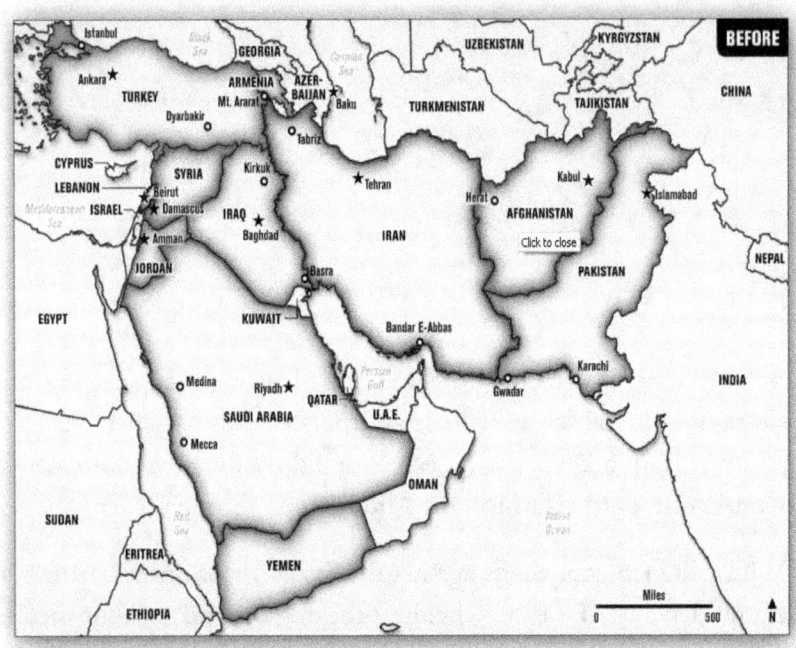

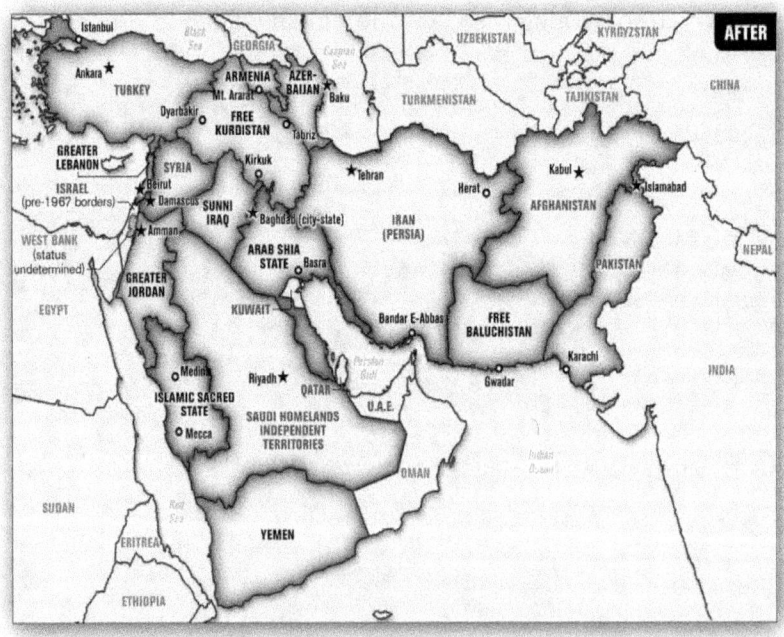

MIDDLE EAST MYTHS

ISLAM HAS ACTED AS THE OBSTACLE IN THE REGION

As the majority of the Middle East consists of Muslims and Islam is seen in many aspects of society and in the relationships between the people the claim has long been made that the lack of development and progress has been due to the Islamic beliefs of the people. Countries such as Saudi Arabia and Iran are Islamic States and many of the other nations in the region take Islam as a main pillar of governance. But on closer examination, the current Muslim countries have aspects of Islamic law being implemented; the most common being parts of family law, but no state derives its laws and policies based exclusively upon Islamic texts.

Saudi Arabia may donate millions of copies of the Qur'an, Islamic books, and a lot of money to build Masājid all over the world, however the Saudi Government rules by a mix of laws, some of which are Islamic and some are man-made. However, to maintain the Islamic perception, it refrains from calling them laws. Saudi uses specific terminologies to differentiate between the Islamic laws and the man-made ones. In a book (in Arabic) on the constitution of Saudi Arabia the author states,

> *'The words 'law (qanoon)' and 'Legislation (Tashree')' are only used in Saudi to refer to the rules taken from the Islamic Shari'ah ..... As for the man-made such as systems (Anthimah)' or ' instructions (Ta'leemaat)' or ' edicts (Awamir)'* ......*'*[cxxxiii]

Aside from this, Saudi Arabia is a hereditary monarchy that uses the religious establishment as a tool to control opposition to its Capitalist and pro-West agenda. Saudi Arabia doesn't take Islam as a basis for its foreign policy it takes nationalism, pragmatism and the preservation of the monarchy as the driving factors in its foreign policy, not Islam. When it comes to legislation The Islamic belief is

239

just one of many sources from where laws are derived. This alone actually makes Saudi Arabia a very un-Islamic state. A monarchy as a form of government also directly contradicts Islamic texts.

The Iranian constitution has many articles which comply with Islam but there are others which directly conflict with it. Article 6 of Iran's constitution states:

> *"The Islamic Republic of Iran, the affairs of the country must be administered on the basis of public opinion expressed by the means of elections, including the election of the President, the representatives of the Islamic Consultative Assembly, and the members of councils, or by means of referenda in matters specified in other articles of this Constitution."*

The Islamic system of governance – the Caliphate is based purely on the Islamic texts. This is not the case with Iran as it says in its constitution

> *"running of the affairs of the country is based on the opinions of the masses through elections".*

In Islam, the running of the affairs of the country is based on the *Shari'ah* itself not on the opinions of the people. Iran like many of the other nations in the region use Islam to give themselves a veneer of legitimacy but pragmatism and Persian nationalism is what defines Iran. Its foreign policy completely contravenes Islam.

With Islam never having been implemented, to accuse Islam of holding the region back is misplaced. The Middle East is composed of nations that are secular in outlook, whether it's a secular dictatorship, secular monarchies or secular democratic nations that have elections. The autocrats in the region pick and choose the laws they want – which in essence is what democracies are, and this has ensured no progress is made as the autocrats with full blessing from the west worked to maintain their own positions. The rulers in the

Middle East relegated Islam to personal worships and some personal relationships and ensured the rule of god played no role in governance and the running of their nations. Islam has thus not been applied in the region to be the cause of holding the region back.

THE MIDDLE EAST NEEDS A REFORMATION

The claim that Islam is backward and has no place in the world today is often built upon the premise that none of the Muslim countries have produced anything in terms of scientific research or technological development. It is often claimed that progress in science and technology occurred in the West when it rid itself of the authority of the Church and separated religion from life. Today this claim has become the criterion to study any alternative value system.

The historical process the West underwent is considered the history of the world and termed modernity, whilst all alternative thoughts are primitive if they do not match Western Liberalism (Capitalism). There are however, some fundamental differences between the history of the West and the struggle with the Church, relative to Islam and its history.

The initial adoption of Christianity by the Roman Empire was not based on the legitimacy of Christianity or on its ability to deal holistically with humanity's affairs. Rather, Christianity was adopted by Constantine in 325 CE simply to preserve the Empire by building a common mentality and loyalty among citizens. Christianity offered blind loyalty to the secular emperors based on the understanding that society could have two separate authorities; one temporal, the other spiritual, and that both authorities could coexist harmoniously. This understanding came from the saying attributed to Jesus (AS):

"Render unto Caesar what is Caesar's and unto god what is god's."[xxxiv]

Despite this, Christianity could not sustain or preserve the Empire and the demise of the Romans as a force meant the Church was able to dominate much of Europe. The domination of the Church meant that all affairs of life had to conform to the dogma of the Church. This caused countless problems given that the Bible, which the Church used as its authoritative text, dealt with only very limited matters. The scope of the Bible, as the Church would be the first to admit, does not and cannot stretch to being used wholly and exclusively to govern a nation or civilisation. Even determined advocates of the Bible fully accept it cannot be the primary source for the derivation of detailed rules, prescripts and guidance on every issue humanity faces. It did give some specific rules related to the Jews in their worships and their foodstuffs. It gave general moral principles for Christians and set norms for their prayers and communal worship. It did not give detailed regulation and direction on economy, accession to ruling, foreign policy, transactions, leasing of land, contracts, representation, judiciary, criminal punishments, the structure, accountability and functioning of government etc.

This meant there was a huge gap in the political landscape and this was an area of constant conflict of interests between kings, feudal barons and priests. During Europe's dark ages it was the priests who dominated life and when they passed judgement all had to submit, even Kings. Yet the judgements of priests were an arbitrary and inconsistent exercise of their authority owing to the lack of comprehensive legislative texts to base their rules upon. It was this random practice that laid the seeds of direct confrontation between the Church and society. With the passage of time, scientific discoveries were made that were at odds with the teachings of the Church. To preserve its authority, the Church took harsh steps against the emergence of such new ideas. Scientists were branded as heretics, infidels and Satan's. In 1633 CE, Galileo was forced to renounce his belief and writings that supported the Copernican theory of heliocentrism that claimed the Earth circumvented the Sun. Instead, the Church adamantly maintained the flawed theory of geocentrism, which stated that the Sun circumvented the Earth.

Other thinkers, such as Bruno, suffered even worse treatment at the hands of the Church. Bruno was imprisoned for 8 years while questioning proceeded on charges of blasphemy, immoral conduct, and heresy. Bruno was eventually burned at the stake.

Also, plenty of evidence exists indicating that hundreds of thousands of women, alleged to be witches were brutally tortured, burnt and drowned. The response to this oppression from the people, especially the scientists, thinkers and philosophers was equally strong. Many began to highlight the contradictions of the Church and reformers such as Martin Luther and John Calvin called for nothing less than the complete separation of the Church from the State. Desperate measures were taken by the Church to deflect the people's criticism, frustration and anger but these measures failed to halt the flames of change that had galvanised the masses. The Church realised that it could no longer remain dominant without reform. The eventual outcome of the struggle for power between the Church, on the one hand, and the scientists, thinkers and philosophers, on the other, was the complete separation of the Church from State. This compromised solution limited the authority of the Church to preserving morals in society and conducting rituals. It left the administration of worldly affairs to the State itself. The Reformation led to the Enlightenment period that bred secularism as a worldview and finally removed the arbitrary authority of the Christian Church. This formed the basis of the liberal Capitalist ideology and sparked the industrial revolution in Europe.

This state of affairs led to an intense intellectual revolution in Europe. European philosophers, writers and intellectuals made considerable efforts for comprehensive change in European ideas with the aim of uniting Europeans under secular liberal democratic thought. Many movements were established and played a great part in the emergence of new opinions about life. One of the most significant events that occurred was the change of the political and legislative systems to the nation state. The spectre of a despotic monarchy gradually disappeared to be replaced by republican systems based on representative rule and national sovereignty. This had the effect of triggering the awakening of Europe from its slumber. The industrial revolution was the centre of the European scene. There were numerous scientific discoveries and inventions springing from Europe. These factors all boosted Europe's intellectual and material progress. This material and scientific progress resulted in Europe finally ridding itself of its medieval culture.

When Europe rid itself of the Christian Church, science and technology came to flourish. Today, advocates of secularism claim Islam needs to go through a reformation process similar to the West whereby Muslims redefine and confine Islam to individual worship rather than a political creed i.e. do away with *Shari'ah, Caliphate and Ummah (one nation)* and adopt allegedly universal values of secularism, freedom, democracy, Human Rights, pluralism and the rule of law. The unfounded claim is that only with such reform cans Muslims progress and makes a transformation just as the West has done. This understanding is flawed due to two reasons:

Liberal thinkers saw Christianity as folklore as well as being part of their cultural heritage. This led them to deny miracles, revelation, prophets and other religious beliefs. This was because for them the Christian creed, which all these ideas and beliefs were based upon, was diametrically opposed to rationality.

For Western thinkers the Church and enlightened thought cannot meet. Martin Luther the famous Christian reformer said,

> *"Among Christians the rule is not to argue or investigate, not to be a smart aleck or a rationalistic know-it-all; but to hear, believe, and persevere in the Word of god, through which alone we obtain whatever knowledge we have of god and divine things. We are not to determine out of ourselves what we must believe about him, but to hear and learn it from him."* (LW. 13.237; Q. in Wood, 120).

This means Christianity is not based on intellectual thought, rather even if the scripture contradicts the clear mind, the scripture must always take precedence.

Defining all religions like Christianity and Islam as in the dark ages is a disservice to critical debate. It deflects any potential debate on secular liberal values and demonstrates clear insincerity in discussing which way humanity should move forward.

The history and struggle of the West was an event that occurred in Europe and was not the only event taking place in the world. When secularists study Islam, they view it through the lens of their history, which was their struggle to remove the authority of the church. For them Islam is no different to the church - irrational, medieval etc., and therefore it needs a reformation, just as the Christian Church went through. Only then can Islam be considered to have met the criteria for modernity.

Thus for the West 'modernity' carries specific connotations of the Enlightenment mission, defined as emancipation from self-imposed infancy i.e. from religion. This mission resulted in the development of secularism and the banishing of the Church, its teachings and its dogma to the private sphere. This was in addition to human rights, equality and freedom. Soon this historical process was termed 'modernism'. For secularists, the adoption of secular liberal values is termed modern and anything not compatible with such values is backward and no different to the medieval Church.

The issue at hand is an alternative ideology and an alternative way of organising life's affairs to the current secular model. There exists some fundamental differences between the two models - the secular and Islamic models are not the same. They do not overlap as they do not stem from the same fundamental ideas. They will therefore have entirely different impressions on how society should look. These differences lead to each viewing the other as a potential challenger to its superiority. Since secularism and Islam do not agree at the basis it is wholly inappropriate to judge this alternative using the secular model as a benchmark. Doing so would inevitably lead to the elimination of any methodology not in agreement with secularism before the discourse even commenced. No debate on secularism would ever take place!

If Islam is an alternative way to organise life it will inevitably have solutions which are the complete opposite to the secular model. However a non-agreement with the secular basis is not proof in itself to render a thought invalid. Consider the following:

- Would we consider the development of China wrong because it was not entirely built upon the free market model, even though it's on course to become the largest economy on the planet within 30 years?
- Would it be wrong for Indian companies to offer free medical alternatives to its poor because the free market abhors state intervention in the economy?
- Would we consider state handouts to the poor wrong because the free market advocates leaving the wellbeing of citizens to the market?

What must also be agreed is that time alone is not enough to render a thought invalid; this is because ideas are never time specific. The revival of ancient Greek philosophy, art and culture was termed a renaissance in 16th Century Europe. Most of the legislation we find today across Western Europe has their traditions in writings three millennia old, which are still considered valid today. For example:

- The US Bill of Rights, passed in 1791, reflects the guarantee of due process which was taken from the Magna Carta in 1215.
- Western scholars and jurists study the thoughts of Aristotle, Plato, Machiavelli, Locke and Nietzsche with no qualms that these people lived a long time ago.

246

- Modern civil law was developed upon the theory of liability which has its origins in Roman law
- Common law, which is the principle of deciding cases by reference to previous judicial decisions has its origins in the Middle Ages in Roman law and influenced by Norman Saxon custom. Today, it remains a source of legislation for the UK, US and Canada.

From this perspective democracy would definitely be backward and primitive due to its ancient origins. So the fact Islam emerged in seventh century Arabia is not an argument to suggest modern inapplicability. Capitalism's universality in reality is a Western specific ideology, an event which cannot be used to measure alternative thoughts as it is not a neutral measure. So it would be incorrect to place Islam on the West's political spectrum as this is a Western construct which follows their historical process.

ISLAM HAS CAUSED EXTREMISM IN THE MIDDLE EAST

The attacks on 9/11 in the US thrust extremism into the global vocabulary. Graphic scenes beamed all over the world from the World Trade Centre in New York and the Pentagon in Virginia remains with much of the world today. The sight of two jumbo jets colliding into the Twin Towers, for many, proves there were people in the world who are prepared to undertake extreme measures in order to make their point. Holding extremist views caused fanaticism and this in turn caused the slaughter of untold innocents in the process.

Al-Qaeda and ISIS are held as two examples that highlight what can happen when extremism is allowed to fester. Osama bin laden, who was the leader of al-Qaeda for much of its history, constantly degenerated the west and made his struggle against the west an Islamic obligation, something that he believed all Muslims needed to support. This is usually held as proof of Islam's direct contribution towards extremism, which led to terrorism. Western leaders have almost exclusively assigned extremism and terrorism to Islam. UK Prime Minister, David Cameron in a security conference in Slovakia, June 2015 stated:

> *"The cause is ideological. It is an Islamist extremist ideology, one that says the West is bad, that democracy is wrong, that women are inferior, that homosexuality is evil."*

George W Bush in Bush, in a speech to the American nation in October 2005 stated:

> *"The militants believe that controlling one country will rally the Muslim masses, enabling them to overthrow all moderate governments in the region, and establish a radical Islamic empire that spans from Spain to Indonesia."*

Similarly, Tony Blair made his infamous speech, two weeks after 7/7, describing the sole cause behind the attacks was an *"evil ideology."* He then went on to describe what some aspects of this evil ideology consisted of, he said:

> *"the establishment of effectively Taliban states and Sharia law in the Arab world on route to one caliphate of all Muslim nations."*

These points were later echoed by his then Home Secretary Charles Clarke in October 2005,

> *"What drive these people on are ideas… However there can be no negotiation about the re-creation of the Caliphate; there can be no negotiation about the imposition of Shari'ah law; there can be no negotiation about the suppression of equality between the sexes; there can be no negotiation about the ending of free speech. These values are fundamental to our civilisation and are simply not up for negotiation."*

All these statements point towards a linear relationship between extremist ideas, fanaticism, and terrorism and then mass slaughter and these extremist ideas, in origin, are the Caliphate, promoting Sharia law, armed resistance anywhere in the world and especially against the Israeli military and also the failure to condemn the killing of western troops in Iraq or Afghanistan.

The argument that terrorism is a result of extremism and radicalisation and is purely motivated by the Islamic ideology, irrespective of the political circumstances, where individuals will inevitably undertake violent acts, conveniently absolves the West of any policies or actions they have undertaken in the Middle East. This view also does not stand-up to academic scrutiny.

The prominent terrorism expert, John Horgan, who was the director of the International Centre for the study of terrorism in the University of Pennsylvania from 2007-2013 stated:

> *"The idea that radicalization causes terrorism is perhaps the greatest myth alive today in terrorism research ... [First], the overwhelming majority of people who hold radical beliefs do not engage in violence. And second, there is increasing evidence that people who engage in terrorism don't necessarily hold radical beliefs.'*[lxxxv]

French sociologist Olivier Roy argued that

> *"the process of violent radicalisation has little to do with religious practice, while radical theology, as Salafism, does not necessarily lead to violence."*

The *"leap into terrorism"* is not religiously inspired but better seen as sharing

> *"many factors with other forms of dissent, either political (the ultra-left), or behavioural: the fascination for sudden suicidal violence as illustrated by the paradigm of random shootings in schools (the 'Columbine syndrome')."*

Marc Sageman, a former CIA Operations Officer, who previously held a position that supported this theory but then changed his position, suggested that governments should

> *"Stop being brainwashed by this notion of radicalisation, there is no such thing. Some people when they're young acquire extreme views; many of them just grow out of them. Do not overreact – you'll just create worse problems."*[cxxxvi]

All the theories propagated about extremism by western governments, completely discount the political context the attacks take place in. Attacks are presented as random acts, coming out of thin air. Numerous politicians have argued you cannot negotiate with Islamic extremists as they have no specific cause and just want to kill people, only those with legitimate aims can be negotiated with. All of this absolves the West for the century of anarchy they have created in the Middle East. Such people would argue that the march 2015, Washington DC-based Physicians for Social Responsibility (PRS) landmark study, that concluded that the death toll from 10 years of the "War on Terror" since the 9/11 attacks was at least 1.3 million, and could be as high as 2 million has absolutely nothing to do with radicalising or making some people to resort to violence.[cxxxvii] They would deny the 4 million Muslims killed since the first gulf war in 1991 had no impact on those who resorted to violence as a means of dealing with this slaughter. It should also be remembered the Iraq war in 2003, was predicated on a lie of WMDs in order to gain access to the country's coveted oil fields, which caused untold deaths and destruction in Iraq and the region, which still continues today, these factors have directly contributed towards many taking up arms against the Western forces who are seen as occupiers. It also led some to conduct attacks in western capitals. The actual driving factors that led to such acts have nothing to do with Islam.

Osama bin Laden, for many, represents the fanatic who embodied the extremist narrative. Originally trained by the CIA, he came to lead the *Mujahedeen* against the Soviet invasion of Afghanistan in the 1980's. After the war he realised he was used as a pawn in the ideological struggle between Capitalism and Communism, he also realised Saudi Arabia was not as Islamic as it made itself out to be. These led him to turn against both the Saudi regime and as US strikes began to increase in the Islamic world he and his organisation al-Qaeda entered into a protracted struggle in the Middle East and beyond, culminating, eventually with 9/11.

In October 2001 Al-Jazeera television correspondent Tayseer Alouni interviewed Osama Bin Laden, in which he explained his methods and motives. Osama bin laden was asked by the al- Jazeera correspondent why he advocated killing civilians and targeting them in war. Bin Laden highlighted:

> *"Yes, the prophet forbade this in the authentic Islamic texts,"* i.e. killing women and children, *"but these laws not set in stone, (i.e. not absolute) the Qur'an says you should fight them as they fight you."*[xxxviii]

Osama bin Laden went further and reiterated this gave him a licence to imitate the west in military tactics. For this he cited the nuclear attack on Hiroshima and Winston Churchill's bombing of German civilians in WW2, as his model, not the Prophet Muhammed (saw). He continued that terrorism is a logical response to western occupation and propping up of client regimes and he cited the west as his model of imitation.

ISIS is also another result of a western war in the Muslim world. The Government and political architecture the US created in Iraq put Iranian Shia proxies in power. Their neglect and oppression of the Sunni minority led them to eventually lead a rebellion against the Nouri al-Maliki government. This uprising was organised by the Sunni tribes in 2013 when matters reached boiling point between the Malaki government and the Sunni's. A senior tribal leader Major General Montasir Al-Anbari confirmed:

"the decision to form the Sunni fighting groups was taken by clerics and tribesmen in the wake of the Hawija Protest Massacre, which was carried out by the Iraqi army; dozens were killed and wounded in the incident."[cxxxix]

Al-Anbari also confirmed that the formation of the fighting groups was decided in a meeting of all Sunni groups apart from ISIS. ISIS, he said, asked to join the groups several months after their formation and asked to be part of the Sunni military action. Many reservations were expressed, claimed Al-Anbari, before it was agreed to accept the ISIS request. He went further:

"In any case, ISIS only forms around 30% of the rebel fighters but it is linked to us by certain agreements and recognizes that it cannot face other fighting groups."[cxl]

The fighters that made up ISIS consisted of many former Saddam Hussein officials, former secret service personnel and army officials. Most of the ISIS personnel were former Ba'athists, who were intent on gaining back their country and saw the rebellion by the Sunni tribes of making a comeback. ISIS effectively hijacked the rebellion to expand its territorial control. Major General Montasir Al-Anbari highlighted:

"Without doubt, though, we are worried about unilateral movements of ISIS because they attacked the city of Telafer and kidnapped the Turkish consul, and they are threatening to head to Baghdad, Karbala and Al-Najaf. All of this, violates the agreement reached between the Sunni rebel groups. However any political solution on the ground that meets the demands of the Sunnis and saves them from Al-Maliki's oppression will be accepted."[cxli]

ISIS has used the veneer of Islam as cover to achieve its political aims and reclaim past glories. Their actions on the whole contradict Islam be it suicide attacks, slavery, mass killings, their treatment of non-Muslims and heretical treatment of other Muslims. Political ambition rather than Islam is the source of extremism by ISIS.

Using Islam for political gains has been a constant trend with violent groups. This was confirmed by a Arizona university report in 2012, where its centre for communications examined over 2000 Islamic texts, to determine what motivated the extremists, between 1998 and 2007. The report titled 'How Islamist Extremists Quote the Qur'an' found terrorists were not aiming to destroy western civilisation, but perceived themselves fighting a defensive war. The authors concluded the verses extremists cite from the Qur'an do not suggest an aggressive or offensive foe, seeking conquest or domination of non-believers as is commonly assumed, instead the verses deal with themes of victimisation, dishonour and retribution.

Many of the extremists and terrorists have stated their aims and motivations when they were put on trial. The report of the official 9/11 commission, confirmed that Khalid Sheikh Mohammed, the ringleader of the al-Qaeda cell who orchestrated 9/11 had intended to *"deliver a speech excoriating US support for Israel . . . and repressive governments in the Arab world."* British-born Mohammad Sidique Khan, from West Yorkshire, who was considered the ringleader of the July 7th 2005 bombing attacks in London highlighted in his video the killing of 52 people was directly linked to Tony Blair's foreign policy, he mentioned civilians were legitimate targets because of the policies of the UK government. He said:

> *"Your democratically elected governments continuously perpetuate atrocities against my people and your support of them makes you directly responsible, just as I am directly responsible for protecting and avenging my Muslim brothers and sisters. Until we feel security, you will be our target. Until you stop the bombing, gassing, imprisonment and torture of my people, we will not stop this fight.*"[xlii]

Asked by the judge at his trial in 2010 how he could justify planting a bomb in a crowded public place, the "Times Square bomber," Faisal Shahzad, raised the impact of US drone strikes in his

253

native Pakistan that *"kill women, children, they kill everybody."*[xliii] Umar Farouk Abdulmutallab, the "underwear bomber" who tried to blow up a US-bound airliner in December 2009, told the judge in his trial that he had worn an explosive device *"to avenge the killing of my Muslim brothers and sisters"* against *"the tyranny of the United States."*[xliv] The Boston Marathon Bomber, Dzhokhar Tsarnaev, according to the Washington Post, *"told interrogators that the American wars in Iraq and Afghanistan motivated him and his brother to carry out the attack."* In the murder of Drummer Lee Rigby in the UK in 2013, Michael Adebolajo, straight after the murder, on camera, said:

> *"The only reason we killed this man . . . is because Muslims are dying daily, this British soldier is an eye for an eye, a tooth for a tooth."*[xlv]

Whilst 9/11 preceded both the invasions of Iraq and Afghanistan as well as Obama's drone war in Pakistan, the west's support for Israel's oppression of the Palestinians preceded 9/11 as did the Anglo-American sanctions against Iraq. In fact, the mastermind of the first al-Qaeda attack on the Twin Towers in 1993, Ramzi Yousef, at his trial in 1998 said:

> *"You have [a] so-called economic embargo [on Iraq] which kills nobody other than children and elderly people."*[xlvi]

Dame Eliza Manningham-Buller, who was the head of the British secret services until her retirement in 2007, explained unequivocally to the Chilcot enquiry, what was causing extremism, she said:

> *"our involvement in Iraq, for want of a better word, radicalised a whole generation of young people"* and *"spurred some young British Muslims to turn to terror."*[xlvii]

Muslim extremists usually cite political, not theological, justifications for their actions. Iraq has been invaded four times, whilst Afghanistan has been invaded three times, this political context is the main motivator for extreme acts, Muslim terrorist are not motivated by Islamic ideology, as many a western leader would like us to believe.

Almost all academic and non-Muslim studies, surveys and analysis into terrorist literature and justifications prove that terrorists overwhelmingly justify their cause, not by reference to a 'war on all infidels' or 'to conquer the world' – but actually as a defensive, deterrent or retaliatory measure against Western foreign policy or the policies of Western-Puppet Muslim regimes. The term "extremism" is now the secular word for heretic and used selectively and inconsistently to construct Muslims as a suspect community and to discourage the expression of alternative opinions.

THE WEST FACES A MAJOR TERRORIST THREAT FROM THE MIDDLE EAST

Successive intelligence reports and associated hearings place terrorism as the biggest threat to the west. The number of terrorists on trial, the number of successful plots and the thousands, we are told the security agencies across the west foiled, are unprecedented in history. On this basis, the west face an existential threat, which requires significant counterterrorism focus and significant curtailment of freedom, privacy and state snooping, if the west is to succeed. Al-Qaeda, ISIS, lone wolfs, transnational terrorists, sleeper cells and foreign fighters, largely from the Muslim world are plotting attacks on western soil. On closer scrutiny of the evidence, background of attackers and statistics much of this is mere noise, rather than substance.

Terrorism from a global perspective in not aimed at the West, but is primarily Muslim-upon-Muslim, in the Muslim world. The Global Terrorism Index (GTI) is maintained by the Institute for Economics and Peace and their annual report which asses global terrorist attacks is based on data from the University of Maryland's Global Terrorism Database. The Global Terrorism Database (GTD) is considered to be the most comprehensive dataset on terrorist activity globally and has codified over 125,000 terrorist incidents between 1970 and 2013. In their most recent report, for 2014, it was confirmed that 82% of terrorist attacks were in just five nations: Iraq, Afghanistan, Pakistan, Nigeria, and Syria. These countries are in the middle of wars, in some cases civil wars. The analysis also found that over 80% of terrorist attacks, every year in the 21st century was in just these five nations, not the US or Europe. To put this into perspective, homicide claims 40 times more lives globally, then terrorism.

In Europe terrorism is a relatively minor threat to people, but due to terror attacks receiving significantly more media coverage than other causes of deaths, terrorist attacks have been magnified. Official data from Europol, which is the European Union's law enforcement agency, who publish an annual terrorism report, EU Terrorism Situation and Trend Report (TE-SAT), shows that more people die from car accidents and burning fires than they do in terrorist's attacks. It also found in 2006, 2007, and 2008 only 0.4% of terrorist attacks in the European Union were committed by Muslims. In 2009 and 2010 there were a total of 543 terrorist attacks, of which only 4 were committed by Muslims. This means that only 0.7% of terrorist attacks (less than 1%) were committed by Muslims. At the same time separatist groups in Europe committed 397 terrorist attacks, or 73% of terrorist attacks overall. In other words, separatist groups committed 99.2 times (nearly 100 times) more terrorist attacks than Muslims. Statistically speaking, there is a very small threat from a Muslim terrorist attacks and even smaller from the Middle East.

The US terror situation is also the same. The National Consortium for the Study of Terrorism and Responses to Terrorism (START) in its report: '9/11, ten years later,' noted, excluding the 9/11 atrocities, fewer than 500 people died in the US from terrorist attacks between 1970 and 2010.[cxlviii] Since 9/11, a total of 238 American citizens died from terrorist attacks. According to the Consumer Product Safety Commission, the average American is as likely to be crushed to death by televisions or furniture as they are to be killed by a terrorist.[cxlix] Whether Europe or the US more people die every year in car accidents, drown in a bathtub, die in a building fire and are struck by lightning then in a terrorist attack.[cl]

Despite US officials and agencies speaking of foiled plots and the threat of terrorism originating from the Middle East, being greater than ever, upon scrutiny this claim does not stack up. The percentage of terror attacks committed by Muslims is almost as miniscule as in Europe. An FBI study looking at terrorism committed on US soil between 1980 and 2005 found that 94% percent of the terror attacks were committed by non-Muslims. In actuality, 42% of terror attacks were carried out by Latino-related groups, followed by 24% perpetrated by extreme left-wing actors.[cli] A 2014 study by University of North Carolina found, since the 9/11 attacks, Muslim-linked terrorism has claimed the lives of 37 Americans. In that same time period, more than 190,000 Americans were murdered.[clii]

The reality is terrorism is a relatively minor threat to most people wherever they are in the world, especially America. For the past century, the American people have been incredibly sheltered from violence. Whilst Pancho Villa conducted a raid on Columbus, New Mexico, in 1916, and there was Pearl Harbour and the 9/11 attacks, but, by and large, war and political violence is something that happens elsewhere. When the US suffers an incident like Columbus, Pearl Harbour or 9/11, they have a tendency to invade other countries to ensure that there will be no repeat performance.

Domestic terrorism has always been a simmering problem in the US and forms the bulk of terror attacks, not Muslims or transnational attacks originating from the Middle East. But most domestic terrorist attacks have been more like Ted Kaczynski's or Daniel Andreas' San Diego pipe bombs than Timothy McVeigh's truck bomb. Most terror attacks in the UK are small scale and it's the exception, when a large scale attacks is successful. The US has not suffered the same level of war or terrorism as most countries in the world. What makes many Americans assume the terrorist threat is bigger than it really is, is the fact that many aspects of US society frequently magnify the real threat of terrorism.

The proliferation of 24-hour television news networks and Internet news sites magnifies this relatively minor threat. The need to fill the airwaves and compete with a plethora of channels has led to bad reporting and misunderstanding that has hyped terror. The outlandish and startling terrorism stories have led to the audience to become impacted by the propaganda leading to the deed becoming far larger than it really is. On September 11th, 2001, millions of people in the US and around the world watched live as the World Trade Centre, came crashing down and people leapt to their deaths to escape the raging fires. Watching this sequence of events in real time profoundly affected many people. Such theatrical attacks exert hold over the human imagination. The sense of terror they create can dwarf the reaction to natural disasters many times greater in magnitude. For example and without belittling any deaths, more than 227,000 people died in the 2004 Indian Ocean tsunami compared to fewer than 3,000 people on 9/11. Yet the 9/11 attacks spawned a global sense of terror and a geopolitical reaction that had a profound and unparalleled impact upon world events over the past decade.

One person losing their life is a tragedy, no matter the motive. I do not mean to trivialize the loss of life nor the burden on families. However, in the big picture, the number of people killed by US gang warfare dwarfs the number killed by al-Qaeda or ISIS— even accounting for the huge number of deaths on 9/11. Yet terrorist attacks continue to generate hysteria that far outweighs their real impact. Scott Stewart who was a special agent with the US State Department for 10 years and was involved in hundreds of terrorism investigations and now supervises Strategic Forecast (Stratfor), a US based geopolitical intelligence firm, terrorism and security issues team, he highlighted:

"Five dead at multiple crime scenes involving street gangs is a bad night in Chicago or Detroit, but it hardly gets noticed in the national and international media. But five dead at multiple crime scenes in which a Muslim gunman is involved becomes immediate fodder for round-the-clock cable news."[xliii]

Alongside this the entertainment industry through film and drama have taken the issue of terrorism and built multiple myths around the issue. Films such as under siege, the Kingdom, United 93, Olympus has fallen etc. have all contributed to the myth that many Muslims are involved in sleeper cells and plotting spectacular attacks on Western targets. TV series' such as Homeland and 24 sensationalised the possibility if a WMD's being snatched by Islamic radicals from a secure, secret facility in order to hold America hostage. When compared to the facts official FBI records showed 94% of terrorist attacks on American soil from 1980 to 2005 were perpetrated by non-Muslims.[cliv]

Even US president Barack Obama confirmed the terror threat being overblown, in a BBC interview in July 2015 he confirmed:

"And you know, if you look at the number of Americans killed since 9/11 by terrorism, it's less than 100. If you look at the number that have been killed by gun violence, it's in the tens of thousands."[xlv]

On a final point on the terror threats in the US, there are some serious question marks about the plots that are foiled on the US continent, the role of the government and the FBI that leads on domestic terrorism. This is because there is plenty of evidence that the FBI is responsible for more terrorism plots in the US than any other organisation. The University of California, Berkeley, funds various programs in its Investigative Reporting Program, which analyses terrorism prosecutions in the decade after 9/11. The program has found in the decade after 9/11, the FBI nabbed 158 defendants in sting operations, in which, to varying degrees, an FBI agent or informant provided the means and/or opportunity for a terrorism plot.[clvi] The FBI has been provided with multiple opportunities to challenge the accuracy of this data — which the Bureau has never done — and Human Rights Watch incorporated this data into its Illusion of Justice report.

In the 14 years after 9/11, there were around six real terrorist attacks in the United States that can be counted. These include the Boston Marathon bombings in 2013, as well as failed attacks, such as the Times Square car bomber Faisal Shahzad, as well as two attackers who were not tried in federal courts, Fort Hood shooter Nidal Hasan and Hesham Mohamed Hadayet, who attacked the El-Al ticket counter at Los Angeles International Airport. But despite just a handful of attacks in the 14 years after 9/11, the FBI has bragged about how it's foiled dozens of terrorist plots. In all, the FBI has arrested more than 175 people in aggressive undercover counter terrorism stings, 158 defendants were caught in counter terrorism stings.

The FBI was told to ensure another attack on US soil never occurs after 9/11. FBI agents were told to find terrorists before they strike. To do this, agents recruited a network of more than 15,000 informants nationwide — all looking for anyone who might be dangerous. An informant could earn $100,000 or more for every terrorism case they bring to the FBI. Shahed Hussian was paid $96,000 for his work in a New York sting,[clvii] Robert Childs took in more than $90,000 for a Seattle operation,[clviii] and Mohammad Hammad collected more than $380,000 for his work for the FBI in Southern California.[clix] These informants nabbed people, Abu Khalid Abdul-Latif and Walli Mujahidh who were paid six figure sums to inform on the Muslim community. These informants provide the means and the opportunity and the idea for mentally ill and economically desperate people to become what is now called terrorism. The FBI has paid informants with dubious background which include former criminals and conmen to spy on US communities, but mostly Muslim communities. Abu Khalid Abdul-

Latif and Walli Mujahidh both are mentally ill. Abdul-Latif had a history of huffing gasoline and attempting suicide. Mujahidh had schizoaffective disorder, he had trouble distinguishing between reality and fantasy. In 2012, the FBI arrested these two men for conspiring to attack a military recruiting station outside Seattle with weapons provided, by the FBI. The FBI's informant was Robert Childs, a convicted rapist and child molester who was paid $90,000 dollars for his work on the case. In 2009, an FBI informant who had fled Pakistan on murder charges led four men in a plot to bomb synagogues in the Bronx. The lead defendant was James Cromitie, a broke Walmart employee with a history of mental problems. And the informant had offered him $250,000 dollars if he participated in that plot.

In a counterterrorism sting in Tampa involving Sami Osmakac, a young man who was living near Tampa, Florida. Osmakac also had schizoaffective disorder. He was broke, and he had no connections to international terrorist groups. Nonetheless, an FBI informant gave him a job, handed him money, introduced him to an undercover agent posing as a terrorist, and lured him in a plot to bomb an Irish bar. But the lead undercover agent would go back to the Tampa field office with his recording equipment on. Behind closed doors, FBI agents admitted that what they were doing was farcical. Behind closed doors, the lead agent, the squad supervisor, described their would-be terrorist as a "retarded fool who didn't have a pot to piss in."[clx] They described his terrorist ambitions as wishy-washy and a pipe dream scenario. But that didn't stop the FBI. They provided Sami Osmakac everything he needed. They gave him a car bomb, they gave him an AK-47, they helped him make a so-called martyrdom video, and they even gave him money for a taxi cab so that he could get to where they wanted him to go. As they were working the sting, the squad supervisor tells his agents he wanted a Hollywood ending. And he got a Hollywood ending.[clxi] When Sami Osmakac attempted to deliver what he thought was a car bomb, he was arrested, convicted and sentenced to 40 years in prison. Sami

Osmakac isn't alone. He's one of more than 175 so-called terrorists, for whom the FBI has created Hollywood endings.

In almost all the 175 arrests, informants were involved and played the role of an agent provocateur by providing the means and opportunity. Prior to the informants arranging the sting operation the victims had no connections to international terrorists or any plans to go abroad. The FBI has been entrapping individuals in the name of terrorism. The FBI is responsible for more terrorist attacks in US then then al-Qaeda, al-Shabab and ISIS combined.

It should also be remembered that despite what the west say, terrorism, the use of terror or violence is a tactic utilised by a wide array of individuals, groups and states and something that has existed throughout history. Terrorism did not come into existence on September 11th, 2001. Terror or violence transcends across various fault lines and there is no single creed, ethnicity, political persuasion or nationality with a monopoly on terrorism. Individuals and groups of individuals from almost every conceivable background from late Victorian-era anarchists to tribal clansmen to North Korean intelligence officers - have conducted terrorist attacks. But on the whole terrorism is a low level threat, with most deaths around the world, Europe and the US due to reasons other than terrorism.

SECULARISM IS NEEDED TO TAME SECTARIANISM IN THE REGION

Of the total Muslim population, 10-13% are of a Shia denomination and 87-90% are of a Sunni denomination. Most Shias (between 68% and 80%) live in just four countries: Iran, Pakistan, India and Iraq. For many the Shia and Sunni schism represents an unresolved conflict and a source of continuous tension in the Middle East. For the West this schism is touted as proof that the concept of one Ummah (one nation) is outdated and unable to deal with sectarian differences. Liberals have contended that the concept of an Islamic political system, one capable of ruling over both Shia and

262

Sunni, is considered a figment of the Ummah's imagination. Olivier Roy's mid-nineties book, 'The Failure of Political Islam' declares,

> *"...the attempt to create a universal Islamist state is doomed to failure because of the conflicts between Sunni and Shia forms and other ethnic differences in the Islamic world..."*

Western views towards sectarianism have been shaped by their own bloody history. The idea of Secular Liberal Democracy was born in an era where monarchies used religion to oppress any dissent and justify an absolute monarchy. The growing voice of the people tied together with thinkers and activists of the time resulted in a secular liberal revolution which would supposedly put an end to the tyranny caused upon minorities by the monarchical structure of ruling. The argument put forward was that all religions could coexist under a secular political system that would act as a neutral platform for all peoples and their beliefs.

Origins

The Sunni-Shia schism has dominated discourse in the Middle East for the last century. The origin of the issue arose as a result of leadership of the Muslim world after the death of the Prophet Muhammed (saw). Today, the vast majority of Muslims hold that the Prophet did not appoint a successor to himself and to the Islamic system he had established during his lifetime. Hence, for the majority of Muslims throughout Islamic history, the issue of leadership was left to the popular will. The Shia on the other hand believe that the Prophet appointed Ali (ra), his cousin, as his successor. They further concluded that all subsequent rulers should be from Ali (ra) bloodline, as only then will they be *ma'soom* (infallible). Whilst the Shia like the Sunni's are not one homogenous group, the *ithna ashariyya* (twelvers) is the largest grouping within the Shia, other smaller branches include those who dispute the lineage of the Imams. Mainstream Shia believe that these rulers number twelve, the twelfth of which, Mohammed ibn Hasan al-Askari, has gone into a period of *ghaybah* (occultation), and will reappear at some unspecified time in the future.

Fundamentally, this is where the difference between some Muslims occurred in the past and like the many differences Muslims globally have over the branch issues of the Islam. This difference however developed into a political movement which continues to plague the Muslim world today. It is not the Islamic position on ruling but a number of political issues and unfortunate historical events that have so loaded the Sunni-Shia issue:

The **first** of these was Ali's (ra) confrontation with Mu'awiyah (another cousin of the prophet (saw). The murder of Uthman (ra) resulted in Mu'awiyah, as the leader of the Ummayads to withhold *bay'ah* to Ali (ra) until the guilty group was brought to justice. This was also the view of Ayesha (ra), Talhah (ra) and Al-Zubayr (ra). This severely undermined Ali (ra), the confrontation with Mu'awiyah while he was the *wali* (governor) of Syria, eventually turned violent.

The **second** was with Ali (ra) son, Hassan ibn Ali (ra). When he became the Caliph after his father's death he was effectively pressured as the Caliph to relinquish the role – which he did after six months in power. Mu'awiyah then took the position for himself.

The **third** was the innovation by Mu'awiyah of appointing a successor and thus instituting hereditary rule. Mu'awiyah's son Yazid had no mandate from the people, whether Shia or Sunni as he was forced upon the people. This episode led to considerable tension, as the Muslim world at the time did not recognise his rule and fought to remove him.

The **fourth** was Hussain's confrontation with Yazid over his usurpation of power. The Muslims gathered around Hussain (ra) in order to end the innovation of hereditary rule. Hussain (ra) and his small band of supporters were murdered at Karbala, now in modern day Iraq, at the hands of Yazid's army headed by Obaidallah ibn

Zeyad on the day of Ashura, the 10th Muharram 61 AH. The Shia have ever since, commemorated the tragic death of Hussain yearly on the day of Ashura. The Umayyad period, which followed directly from the era of Mu'awiyah and Yazid suffered from the fallout of these events. Shia were treated with suspicion by some of the Ummayyads and some Abbasid Caliphs, endured brutal persecution as a result.

A deeper scrutiny of these tragic events reveals that both the Sunni and Shia hold similar positions on them. The Sunnis reject all the attempts by Mu'awiyah to consolidate political power within his own family. In the confrontation between Mu'awiyah and Ali, the view amongst the Sunnis is that Mu'awiyah's condition of bringing to task those who murdered Uthman (ra) for ba'yah was unacceptable and that the actions of Ali (ra) were mandated by Islamic rule. The Sunnis historically believe that Yazid had usurped power illegitimately and that he was never a legitimate Caliph, it was Abdullah ibn Zubair (ra), whilst not as the Caliph, who led the Muslims in reversing this innovation instigated by Mu'awiyah. On the issue of persecution, some Sunnis went as far as to support the Shia in their stand against those in power. Imam Abu Hanifah, who established his own school of thought provided active verbal, and financial, support to Ibrahim ibn Abdullah (d. 145 AH) who led a campaign against the Caliph al-Mansur, support for which Abu Hanifah was sent to prison where he was eventually poisoned. The persecution by some Umayyad and Abbasid Caliphs was not sanctioned by any school of thought, whether Sunni or Shia, and is seen as a clear deviation from Islam.

Other events over the expanse of Islamic history have also acted to skew perceptions of the core doctrinal differences between of the Sunni and Shia. Until the creation of the Safavid state in Persia in the 16th century, bar a few previous glimpses of autonomy, the Shia had lived under the Caliphate contributing to Islam's "Golden Age" under the Abbasids, some assuming various governmental roles as individuals but on the whole confining their activities to religious education, spiritual and moral guidance after the onset of the *ghaybah*. The Safavid's encouraged the Shia, who until then had been scattered across the Islamic world, to migrate and settle in Persia and institutionalised Shia doctrine and jurisprudence. The Safavid rule contradicted Shia thinking. A fallible (i.e. not *ma'soom*) ruler not from amongst the twelve Imams lacked legitimacy in Shia doctrine, consequently even though some Shia scholars welcomed opportunities made available to them, they remained cautious and represented a body outside of government acting principally to advise the Safavid rulers on matters of morality and justice. Although in this sense Shia scholars remained quite distinct from Safavid rule, some have chosen to interpret Safavid policies as sanctioned by Shia thought. The Safavid attack on Baghdad whilst the Ottoman Caliph Sulayman the magnificent (d. 1566) laid siege on Vienna was believed to have contributed to its failure as Sulayman marched to defend Baghdad after his retreat, an event some popularised as a Shia - as opposed to a Safavid – attack which curtailed Islamic advances.

The emergence of Wahhabism in the 18th century CE, which adopted a literalist approach to jurisprudence and doctrine, drew on works by like-minded literalists to publicise the illegitimacy of Shia thinking. Their attack on the Shia was fierce and considerable; many of their anti-Shia arguments are still vociferously publicised by Wahhabi scholars, particularly those in Saudi Arabia, and contribute considerably to Sunni rhetoric and stereotypes of the Shia in the Islamic world today. However, the Wahhabi attack on the Sunni schools of thought was just as fierce. They provided justification to attack the Sunni Ottoman Caliphate on grounds of deviancy, wresting control of the holy sites of Mecca and Medina despite much bloodshed. The promotion of Wahhabi material has served to skew history and perceptions of the Shia, as it has also served to confuse the Shia *ithna ashariyya* with other sects who the Shia themselves consider outside the fold of Islam.

Politics

Differences between Shia and Sunni relate to the qualities and characteristics of those who rule, not whether Islam should be divorced from ruling. For the Shia traditionally the head of state is infallible and divinely appointed; for the Sunni he is fallible and selected by the people, but for both ruling is based on Islamic rules and principles. Indeed, the very origin of their dispute refers to the rightful successors of the Prophet Muhammad in their role as heads of state (and spiritual guide for the Shia.)

The Shia opinions towards politics and ruling during the occultation, has been a point of contention amongst Shia scholars for centuries. This is because if no one can rule during the occultation, someone else will and there is no guarantee they will do so according to Islam. The absence of the twelfth Imam gained prominence during the Safavid Empire and was the catalyst for the Iranian Grand Ayatollah, Ayatullah Ruhullah Khomeini, to lead the Iranian revolution in 1979.

It was under Safavid rulers that Shia thinking began to develop and expand and formalise beyond its traditional scope. The current Shia hierarchy of *talib-ul-ilm* (student) progressing to *hujjat-ul-Islam* (teacher) to Ayatollah, following the establishment of centres of learning at Isfahan and Najaf were developed and formalised under Safavid rule. Shia thinking developed to afford the grand ayatollah greater power and rights which were previously the reserve of the twelve Imams, such as collecting charity, adjudication in certain civil cases and issuing fatwa's. Grand ayatollahs came to be seen as proxies of the twelfth Imam through which they were afforded greater responsibilities. It was during this period that the notion of *Wilayat ul-Faqih* - the rule of the jurist - emerged, particularly through the writings of Mullah Ahmad al-Naraqi.

It was however Ayatullah Khomeni's publication of *al-Hukumat al-Islam Wilayat ul-Faqih* (Islamic government: *Wilayat ul-Faqih*) that included the right of a fallible but upright jurist to govern as a proxy to the twelfth Imam in the Imam's absence. Khomeini challenged the notion that Islam should be absent from ruling even if it was temporary until the return of the twelfth Imam, stating,

> *"From the time of the Lesser Occultation down to the present (a period of more than twelve centuries that may continue for hundreds of millennia, if it is not appropriate for the Occulted Imam to manifest himself), is it proper that the laws of Islam be cast aside and remain unexecuted, so that everyone acts as he pleases and anarchy prevails? Were the laws that the Prophet of Islam laboured so hard for twenty-three years to set forth, promulgate, and execute valid only for a limited period of time? Did god limit the validity of His laws to two hundred years? Was everything pertaining to Islam meant to be abandoned after the Lesser Occultation?"*

He in essence proposed *Wilayat ul Faqih*, i.e. a ruler who is a *mujtahid* (competent scholar) to rule with the belief that the Islamic system cannot be suspended. By arguing that the Shia must accept a fallible individual to rule as a proxy to the Imams, Khomeini filled the gap in Shia Islamic political thought that arose from a literal interpretation of the *ithna ashari* doctrine. Hence remaining passive until the twelfth imam re-appears, has been challenged for over two centuries, well before Khomeni. One of the strongest Shia advocates of Islamic rule during the occultation, was the Iraqi Grand Ayatullah Mohammed Baqir al-Sadr. Forming the movement *Hizb ad-Da'wah* (Party of the Islamic Call), he opposed communist influences in Iraq and engaged in open political opposition to the secular Ba'athist regime with a view to establish, not an Iraqi, but an Islamic state that encompassed the whole of the Islamic world. Baqir al-Sadr, uncle of Moqtada al-Sadr the hostile opponent of US presence in Iraq, wrote a number of key works on various elements of the Islamic system, including titles such as "Our Economics", "Sources of Power in the Islamic State" and a series of essays later called "al-Islam Yaqud al-Hayat" (Islam Governs Life). He challenged the traditional political passiveness of some Shia in the *Hawza al-Ilm* (religious institution) of

268

Najaf where he was a student, teacher and granted status as *marjah* (supreme legal authority). He remained steadfast to this view even under house arrest because of his opposition to Ba'athism and non-Islamic rule in Iraq.

The principle difference between the Shia and Sunni is over the virtues and qualities of those who rule, not whether Islam should rule in the first instance. Disagreements over the criteria for selecting a ruler is an area of differences, whilst the Sunnis hold at least seven core conditions, the Shia during the absence of the twelfth Imam insist on his credentials as a jurist. Shia and Sunni have articulated Islamic ruling in very similar terms. Following the destruction of the Caliphate in 1924, Sunnis advocating its re-establishment worked with Baqir al-Sadr and made contact with Khomeni, however Khomeini's post-Iranian revolution constitution never matched his earlier writings on the subject of *Wilayat ul-Faqih*. Aside from this both Shia and Sunni therefore hold identical conceptions of Islam: that Islam is a spiritual and a political system.

Whilst episodes of historical animosity have resulted in rebellion and secession, the Sunni-Shia schism remained dormant for many centuries and may have remained if only academic interest if it were not exploited by foreign powers to promote further fractures in the Muslim world. There has been a concerted campaign by western policy centres to use the Sunni-Shia dispute as a propaganda weapon to challenge key Islamic notions such as the *"Ummah,"* "unity" and Islamic rule. According to Graham Fuller of the RAND Corporation

> *"To speak of the Shia of the Arab world is to raise a sensitive issue that most Muslims would rather not discuss."*

According to Francke

> *"The Shia...present a sensitive problem that assails to the core of Muslim unity and undermines the traditional historiography of the Muslim state..."*

The Library Journal suggests, "...the attempt to create a universal Islamist state is doomed to failure because of the conflicts between Sunni and Shia forms..." And so on...

Islamic thought is what unites Shia and Sunni and Islamic jurisprudence addresses the differences between them. Secularism is foreign to both Sunni and Shia. Saudi Arabia and Iran have also contributed towards sectarianism in the Middle East as they have used both sects for their own national aims, rallying upon a sectarian basis has allowed them to gain support from their respective sects.

THE WEST HAS ALWAYS SUPPORTED DEMOCRACY IN THE MIDDLE EAST

Democracy promotion has been a buzzword by western governments and officials for long in the Middle East. Successive U.S. administrations and presidents have made supporting democracies in the Middle East a key foreign policy aim. However, a century on the west as a mixed record, whilst within the region the west is viewed as constantly supporting non-democratic leaders.

It is always explicit or implicit in the rhetoric of Western foreign policy that Western states aim to promote their grand principles of democracy, peace, human rights and overseas development. However, these same Western states are systematic violators of these principles and of international law. They consistently condone rights abuses and are key allies of repressive and dictatorial regimes.

There has long been an ignominious association between 'democratically elected' Western governments and 'dictatorial regimes' around the world. When benefit is the axiom around which politics in the West is conducted, international law, principles and 'ethical' foreign policies are conveniently discarded. Given this, it is of no surprise that the UK and US have been at the forefront of courting alliances with the most brutal of dictatorships over the best part of the last century and continue to do so today. In many instances they have installed, supported and removed leaders according to their respective national interests. Their alliance with the world's most reprehensible regimes has been excused under euphemisms related to strategy, geo-politics and the like. Thomas Jefferson was correct when he said,

"We believe no more in Bonaparte's fighting merely for the liberties of the seas than in Great Britain's fighting for the liberties of mankind. The object is the same, to draw to themselves the power, the wealth and the resources of other nations."

Peter de la Billiere, the UK commander in the first Gulf War, explicitly explained the importance of keeping these dictators in power in the Muslim world. He talked of the need to maintain the Saudi regime:

"As we, the British, had backed the system of sheikhly rule ever since our own withdrawal from the Gulf in the early 1970s, and seen it prosper, we were keen that it should continue. Saudi Arabia was an old and proven friend of ours…It was thus very much in our interests that the country and regime should remain stable after the war."

Western leaders, their think tanks and media have for long justified supporting dictators and autocrats in the Middle East. The West has supported autocrats because they are the only force capable of stemming the tide towards Islam, which represents the basic value system of the region and they ensure a regular supply of oil security. Supporting autocrats for 'security,' is the same one used by Arab autocrats to keep their domestic audiences in line. In Egypt, after the military coup that removed the Muslim Brotherhood from power, the military embarked on a campaign of severe repression against its opponents. This strategy was not only aimed at suppressing the Brotherhood, a spent force politically, it aimed at polarising the political system in a manner that ensured support for the military among the urban middle classes.

271

In Iraq, the US after the invasion proceeded to create a political order based on an exclusive rather than inclusive elite bargain; igniting resistance across the country. They created the ensuing chaos with dismantling the Iraqi army, the low number of combat coalition troops, and the aggressive policy of de-Ba'athification served to push the country towards a state of collapse, and paved the way for the rise of Sunni extremism that eventually led to the rise of ISIS. During this, over a decade-long, process of state collapse, insurgency and terrorism, the US and its allies continued to support an openly sectarian regime, which committed acts of sectarian killing and state-sponsored terrorism no less atrocious than the acts of ISIS.

The notion that oil producers would shut off oil supply if friendly relations are not maintained is ludicrous to say the least. In reality, the west is not dependent on Arab oil producers; it is the other way around. First, the survival of the Gulf monarchies depends on their ability to provide a certain standard of welfare in exchange for political obedience from their citizens. In essence, the ability of Gulf States to survive as *rentier* states without democratising their political systems depends on their ability to sell oil on the international market. Thus, the ability of Gulf States to cut the supply of oil is restricted by this fact. The dependency of the west on Arab oil is restricted by its bargaining power as the major consumer in the world.

Stratfor founder George Friedman encapsulated why autocrats are regularly supported in the Middle East.

"The case of Egypt raises an interesting and obvious question regardless of how it all turns out. What if there are democratic elections and the people choose a regime that violates the principles of Western human rights? What happens if, after tremendous Western effort to force democratic elections, the electorate chooses to reject Western values and pursue a very different direction — for example, one that regards Western values as morally reprehensible and aims to make war against

them?........but the general assertion is a form of narcissism in the West that assumes that all reasonable people, freed from oppression, would wish to emulate us.'[clxii]

Friedman recognises the people of the Middle East are culturally different and therefore have not necessarily embraced western values. Whilst elections, security, ownership and rule of law are universal values, democracy, freedom and secularism are not and have their origins in Europe and the struggle between the church and the people. This cultural difference has led to the failure of western values becoming widespread in the Middle East and it is here the autocrats are needed to ensure the region doesn't return to its own governance and dominate one of the world's most strategic regions and expel the west.

Egypt has played a key role as a dictatorship, who has maintained western influence in the region. Egypt's military was "restoring democracy," according to US Secretary of State John Kerry when it overthrew the democratically elected Muslim Brotherhood government in July 2013. America's massive financial assistance to the Field Marshal continues despite the technicality that "restoring democracy" occurred through an undemocratic, and very bloody, military coup against a democratically elected government. While America has criticised some actions of the military dictatorship, its legitimacy has not been criticised. This is despite the fact that many of America's political commentators have highlighted the contradiction inherent in American support for the Egyptian army's coup. The New York based Human Rights Watch (HRW) complained about the arrest of those opposing the army's will for a 'yes' vote in the next day's constitutional referendum: *"Egyptian citizens should be free to vote for or against the new constitution, not fear arrest for simply campaigning for a 'no' vote."* The next day, the Washington Post ran an opinion piece entitled: *"Egypt's bogus democracy doesn't deserve U.S. aid."*

The Brookings Institute and The Carnegie Endowment for International Peace published numerous opinion pieces from their 'fellows' and 'associates' highlighting the anti-democratic reality of Egypt's military government, but they also pointed out that the main concern is not human rights or democracy itself, but rather that if the Egyptian Army does not succeed in controlling the country, "Islamist extremism" will be fuelled, and by noting that "what is going on in Egypt now is very popular among Egyptians" democratic legitimacy was offered to a military institution that was not democratic in any sense of the word.

The Gatestone Institute, questioned whether Egypt's Elections were Democracy? It said:

> *"From reading the American press, you would believe that if Middle Eastern Muslims were allowed to govern themselves by having free elections, this would be the route to democracy. This is a fallacy.* They argued that opinion polls showed that Muslims in Egypt and throughout the Middle East overwhelmingly preferred Islam to Democracy. Their conclusion was: *"If there is ever to be anything approximating democratic transformation in Egypt the only way it is going it happen is if Egypt has a respected institution, such as the military, that governs the country".* [clxiii]

The Gatestone view placed Egypt's vicious military dictatorship as well as the autocrats in the region, at the head of democratic institutions even though it stands against the will of the people, because the will of the people was for Islam.

It is not democracy the west has always supported but dictatorship is what has been the key export from the West to the Middle East. This is fundamentally because their values have not found fertile ground in the region as the people are culturally different and after a century have not subscribed to western values. This is why the west supports autocrats to ensure the masses do not succeed in instilling their own values, which would include expelling

274

the west.

THE MIDDLE EAST AND THE WORLD WOULD HAVE BEEN A MUCH BETTER PLACE IF ISLAM HAD NEVER EXISTED

Islam is presented as the cause of some of the world's key problems. Clash of civilisations, holy wars, terrorism and 9/11 are presented almost daily in news headlines and the common denominator between them is Islam. Is seems to lay behind a broad range of international disorders: suicide attacks, car bombings, military occupations, resistance struggles, riots, fatwas, Jihads, guerrilla warfare, threatening videos, and 9/11 itself. For some, "Islamofascism" is the West's sworn foe in a looming "World War III."

The intense focus on terrorism, war, and rampant anti-Americanism — some of the most emotional international issues of the day all relate to Islam. A Middle East without Islam would most likely have spared many of the current challenges in the world, the Middle East would be much more peaceful, East-West relations would have been very different. In fact, advocates of 'Is Islam the source of all problems' argue the international order would have been a very different picture today had Islam never have existed.

What if there was no such thing as Islam? What if there had never been a Prophet Muhammed (saw), no saga of the spread of Islam across vast parts of the world? In an exercise of historical imagination let's assess how the world would have evolved without Islam and events would have turned out and where they would be today.

Islam culturally shaped the Middle East as well as its politics from the earliest days of a broader Middle East. Without Islam, the face of the region still remains complex and conflicted. The dominant ethnic groups of the Middle East — Arabs, Persians, Turks, Kurds, Jews, even Berbers and Pashtuns — would still dominate politics. Long before Islam, successive Persian empires pushed to the doors of Athens and were the perpetual rivals of whoever inhabited Anatolia. Contesting Semitic peoples, too, fought the Persians across the Fertile Crescent and into Iraq. And then there are the powerful forces of diverse Arab tribes and traders expanding and migrating into other Semitic areas of the Middle East before Islam. Mongols would still have overrun and destroyed the peoples of Central Asia and much of the Middle East in the 13th century. Turks still would have conquered Anatolia, the Balkans up to Vienna, and most of the Middle East. These struggles — over power, territory, influence, and trade — existed long before Islam arrived.

From a religious perspective if Islam had never emerged, most of the Middle East would have remained predominantly Christian, in its various sects, just as it had been at the dawn of Islam. Apart from some Zoroastrians and small numbers of Jews, no other major religions were present. So the question is would harmony with the West have reigned if the whole Middle East had remained Christian? Would the restless and expansive medieval European world not have projected its power and hegemony into the neighbouring East in search of economic and geopolitical footholds? The Crusades was a Western adventure driven primarily by political, social, and economic needs. The banner of Christianity was little more than a potent symbol, a rallying cry to bless the more secular urges of powerful Europeans. In fact, the particular religion of the natives never figured highly in the West's imperial march across the globe. Europe may have spoken in an uplifting way about bringing "Christian values to the natives," but the patent goal was to establish colonial outposts as sources of wealth for the metropole and bases for Western power projection. So it's unlikely that Christian inhabitants of the Middle East would have welcomed the stream of European fleets and their merchants backed by Western guns. Imperialism would have prospered in the region's complex ethnic mosaic — the raw materials for the old game of divide and rule. And Europeans still would have installed the same pliable local rulers to accommodate their needs.

Move the clock forward to the age of oil in the Middle East. Would Middle Eastern states, even if Christian, have welcomed the establishment of European protectorates over their region? The West still would have built and controlled the same choke points, such as the Suez Canal. It wasn't Islam that made Middle Eastern states powerfully resist the colonial project, with its drastic redrawing of borders in accordance with European geopolitical preferences. Nor would Middle Eastern Christians have welcomed imperial Western oil companies, backed by their European vicegerents, diplomats, intelligence agents, and armies, any more than Muslims did. Look at the long history of Latin American reactions to American domination of their oil, economics, and politics. The Middle East would have been equally keen to create nationalist anticolonial movements to wrest control over their own soil, markets, sovereignty, and destiny from foreign grips — just like anti-colonial struggles in Hindu India, Confucian China, Buddhist Vietnam, and a Christian and animist Africa.

The French would have just as readily expanded into a Christian Algeria to seize its rich farmlands and establish a colony. The Italians, too, never let Ethiopia's Christianity stop them from turning that country into a harshly administered colony. In short, there is no reason to believe that a Middle Eastern reaction to the European colonial ordeal would have differed significantly from the way it actually reacted under Islam.

Would the Middle East have been more democratic without Islam? The history of dictatorship in Europe itself is not reassuring. Spain and Portugal ended harsh dictatorships only in the mid-1970s. Greece only emerged from church-linked dictatorship a few decades ago. Christian Russia is still not out of the woods. Until quite recently, Latin America was riddled with dictators, who often reigned with US blessing and in partnership with the Catholic Church. Most Christian African nations have not fared much better. Why would a Christian Middle East have looked any different?

With regards to Palestine it was Christians who shamelessly persecuted Jews for more than a millennium, culminating in the Holocaust. These horrific examples of anti-Semitism were firmly rooted in Western Christian lands and culture. Jews would therefore have still sought a homeland outside Europe; the Zionist movement would still have emerged and sought a base in Palestine. And the new Jewish state would still have dislodged the 750,000 Arab natives of Palestine from their lands even if they had been Christian — and indeed some of them were. These Arab Palestinians would have fought to protect or regain their land. The Israeli-Palestinian problem remains at heart a national, ethnic, and territorial conflict, only recently bolstered by religious slogans. It is also worth remembering that Arab Christians played a major role in the early emergence of the whole Arab nationalist movement in the Middle East, indeed, the ideological founder of the first pan – Arab Baa'th party, Michel Aflaq, was a Sorbonne- educated Syrian Christian.

But surely Christians in the Middle East would have at least been religiously predisposed toward the West. Couldn't we have avoided all that religious strife? In fact, the Christian world itself was torn by heresies from the early centuries of Christian power, heresies that became the very vehicle of political opposition to Roman or Byzantine power. Far from uniting under religion, the West's religious wars invariably veiled deeper ethnic, strategic, political, economic, and cultural struggles for dominance.

Without Islam, the peoples of the Middle East would have remained as they were at the birth of Islam — mostly adherents of Eastern Orthodox Christianity. But it's easy to forget that one of history's most enduring, virulent, and bitter religious controversies was that between the Catholic Church in Rome and Eastern

Orthodox Christianity in Constantinople — a rancour that persists still today. Eastern Orthodox Christians never forgot or forgave the sacking of Christian Constantinople by Western Crusaders in 1204. Nearly 800 years later, in 1999, Pope John Paul II sought to take a few small steps to heal the breach in the first visit of a Catholic pope to the Orthodox world in a thousand years. Despite this friction between East and West in a Christian Middle East would have remained much as it is today. Take Greece, for example: The Orthodox cause has been a powerful driver behind nationalism and anti-Western feeling there, and anti-Western passions in Greek politics as little as a decade ago echoed the same suspicions and virulent views of the West that we hear from many Islamic leaning leaders today.

The culture of the Orthodox Church differs sharply from the Western post-Enlightenment ethos, which emphasizes secularism, capitalism, and the primacy of the individual. It still maintains residual fears about the West that parallel in many ways current Muslim insecurities: fears of Western missionary proselytism, a tendency to perceive religion as a key vehicle for the protection and preservation of their own communities and culture, and a suspicion of the "corrupted" and imperial character of the West. Indeed, in an Orthodox Christian Middle East, Moscow would enjoy special influence, even today, as the last major centre of Eastern Orthodoxy. The Orthodox world would have remained a key geopolitical arena of East-West rivalry in the Cold War. Samuel Huntington, after all, included the Orthodox Christian world among several civilizations embroiled in a cultural clash with the West.

Today, the US occupation of Iraq would be no more welcome to Iraqis if they were Christian. The U.S. did not overthrow Saddam Hussein, an intensely nationalist and secular leader, because he was Muslim. Other Arab peoples would still have supported the Iraqi Arabs in their trauma of occupation. Nowhere do people welcome foreign occupation and the killing of their citizens at the hands of foreign troops. Indeed, groups threatened by such outside forces invariably cast about for appropriate ideologies to justify and glorify their resistance struggle. Religion is one such ideology.

A world without Islam would see the Middle East dominated by Eastern Orthodox Christianity — a church historically and psychologically suspicious of, even hostile to, the West. Still riven by major ethnic and even sectarian differences, it possesses a fierce sense of historical consciousness and grievance against the West. It has been invaded repeatedly by Western imperialist armies; its resources commandeered; borders redrawn by Western fiat in conformity with its various interests; and regimes established that are compliant with Western dictates. Palestine would still burn. Iran would still be intensely nationalistic. We would still see Palestinians resist Jews, Chechens resist Russians, Iranians resist the British and Americans, Kashmiris resist Indians, Tamils resist the Sinhalese in Sri Lanka, and Uighurs and Tibetans resist the Chinese. The Middle East would still have the historical model — the Byzantine Empire of more than 2,000 years' standing — with which to identify as a cultural and religious symbol. It would, in many respects, perpetuate an East-West divide.

If there had been no Islam, the Muslim countries of South Asia and Southeast Asia today — particularly Pakistan, Bangladesh, Malaysia, and Indonesia — would be rooted instead in the Hindu world. Europeans were able to divide and conquer numerous African, Asian, and Latin American peoples who then fell singly before Western power. Islamic civilisation provided a common ideal to which all Muslims could appeal in the name of resistance against Western encroachment. Even if that appeal failed to stem the Western imperial tide, it created a cultural memory of a commonly shared fate that did not go away. A united, transnational resistance among those peoples was hard to achieve in the absence of any common cultural symbol of resistance.

In a world without Islam, Western imperialism would have found the task of dividing, conquering, and dominating the Middle East and Asia much easier. There would not have remained a shared cultural memory of humiliation and defeat across a vast area. That is a key reason why the U.S. now finds itself breaking its teeth in the Muslim world. Today, global intercommunications and shared satellite images have created a strong self-consciousness among Muslims and a sense of a broader Western imperial siege against a common Islamic culture. This siege is not about modernity; it is about the unceasing Western quest for domination of the strategic space, resources, and even culture of the Muslim world.

The most urgent issue the West most immediately associated with Islam today is terrorism. Without Islam, 9/11, 7/7 etc. would not have occurred, we are told. This is assuming that the grievances of the Middle East, rooted in years of political and emotional anger at US policies and actions, had been wrapped up in a different banner, things have been vastly different. Not really! September 11, 2001, was not the beginning of history.

In the West's focus on terrorism in the name of Islam, memories are short. Jewish guerrillas used terrorism against the British in Palestine. Sri Lankan Hindu Tamil "Tigers" invented the art of the suicide vest and for more than a decade led the world in the use of suicide bombings — including the assassination of Indian Prime Minister Rajiv Gandhi. Greek terrorists carried out assassination operations against US officials in Athens. Organised Sikh terrorism killed Indira Gandhi, spread havoc in India, established an overseas base in Canada, and brought down an Air India flight over the Atlantic. Macedonian terrorists were widely feared all across the Balkans on the eve of World War I. Dozens of major assassinations in the late 19th and early 20th centuries were carried out by European and American "anarchists," sowing collective fear. The Irish Republican Army employed brutally effective terrorism against the British for decades, as did communist guerrillas and terrorists in

Vietnam against Americans, communist Malays against British soldiers in the 1950s, and Mau terrorists against British officers in Kenya — the list goes on. It doesn't take a Muslim to commit terrorism.

Even the recent history of terrorist activity as has already been noted, see's Islam play virtually no role. Europol's 2015 report on terrorist attacks in Europe saw 201 terrorists' attacks in 2014. Of these, separatist terrorism accounted for the largest proportion, followed by anarchist and left-wing attacks. Only 2 were carried out by Muslims![clxiv] There were a number of foiled attempts in a highly surveilled Muslim community. But these figures amongst many others reveal that Islam plays an extremely minor, although highly reported by the media, role in terror attacks around the world.

Even if Islam as a vehicle of resistance had never existed, Marxism did. It is an ideology that has spawned countless terrorist, guerrilla, and national liberation movements. It has informed the Basque ETA, the FARC in Colombia, the Shining Path in Peru, and the Red Army Faction in Europe, to name only a few in the West. George Habash, the founder of the deadly Popular Front for the Liberation of Palestine, was a Greek Orthodox Christian and Marxist who studied at the American University of Beirut. In an era when angry Arab nationalism flirted with violent Marxism, many Christian Palestinians lent Habash their support.

Peoples who resist foreign oppressors seek banners to propagate and glorify the cause of their struggle. The international class struggle for justice provides a good rallying point. Nationalism is even better. But religion provides the best one of all, appealing to the highest powers in prosecuting its cause. And religion everywhere can still serve to bolster ethnicity and nationalism even as it transcends it — especially when the enemy is of a different religion. In such cases, religion ceases to be primarily the source of clash and confrontation, but rather its vehicle. The banner of the moment may go away, but the grievances remain.

We live in an era when terrorism is often the chosen instrument of the weak. It already stymies the unprecedented might of US armies in Iraq, Afghanistan, and elsewhere. And thus bin Laden in many non-Muslim societies has been called the "next Che Guevara." It's nothing less than the appeal of successful resistance against dominant American power, the weak striking back — an appeal that transcends Islam or Middle Eastern culture.

The world would be vastly different if Islam didn't exist assumes Islam is source of all the problems. It may seem sophisticated to seek out passages in the Qur'an to explain "why they hate us." But that blindly misses the nature of the phenomenon, which is exploring the impact of the massive global footprint of the colonial west. A world without Islam would still see most of the enduring bloody rivalries whose wars and tribulations dominate the geopolitical landscape. If it were not religion, all of these groups would have found some other banner under which to express nationalism and a quest for independence. Sure, history would not have followed the exact same path as it has. But, at rock bottom, conflict between East and West remains all about the grand historical and geopolitical issues of human history: ethnicity, nationalism, ambition, greed, resources, local leaders, turf, financial gain, power, interventions, and hatred of outsiders, invaders, and imperialists.

It should also be remembered that virtually every one of the horrors of the 20th century came almost exclusively from strictly secular regimes: Leopold II of Belgium in the Congo, Hitler, Mussolini, Lenin and Stalin, Mao, and Pol Pot. It was Europeans who visited their "world wars" twice upon the rest of the world — two devastating global conflicts with no remote parallels in Islamic history.

Some today might wish for a "world without Islam" in which these problems presumably had never come to be. But, in truth, the conflicts, rivalries, and crises of such a world do not look any different the ones we know today.

BIBLIOGRAPHY

A Decade Lost Rethinking Radicalisation and Extremism, Professor Arun Kundnani, Claystone, January 2015, http://www.claystone.org.uk/wp-content/uploads/2015/01/Claystone-rethinking-radicalisation.pdf

Arab Human Development Report 2009, challenges to human security in the Arab countries, United Nations Development Programme, http://www.arab-hdr.org/publications/other/ahdr/ahdr2009e.pdf

Arab Human Development Report, Research paper series, Economic Development, Bassam Fattouh & Laura El-Katiri, UN Development programme, 2012, http://www.arab-hdr.org/publications/other/ahdrps/ENGFattouhKatiriV2.pdf

Arab Human Development Report, Research paper series, Population Levels, Trends and Policies in the Arab Region: Challenges and Opportunities, Mirkin, B, UN Development programme, 2010, http://www.arab-hdr.org/publications/other/ahdrps/paper01-en.pdf

Body Count, Casualty Figures after 10 Years of the "War on Terror" Iraq Afghanistan Pakistan, International Physicians for the Prevention of Nuclear War, First international edition, March 2015, http://www.psr.org/assets/pdfs/body-count.pdf

Egypt - The Status of Poverty and Food Security in Egypt: Analysis and Policy Recommendations, May 2013, United Nations' World Food Programme (WFP) and CAPMAS, http://www.wfp.org/content/egypt-status-poverty-food-security-analysis-policy-recommendations-may-2013

EU Terrorism Situation and Trend Reports 2006, 2007, 2008, 2009, 2010, 2011, 2012, 2013, 2014 and 2015, Europol, https://www.europol.europa.eu/sites/default/files/publications/p_europol_tsat15_09jun15_low-rev.pdf

Gareth Stansfield and Saul Kelly, A return to the East of the Suez? UK military deployment to the Gulf, briefing paper, RUSI, April 2013, retrieved 29 May 2015,
https://www.rusi.org/downloads/assets/East_of_Suez_Return_042013.pdf

Gendzier, Irene L. Notes from the Minefield: United States Intervention in Lebanon and the Middle East, 1945–1958. Columbia University Press, 1997

Global Terrorism Index 2014, measuring and understanding the impact of terrorism, Institute for economics and peace, Data is based on Global Terrorism Database (GTD) which is collected and collated by the National Consortium for the Study of Terrorism and Responses to Terrorism (START), University of Maryland, http://economicsandpeace.org/wp-content/uploads/2015/06/Global-Terrorism-Index-Report-2014.pdf

Great Britain & Reza Shah: The Plunder of Iran 1921 - 1941, Mohammed Gholi Majd, 2001, www.kurdipedia.org/books//65502.pdf
Heikal, Muhammad, the Road to Ramadan, 1976, Ballentine Books

How Islamist Extremists Quote the Qur'an, Centre for Strategic Communication, University of Arizona, July 2012, http://csc.asu.edu/wp-content/uploads/pdf/csc1202-quran-verses.pdf
H.R.P. Dickson, Kuwait and Her Neighbours, December 1956, Allen & Unwin

James Barr, A Line in the Sand: Britain, France and the Struggle That Shaped the Middle East, Simon & Schuster, 2012

James Onley, Britain and the Gulf Shaikhdoms, 1820–1971: The Politics of Protection, Occasional paper 4, Centre for international and regional studies, Georgetown University, 2009,
http://socialsciences.exeter.ac.uk/iais/downloads/Onley_Britain_and_Gulf_Shaikhdoms2009.pdf

Keeping Faith: Memoirs of a President, Jimmy Carter, 1982

Mapping the Global future, Report of the National Intelligence Council's 2020 Project, December 2004,
http://www.futurebrief.com/project2020.pdf

Marshal G H Hodgson, Rethinking world History, Essays on Europe, Islam and world history, Cambridge university press,

Measuring Stability and Security in Iraq, November 2006, Report to Congress In accordance with the Department of Defense Appropriations Act 2007 (Section 9010, Public Law 109-289),
http://www.defense.gov/pubs/pdfs/9010Quarterly-Report-20061216.pdf

Muslim Public Opinion on US Policy, Attacks on Civilians and al Qaeda, worldpublicopinion.org,
University of Maryland, April 24, 2007,
http://www.worldpublicopinion.org/pipa/pdf/apr07/START_Apr07_rpt.pdf

Ochsenwald, William, and Sydney Fisher. *The Middle East: A History.* 6th. New York: McGraw-Hill, 2003

Olivier Roy, Al Qaeda in the West as a Youth Movement: the Power of a Narrative, MICROCON Policy Working Paper, 2008,
http://www.microconflict.eu/publications/PWP2_OR.pdf

Rebuilding America's Defenses: Strategy, Forces and Resources for a New Century, *A Report of*
The Project for the New American Century, September 2000

Subsidy Reform in the Middle East and North Africa, Recent Progress and Challenges Ahead, IMF, 2014,
http://www.imf.org/external/pubs/ft/dp/2014/1403mcd.pdf

Tessler, Mark. *A History of the Israeli-Palestinian Conflict.* 2nd ed. Bloomington, Indiana: Indiana University Press, 2009

The Blue Peace, Rethinking Middle East Water, Sundeep Wasler, Strategic Foresight Group (SFG), Geneva, 2011,

The Changing Scenes of Life: An Autobiography, Quartet Books (London), 1983

The Global Religious Landscape, Pew Research Centre, December 2012, http://www.pewforum.org/2012/12/18/global-religious-landscape-muslim/

Water Scarcity Challenges in the Middle East and North Africa (MENA), Human Development Report - Water for Human Development, 2006, http://hdr.undp.org/sites/default/files/siwi2.pdf

World Employment and Social Outlook, trends 2015, international labor organization, 2015, retrieved 13 July 2015, http://www.ilo.org/wcmsp5/groups/public/---dgreports/---dcomm/---publ/documents/publication/wcms_337069.pdf

NOTES

[i] See, http://english.al-akhbar.com/node/16132

[ii] See, https://now.mmedia.me/lb/en/commentary/565599-all-fall-down

[iii] The Global Religious Landscape, Pew Research Centre, December 2012, retrieved 20 March 2015, http://www.pewforum.org/2012/12/18/global-religious-landscape-muslim/

[iv] Arab Human Development Report 2009, challenges to human security in the Arab countries, United Nations Development Programme, 2009, accessed March 2015, http://www.arab-hdr.org/publications/other/ahdr/ahdr2009e.pdf

[v] Marshal G H Hodgson, Rethinking world History, Essays on Europe, Islam and world history, Cambridge university press, 1993, pg 97

[vi] Gibbon, Edward, The Decline and Fall of the Roman Empire, Battle of Tours, Chapter 52, http://www.ccel.org/g/gibbon/decline/volume2/chap52.htm

[vii] Crawley, R, Constantinople: The Last Great Siege, 1453, Faber, 2006

[viii] Goodwin, J, Lords of the Horizons : A History of the Ottoman Empire, Vintage, 1999, pg 60

[ix] Jaques Benoist-Mechin, The End of The Ottoman Empire pg 104

[x] Prime Minister Henry Campbell-Bannerman, Campbell-Bannerman Report, 1907

[xi] See, http://english.al-akhbar.com/node/22253

[xii] Fromkin, David, A Peace to End All Peace: Creating the Modern Middle East, 1989,

[xiii] As cited by Daniel Yergin, The Prize (New York, 1991), p. 188

xiv The Report: Emerging Jordan 2007, Oxford Business Group, London, Apr. 2007.

xv "Great Britain & Reza Shah: The Plunder of Iran 1921 – 1941," Mohammed Gholi Majd, 2001, www.kurdipedia.org/books//65502.pdf

xvi The Post-American World, And the rise of the rest, Fareed Zakaria, Penguin books, 2009, pg 179

xvii U.S. Department of State. Foreign Relations of the United States. 1945, viii, 45, cited in Joyce and Gabriel Kolko, *The limits of power*, Harper & Row, 1972, which provides a comprehensive analysis of the development of U.S. policy at the time.

xviii New Statesmen interview with Jack Straw, November 2002, http://www.newstatesman.com/node/144241

xix See, http://www.nybooks.com/articles/archives/2011/aug/18/egypt-who-calls-shots/

xx http://news.nationalgeographic.com/news/2013/07/130705-egypt-morsi-government-overthrow-military-revolution-independence-history/

xxi Egypt may not need fighter jets but US keeps sending them anyway, NPR.org, August 2008, http://www.npr.org/blogs/money/2013/08/08/209878158/egypt-may-not-need-fighter-jets-but-u-s-keeps-sending-them-anyway

xxii See, ttp://killerapps.foreignpolicy.com/posts/2013/07/02/soldiers_trained_by_us_threatening_to_overthow_egypt

xxiii Egypt may not need fighter jets but US keeps sending them anyway, NPR.org, August 2008, http://www.npr.org/blogs/money/2013/08/08/209878158/egypt-may-not-need-fighter-jets-but-u-s-keeps-sending-them-anyway

xxiv Mubarak family fortune could reach $70bn, says expert, Guardian, February 2011, retrieved 5 August 2015, http://www.theguardian.com/world/2011/feb/04/hosni-mubarak-family-fortune

xxv Egypt - The Status of Poverty and Food Security in Egypt: Analysis and Policy Recommendations, May 2013, United Nations' World Food Programme (WFP) and CAPMAS, retrieved 14 may 2015, http://www.wfp.org/content/egypt-status-poverty-food-security-analysis-policy-recommendations-may-2013

xxvi See, http://www.hrw.org/news/2013/08/19/egypt-security-forces-used-excessive-lethal-force

xxvii Egypt sends Mursi to trial as new constitution advances, Reuters, September 2013, http://www.reuters.com/article/2013/09/01/us-egypt-protests-mursi-idUSBRE9800EI20130901

xxviii Aron S. Klieman, *Foundation of British Policy in the Arab World: The Cairo Conference of 1921* (The Johns Hopkins University Press, 1970), 51.

xxix Daniel Pipes, Greater Syria: The History of an Ambition, Oxford University press, 1992, Pg 166

xxx Ibid

xxxi Douglas Little , "Cold War and Covert Action: The United States and Syria, 1945-1958". *Middle East Journal* 44 (1). 1990, retrieved April 18 2015, http://coat.ncf.ca/our_magazine/links/issue51/articles/51_12-13.pdf and Gendzier, Irene L. (1997). *Notes from the Minefield: United States Intervention in Lebanon and the Middle East, 1945–1958.* Columbia University Press. p. 98

xxxii Fearful Alawites pay sectarian militias in battered Homs, Reuters, Sep 25, 2012, http://www.reuters.com/article/2012/09/25/syria-shabbiha-extortion-idUSL5E8KP4AZ20120925

xxxiii MAFIA-STYLE SHOOT-OUT EXPOSES THREAT TO SYRIA'S ASSAD, FRANCE 24, OCTOBER 2012, http://www.france24.com/en/20121003-shoot-out-syria-corleone-exposes-new-threat-bashar-mohammed-al-assad-alawite

xxxiv Bashar al-Assad's inner circle, BBC Online, 30 July 2012, http://www.bbc.co.uk/news/world-middle-east-13216195

xxxv President in name only, Assad plays for time, David Blair, the Telegraph, 30 July 2012, http://www.telegraph.co.uk/news/worldnews/middleeast/syria/9438240/President-in-name-only-Assad-plays-for-time.html

xxxvi See, http://www.aljazeera.net/programs/pages/fa527ac3-2308-4892-945e-7978486e3ac5 (arabic)

xxxvii See, http://www.meforum.org/research/lsg.php

xxxviii See, http://www.gmu.edu/programs/icar/ijps/vol14_2/SALAMEY%20-%2014n2%20IJPS.pdf

xxxix Full text of document drafted during secret talks, Akiva Eldar, Haaretz, January 2007, http://www.haaretz.com/news/exclusive-full-text-of-document-drafted-during-secret-talks-1.210053

xl Measuring Stability and Security in Iraq, November 2006, Report to Congress In accordance with the Department of Defense Appropriations Act 2007 (Section 9010, Public Law 109-289), retrieved 19 April 2015, pg 20, http://www.defense.gov/pubs/pdfs/9010Quarterly-Report-20061216.pdf

xli See, http://en.wikipedia.org/wiki/Maher_Arar

xlii See, http://wikileaks.org/cable/2009/03/09DAMASCUS179.html

xliii Israeli official: Assad preferable to extremist rebels, The Times of London reports, Haaretz, May 2013, retrieved 18 April 2015, http://www.haaretz.com/news/diplomacy-defense/israeli-official-assad-preferable-to-extremist-rebels-the-times-of-london-reports-1.524605

xliv Israeli Official: Assad Preferable to Extremist Rebels, Haaretz, May 2013

xlv See, http://www.dailystar.com.lb/News/Lebanon-News/2013/Sep-23/232198-kissinger-saw-the-benefits-of-syrian-intervention-in-lebanon.ashx

xlvi Lebanon aghast as return of sectarian kidnappings raises spectre of civil war, Guardian, August 2012, retrieved 25 April 2014,

http://www.theguardian.com/world/2012/aug/15/lebanon-syria-sectarian-kidnappings-warnings

xlvii Palestine Royal Commission Report Presented by the Secretary of State for the Colonies to Parliament by Command of His Majesty, July 1937, Cmd. 5479. His Majesty's Stationery Office., London, 1937. 404 pages + maps

xlviii Alexander C. Diener; Joshua Hagen (January 2010). Borderlines and Borderlands: Political Oddities at the Edge of the Nation-state. Rowman & Littlefield. pg 189

xlix Roger Louis, William (1985), the British Empire in the Middle East, 1945–1951. pp. 348

l Middle East Centre Archive, Oxford, (MEC), Sykes Papers, Sykes to Clayton, 22 July 1917

li Andrew and Patrick Cockburn, excerpt from Out of the Ashes, The Resurrection of Saddam Hussein, 2000. Cited by Tim Buckley, http://www.casi.org.uk/discuss/2000/msg01267.html

lii Malik Mufti (1996), Sovereign Creations: Pan-Arabism and Political Order in Syria and Iraq, Ithaca and London: Cornell University Press

liii Unpeople: Britain's Secret Human Rights Abuses, The massacres in Iraq, 1963, Mark Curtis, February 2007, retrieved 4 may 2015, https://markcurtis.wordpress.com/2007/02/12/the-massacres-in-iraq-1963/

liv Unpeople: Britain's Secret Human Rights Abuses, The massacres in Iraq, 1963, Mark Curtis, February 2007, retrieved 4 may 2015, https://markcurtis.wordpress.com/2007/02/12/the-massacres-in-iraq-1963/

lv "US Secretly Gave Aid to Iraq Early in Its War Against Iran", Seymour Hersh, The New York Times, 1992, www.nytimes.com/1992/01/26/world/us-secretly-gave-aid-to-iraq-early-in-its-war-against-iran.html?pagewanted=all&src=pm

lvi "U.S. Secretly Gave Aid to Iraq Early in Its War Against Iran", Seymour Hersh, The New York Times, 1992,

www.nytimes.com/1992/01/26/world/us-secretly-gave-aid-to-iraq-early-in-its-war-against-iran.html?pagewanted=all&src=pm

lvii The United States and Iran: Sanctions, Wars and the Policy of Dual Containment, Sasan Fayazmanesh, 2008

lviii Unholy Babylon,' Adel Darwish and Gregory Alexander, 1991, Gollancz

lix See, http://www.globalresearch.ca/articles/MAC209A.html

lx See, http://www.richardsilverstein.com/2010/07/13/18-israeli-families-control-60-of-nations-corporate-equity/

lxi From the Campbell-Bannerman Report, 1907

lxii Tessler, Mark. *A History of the Israeli-Palestinian Conflict*. 2nd ed. Bloomington, Indiana: Indiana University Press, 2009. Print. p.266

lxiii Ochsenwald, William, and Sydney Fisher. *The Middle East: A History*. 6th. New York: McGraw-Hill, 2003. Pg 538

lxiv See, http://rt.com/news/israel-west-allies-support-162/

lxv See, http://www.jonathanpollard.org/2005/012805.htm

lxvi See, http://www.larouchepub.com/eiw/public/1981/eirv08n50-19811229/eirv08n50-19811229_036-begin_blowtorches_the_mideast_ma.pdf

lxvii See, http://www.aljazeera.com/indepth/opinion/2014/12/revisiting-british-conquest-je-2014121381243881138.html

lxviii The Changing Scenes of Life: An Autobiography, Quartet Books (London), 1983

lxix Barnett C, 'The Collapse of British Power,' Macmillan, 1972

lxx The Road to Ramadan, Mohamed Heikal, 1976

lxxi H.R.P. Dickson, Kuwait and her neighbours, part 1, p.281

lxxii H.R.P. Dickson, Kuwait and her neighbours, part 1, p.282

lxxiii John Gordon Lorimer, The Gazetteer, Historical Section, Part 6, pp.3770-3776.

lxxiv See, http://www.hrw.org/legacy/backgrounder/mena/saudi/

lxxv The Constitutional Laws of the Arab Countries," chapter "The Constitution of the Kingdom of Saudi Arabia.

lxxvi See, http://www.hrw.org/legacy/backgrounder/mena/saudi/

lxxvii See, http://www.hrw.org/en/news/2011/02/19/saudi-arabia-free-political-activists

lxxviii See, https://www.goodreads.com/author_blog_posts/3885073-50-years-of-the-british-military-mission-to-the-saudi-arabian-national-g

lxxix Strange Menagerie: The Atlantic Charter as the Root of American Entanglement in Iran, & Its Influence Upon the Development of the Policy of Containment, 1941-1946, Gregory J. Rosmaita, 1994, www.hicom.net/~oedipus/us_iran.html

lxxx Strange Menagerie: The Atlantic Charter as the Root of American Entanglement in Iran, & Its Influence Upon the Development of the Policy of Containment, 1941-1946, Gregory J. Rosmaita, 1994, www.hicom.net/~oedipus/us_iran.html

lxxxi The United States, Great Britain, and Mossadegh, David Painter, Georgetown University, 2006, https://americamiddleeast.files.wordpress.com/2012/09/the-us-and-mossadegh-1951-19531.pdf

lxxxii The United States, Great Britain, and Mossadegh, David Painter, Georgetown University, 2006, https://americamiddleeast.files.wordpress.com/2012/09/the-us-and-mossadegh-1951-19531.pdf

lxxxiii US Foreign policy and the Shah: Building a Client State in Iran", Mark Gasiorowski, 1991

lxxxiv Warning to America: 'A False sense of Security will destroy you, (Exclusive Interview with the Shah of Iran) U.S. New World Report, 1976 lxxxv Mission to Iran, William H. Sullivan, 1981

lxxxvi Strange Menagerie: The Atlantic Charter as the Root of American Entanglement in Iran, & Its Influence Upon the Development of the Policy of Containment, 1941-1946, Gregory J. Rosmaita, 1994, pg 76 www.hicom.net/~oedipus/us_iran.html

lxxxvii Ziyara Khassa (Special Visit): Interview with Abul Hassan Bani Sadr, first president of the Iranian Republic", Al Jazeera Aarabic, 2000; "My Turn to Speak: Iran, the Revolution and Secret Deals with the U.S", Abol Hassan Bani Sadr, 2010

lxxxviii Keeping Faith: Memoirs of a President, Jimmy Carter, 1982

lxxxix Al Hawadess, 3 Februari 1979, edition 1161, page 26, through http://islamicweb.com/beliefs/cults/iranian_revolution.htm; also: "Was it Wrong to Support the Iranian Revolution in 1978 (because it turned out badly)", Richard Falk, http://richardfalk.wordpress.com/2012/10/09/was-it-wrong-to-support-the-iranian-revolution-in-1978-because-it-turned-out-badly/ (Richard Falk accompanied Ramsey Clark on the latter's trip to Iran and Paris)

xc Fars News, January 12, 2016

xci Iran and the west: From Khomeni to Ahmedinejad, BBC documentary, 2009, http://www.bbc.co.uk/programmes/b00hmrvt and https://www.youtube.com/watch?v=ZOaGmK8aTHQ

xcii Ibid

xciii Ibid

xciv Iranian support seen crucial for Yemen's Houthis, Reuters, December 2014, http://www.reuters.com/article/2014/12/15/us-yemen-houthis-iran-insight-idUSKBN0JT17A20141215

xcv See, http://www.al-monitor.com/pulse/originals/2015/01/yemen-houthis-obama-administration.html#ixzz3VX9Ndq7x

xcvi Tunisia's Islamists rule out sharia in constitution, France 24, March 2012, retrieved 23 September 2012,

http://www.france24.com/en/20120328-tunisia-islamists-rule-out-sharia-constitution-ennahda

xcvii Tunisia's Islamists rule out sharia in constitution, France 24, March 2012, retrieved 23 September 2012, http://www.france24.com/en/20120328-tunisia-islamists-rule-out-sharia-constitution-ennahda

xcviii Interview with Rachid Ghannouchi, France 24, 13 November 2011, retrieved 11 November 2012, http://alhittin.com/2011/11/13/rashid-al-ghannushi-rejects-the-idea-of-khilafah-wants-reforms/

xcix See, http://www.aljazeera.com/indepth/interactive/2014/10/tunisia-decides-20141021164020540690.html

c Joe Biden, PBS Newshour interview transcript, January 2011, retrieved 5 June 2015, http://www.pbs.org/newshour/bb/politics-jan-june11-biden_01-27/

ci Patrick Brennen, State Department: Morsi 'A Far Cry from an Autocrat,' National Review Online, November 2012, http://www.nationalreview.com/corner/334237/state-department-morsi-far-cry-autocrat-patrick-brennan

cii Obama Urges Egypt's Military to Restore Power to a Civilian Government, Wall Street Journal, 3 July 2013, http://online.wsj.com/article/BT-CO-20130703-710706.html

ciii Egypt army 'restoring democracy', says John Kerry, BBC News, 1 August 2013, http://www.bbc.co.uk/news/world-middle-east-23543744

civ See, http://news.bbc.co.uk/1/hi/uk_politics/3566545.stm

cv See, http://www.state.gov/documents/organization/199157.pdf

cvi See, http://online.wsj.com/article/SB10000872396390444165804578008411144721162.html

cvii See, http://www.economist.com/news/middle-east-and-africa/21596974-power-struggles-are-intensifying-little-celebrate

cviii See, http://www.businessinsider.com/the-cias-man-in-libya-2011-4

cix See, http://www.bbc.co.uk/news/world-africa-30913458

cx See, http://www.al-monitor.com/pulse/tr/security/2014/06/libya-hifter-interview-egypt-parliament.html

cxi See, http://www.mei.edu/content/at/huthi-ascent-power

cxii Yemen president warns of civil war, Aljazeera, 24 September 2014, http://www.aljazeera.com/news/middleeast/2014/09/yemen-president-warns-civil-war-201492313054524108.html

cxiii President Hadi receives UK Ambassador to Yemen, The official website of the President of the Republic of Yemen, 24 September 2014, https://presidenthadi-gov-ye.info/en/archives/president-hadi-receives-uk-ambassador-yemen-2/

cxiv See, http://www.eeas.europa.eu/statements/docs/2014/140922_02_en.pdf

cxv See, http://www.wsj.com/articles/covert-cia-mission-to-arm-syrian-rebels-goes-awry-1422329582

cxvi See, http://www.nybooks.com/articles/archives/2014/nov/06/there-answer-syria

cxvii US dept of state, Hilary Clinton interview with Lucia Annunziata of "In Mezz'Ora," May 2011, http://www.state.gov/secretary/rm/2011/05/162817.htm

cxviii Panetta says when, not if, al-Assad falls, Syrian military should remain intact, CNN, July 30 2012, http://security.blogs.cnn.com/2012/07/30/panetta-says-when-not-if-al-assad-falls-syrian-military-should-remain-intact/

cxix Clinton calls for overhaul of Syrian opposition, Reuters, October 2012, http://uk.reuters.com/article/us-syria-usa-idUKBRE89U1AY20121031

cxx See, http://www.theguardian.com/world/2014/nov/17/john-kerry-isis-bashar-assad-symbiotic

cxxi Dr. K R Bolton, Tunisian Revolt: Another Soros/NED Jack-Up? Foreign policy journal, http://www.foreignpolicyjournal.com/2011/01/18/tunisian-revolt-another-sorosned-jack-up/

cxxii A fatwa from the Council of Senior Scholars in the Kingdom of Saudi Arabia warning against mass demonstrations, Asharq al awsat News, October 2011, retrieved 1 October 2012, http://islamopediaonline.org/fatwa/fatwa-council-senior-scholars-kingdom-saudi-arabia-warning-against-mass-demonstrations

cxxiii The future of the global Muslim population, Pew Research Centre, 2011, retrieved 9 July 2015, http://www.pewforum.org/2011/01/27/future-of-the-global-muslim-population-regional-middle-east

cxxiv Inequality and Arab Spring Revolutions in North Africa and the Middle East, African Development Institute, Vol 3, issue 7, 2012, pg 7, http://www.afdb.org/fileadmin/uploads/afdb/Documents/Publications/AEB%20VOL%203%20Issue%207%20juillet%202012%20ENG_AEB%20VOL%203%20Issue%207%20juillet%202012%20ENG%202.pdf

cxxv What does the Arab world do when its water runs out? Guardian, February 2011, retrieve July 13 2015, http://www.theguardian.com/environment/2011/feb/20/arab-nations-water-running-out

cxxvi Water Scarcity Challenges in the Middle East and North Africa (MENA), Human Development Report - Water for Human Development, 2006, pg 3, http://hdr.undp.org/sites/default/files/siwi2.pdf

cxxvii Albright says U.S. not happy about Turkey's Islamic drift, CNN, February 1997, retrieved 18 July 2015, http://edition.cnn.com/WORLD/9702/12/turkey/

cxxviii How ignorance and prejudice sour the West's view of Islam, Telegraph, August 2001, http://www.telegraph.co.uk/comment/4264802/How-ignorance-and-prejudice-sour-the-Wests-view-of-Islam.html

cxxix Transcript of Speech by Deputy Secretary of Defence Paul Wolfowitz, Luncheon Press Event in Singapore, May 2002, retrieved July 18th 2015, http://www.defenselink.mil/transcripts/transcript.aspx?transcriptid=3472

cxxx National Intelligence Estimate, December 2004, Report of the National Intelligence Councils 2020 project, *Mapping the Global Future,'* Pg 83-92, http://www.futurebrief.com/project2020.pdf

cxxxi Iraq, Jordan See Threat To Election From Iran, Leaders Warn Against Forming Religious State, Washington Post, December 2004, retrieved July 27 2015, http://www.washingtonpost.com/wp-dyn/articles/A43980-2004Dec7.html

cxxxii Forum for the Future: Partnership Dialogue Panel Session, Hillary Rodham Clinton, US Secretary of State, Doha Qatar, January 2011, http://www.state.gov/secretary/20092013clinton/rm/2011/01/154595.htm

cxxxiii "The Constitutional Laws of the Arab Countries," chapter "The Constitution of the Kingdom of Saudi Arabia."

cxxxiv The Bible - NKJ Version (Luke 20:25)

cxxxv John Knefel, "Everything You've Been Told About Radicalization is Wrong," Rolling Stone, May 2013, retrieved 22 July 2015, http://www.rollingstone.com/politics/news/everything-youve-been-told-about-radicalization-is-wrong-20130506

cxxxvi Olivier Roy, Al Qaeda in the West as a Youth Movement: the Power of a Narrative, MICROCON Policy Working Paper 2, November 2008, p. 3, http://www.microconflict.eu/publications/PWP2_OR.pdf

cxxxvii Nafeez Ahmed, 'Unworthy victims: Western wars have killed four million Muslims since 1990, Middle East Eye, April 2015, retrieved 22 July 2015, http://www.middleeasteye.net/columns/unworthy-victims-western-wars-have-killed-four-million-muslims-1990-39149394#sthash.CvjXSgew.dpuf

cxxxviii Transcript of Bin Laden's October interview by Al-Jazeera, October 2001, published by CNN, February 2002, retrieved 22 July 2015, http://edition.cnn.com/2002/WORLD/asiapcf/south/02/05/binladen.transcript/index.html

cxxxix ISIS is less than third of Sunni rebels in Iraq, Middle East monitor, June 2014, retrieved July 23 2015,
https://www.middleeastmonitor.com/news/middle-east/12174-isis-is-less-than-third-of-sunni-rebels-in-iraq

cxl Ibid

cxli Ibid

cxlii Video of 7/7 ringleader blames foreign policy, Guardian, September 2005, retrieved 23 July 2015,
http://www.theguardian.com/uk/2005/sep/02/alqaida.politics

cxliii US drone attacks are no laughing matter, Mr Obama, Guardian, December 2010, retrieved July 23 2015
http://www.guardian.co.uk/commentisfree/cifamerica/2010/dec/28/us-drone-attacks-no-laughing-matter

cxliv Underwear bomber surprises with sudden guilty plea, USA Today, December 2011, July 23 2015,
http://usatoday30.usatoday.com/news/nation/story/2011-10-12/underwear-bomber-trial/50742774/1

cxlv Boston bombing suspect cites U.S. wars as motivation, officials say, *The Washington Post*, April, 2013, retrieved July 23 2015,
http://www.washingtonpost.com/national/boston-bombing-suspect-cites-us-wars-as-motivation-officials-say/2013/04/23/324b9cea-ac29-11e2-b6fd-ba6f5f26d70e_story.html

cxlvi Excerpts From Statements in Court of the Ramzi Yousef trial, New York Times, January 1998, retrieved July 23 2015,
http://www.nytimes.com/1998/01/09/nyregion/excerpts-from-statements-in-court.html

cxlvii Former MI5 chief delivers damning verdict on Iraq invasion, Guardian, July 2010, retrieved 24 July 2015,
http://www.theguardian.com/uk/2010/jul/20/chilcot-mi5-boss-iraq-war

cxlviii See,
http://www.start.umd.edu/sites/default/files/files/announcements/BackgroundReport_10YearsSince9_11.pdf

cxlix See, http://www.cpsc.gov/PageFiles/108985/tipover2011.pdf

cl See, http://danger.mongabay.com/injury_death.htm

cli See, https://www.fbi.gov/stats-services/publications/terrorism-2002-2005/terror02_05#terror_05sum

clii See, http://sites.duke.edu/tcths/files/2013/06/Kurzman_Muslim-American_Terrorism_in_2013.pdf

cliii Terrorism: When Reality Meets Unrealistic Expectations, Security weekly, Scott Stewart, Strafor, July 2015, https://www.stratfor.com/weekly/terrorism-when-reality-meets-unrealistic-expectations

cliv See, https://www.fbi.gov/stats-services/publications/terrorism-2002-2005/terror02_05#terror_05sum

clv Full transcript of BBC interview with President Barack Obama, BBC, 24 July 2015, http://www.bbc.co.uk/news/world-us-canada-33646542

clvi Terror Trials by the Numbers, Stings, informants, and underwear bombs: Digging through the data from federal terrorism cases, Mother Jones, September/October 2011 Issue, http://www.motherjones.com/politics/2011/08/terror-trials-numbers and Profiles in Terror, http://www.motherjones.com/fbi-terrorist

clvii See, https://www.documentcloud.org/documents/230985-8-25-10-fuller.html

clviii See, http://old.seattletimes.com/text/2020640693.html

clix Trever Aaronson, Double Agent, An FBI Informant Makes a New Career as a Defense Expert, The Intercept, May 2015, https://firstlook.org/theintercept/2015/05/20/craig-monteilh/

clx See, https://firstlook.org/theintercept/2015/03/16/howthefbicreatedaterrorist/

clxi Ibid

clxii George Friedman, Egypt and the Idealist-Realist Debate in U.S. Foreign Policy, Stratfor, December 2011, http://www.stratfor.com/weekly/20111205-egypt-and-idealist-realist-debate-us-foreign-policy

clxiii MacCarthy A, Egypt: Are Elections "Democracy"? Gatestone Institute, January 2014, http://www.gatestoneinstitute.org/4145/egypt-elections-democracy

clxiv EU Terrorism Situation and Trend Report 2015, Europol, July 2015, pg 8, https://www.europol.europa.eu/sites/default/files/publications/p_europo l_tsat15_09jun15_low-rev.pdf

www.ingramcontent.com/pod-product-compliance
Lightning Source LLC
Chambersburg PA
CBHW070104290526
45789CB00005B/1924